VISIONARY
CAPITALISM

VISIONARY
CAPITALISM

Financial Markets and
the American Dream
in the Twentieth Century

CHARLES R. GEISST

New York
Westport, Connecticut
London

Library of Congress Cataloging-in-Publication Data

Geisst, Charles R.
   Visionary capitalism : financial markets and the American dream in
the Twentieth century / Charles R. Geisst.
     p.   cm.
  Includes bibliographical references.
  ISBN 0-275-93283-4
  1. Capital market—United States—History—20th century.
2. Finance—United States—History—20th century. 3. Capitalism—
United States—History—20th century. I. Title.
HG4910.G45   1991
332.63'2'09730904—dc20   90-37789

British Library Cataloguing in Publication Data is available.

Library of Congress Catalog Card Number: 90-37789
ISBN: 0-275-93283-4

First published in 1990

Praeger Publishers, One Madison Avenue, New York, NY 10010
An imprint of Greenwood Publishing Group, Inc.

Printed in the United States of America

The paper used in this book complies with the
Permanent Paper Standard issued by the National
Information Standards Organization (Z39.48-1984).
10 9 8 7 6 5 4 3 2 1

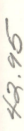
For Margaret Ann Geisst

Contents

Introduction

The idea of an American dream has been one of the most compelling notions of the nineteenth and twentieth centuries. Embodied in the dream are the visions of political freedom, home ownership, the accumulation of wealth, and the freedom from want. This combination of political and economic ideals was the magnet that drew millions of immigrants during the nineteenth century. Although sometimes dominated by economic aspiration, at its very center is the political ideal. The American experiment has evolved over the years as a process through which economic ideals are protected and nourished by a form of government that both shares and recognizes the economic dream as essential to stability and growth.

In order to arrive at the more material aspects, government has to share in the same dream and not stand in its way. By encouraging an atmosphere of industriousness and growth, the U.S. government usually has allowed the marketplace a remarkably free reign. Pragmatically, the ideal atmosphere can be best summed up in the words of Thoreau: that government is best which governs least. But in American political history, that idealistic stance has not always been possible. The realistic side of American history has seen governments play a strong, central role in defining and fashioning this persistent dream, especially when political and economic factors become too overwhelming for the marketplace.

The financial markets have played a central role in helping to shape and define the American dream over the decades. Naturally, their role has been confined to the material side rather than the political but their own development has had strong political implications. The markets could not have developed without governmental influence, sometimes loose while at other times strong. In this respect, their own history parallels developments in society as a whole. But financial markets usually are understood as places in which corporations and governments raise capital—not the sort of places one looks to for social developments. However, the U.S. financial markets have played a central role in furthering the American dream.

During the course of the twentieth century, the American dream has taken on more and more of a material significance. The central, economic part of the dream is still home ownership, but that has taken on additional baggage over the years. After World War I, higher education became integrated into the vision and became more firmly entrenched in the 1950s. Agricultural production has always found itself in the dream as well, representing freedom from hunger and want. In order to ensure these basic economic ideals, homeowners, farmers, and students had to find forms of financing similar to that of corporations. Regardless of the sector of the economy involved, as the vision became more extended, the financial markets began to play a crucial role in the development of the ideal. But their involvement was in keeping with the spirit of market capitalism in that investment risks and returns would still be present. Government and the markets together would find a common ground whereby the good economic life could be achieved. Government's role would be to provide direction and regulation of the markets so that the capital-raising process would not be left solely in the hands of the relative few without constraints on their activities. The markets in turn would provide capital to many sectors of the economy that government itself was ill equipped to intervene in for both practical and ideological reasons.

The American dream has undergone two distinct stages of development. In the contemporary sense, it means the accumulation of wealth, ownership of one's home, the opportunity for higher education, and basic freedom from hunger. As society becomes more developed, the last factor is mentioned less frequently. However, it still appears during periods of agricultural crisis and therefore needs to be included although it has come to be taken for granted. But when the dream was first beginning to take shape in the nineteenth century, it had a more simple connotation. Originally, the American dream was directly associated with the acquisition and protection of property.

Alexis de Tocqueville perhaps best summarized the meaning of property in America and how it differed from the European notions preceding it. Comparing a man's perceptions of possessions to that of a child who initially tends to seize everything around him as his own, de Tocqueville offered his own developmental view of the way in which individual property comes to be recognized: "The principle which the child derives from the possession of his toys is taught to the man by the objects which he may call his own. . . . As everyone [in America] has property of his own to defend, everyone recognizes the principle upon which he holds it."[1] The principle quickly became embedded in political rights. When all men have property, they tend to refrain from attacking that of others so they are not attacked themselves in turn.

The danger with property is that it could also be construed as a test or qualification to exclude those not possessing it from political rights or participation in the political process. James Fenimore Cooper, better known for his novels of early American frontier life, was only one of many writers and commentators recognizing this darker use of property in the early American political system. In *The American Democrat*, published in 1838, he pointed out the dangers of making property a qualification for political participation: "Property always carries with it a portion of indirect political influence, and it is unwise to . . . strengthen this influence by adding to it constitutional privileges."[2] Early political writers seeking to define the uniqueness of American civilization were quick to recognize the central role of property in this new society. Commentators ranging from the authors of the *Federalist Papers* to Tom Paine and Cooper all pointed out that the protection of that one basic freedom, if granted undue emphasis in the new democracy, would only lead to further inequities if the non-propertied were treated as less than first class citizens. But while these sorts of statements make a blanket case for property not being a qualification for political participation, it is obvious that certain segments of the population were still excluded by state and federal practices from full political rights. Nineteenth- and twentieth-century political history would record the often tortuous process by which all would finally be included in this basic element of the dream.

While the full principle of political equality would still require many years to become reality for all, the early writings of the nineteenth century were still reiterating principles found in the constitutional writings of the prior century. But while the American dream would always revolve around the principle of property, it would require other popular proponents if it were to become accepted as a vision that was uniquely American. Rallying cries may find their origins in theory but require more popular exponents to carry it to the mass of people who may have never read *The Federalist*. These people would nevertheless share the dream and come to embrace it as their own.

Henry James once remarked that it takes a great deal of history to produce a little literature. The Anglo-American tradition of property produced a great deal of political upheaval centering around property rights, but by the mid-nineteenth century the literature was still mainly theoretical. If one could summarize briefly the American concept of property it would be no different from that of John Locke, who had written two centuries before. Property was a right of man that was an extension of his labor, and that right was to be protected by government. While this idea had come to be ingrained through legal theory and practice, it did not form the visionary part of the American dream that hard work would bring with it fruits to be enjoyed.

That part of the American dream was more popular and could not be directly attributed to political or legal theory.

Where then did the more tangible part of the American vision originate? Turning Henry James's phrase on its head for a moment gives some indication. In this case, a great deal of history did produce a great deal of literature and it was this literature that gave the dream its most tangible form. But this was not the vision implanted by Edward Albee, Theodore Dreiser, or Norman Mailer in the twentieth century. In those cases, the literary representations of the American dream mainly discussed how it had gone wrong, how individuals had turned the idea upside down for their own selfish, ill-conceived ends. The vision had become identified, either through positive or negative interpretation, with hard work, success, and the will to strive for economic betterment. In the nineteenth century, this popular notion attached itself to individuals such as Benjamin Franklin and Abraham Lincoln. Both were common men who had turned their visions to higher goals and succeeded. But what about average people, whose goals may have been somewhat more mundane? Where did their visions originate?

The popular nineteenth-century view of hard work and its subsequent economic success was given widespread popularity in the works of Horatio Alger. A former divinity student and Unitarian minister, Alger took up writing shortly after the Civil War. Between 1866 and his death in 1899, he produced over 100 books revolving around a central theme: young boys facing the harshness of life in industrial society and overcoming its obstacles. While hardly examples of the best American literature of their time, Alger's works nevertheless gave the American dream more of a tangible, prosaic form than any other contemporary source. The best known of them remains *Ragged Dick, or Street Life in New York*, published in 1867.

The hero was Dick Hunter, a New York bootblack who, through a series of trials and successful tribulations, became a rich man through hard work and more than a bit of luck. Along with his numerous other novels and short stories, Alger almost single-handedly created the literary equation of hard work, good fortune, and success. The popularity of his works was unprecedented. He became the best known and most widely published author in America at the time, a distinction that still remains despite competition from contemporaries such as Harriet Beecher Stowe and Lew Wallace. Through the sheer volume of his writings, he rivaled Stowe in imprinting a simple but compelling idea upon the American mind. While the social significance was less compelling, his works became a central part of the American literary landscape and the popular imagination. Although frequently republished, his works started to become less popular after 1930. However, their impact on two generations, spanning the post–Civil War years to those following World War I, is not disputed.

The accessibility of property, potential riches, and the good life, whether represented by experience or by Alger's works, became a strong magnet by which many immigrants and first generation Americans were drawn into the American industrial culture of the nineteenth century. But the popularity of his books reached across all social groups. Among avid Alger readers were many businessmen, politicians, and other writers, among them Al Smith, Governor Herbert Lehman, and Ernest Hemingway, to name but a few. These simply written books, reflecting and contributing to the popular mind, had captured the quintessential American spirit of the nineteenth and early twentieth centuries.

After a century of growth and the end of relative isolation after World War I, the American dream would explode in the 1920s. Success in the war led to a domestic economic expansion at home that put great strain on the economic infrastrucutre of the country. The radio was mass produced, greater numbers of people were attending colleges and universities, home ownership expanded rapidly, and the stock market was booming. If any one decade could be characterized as that of the American dream, it was undoubtedly the 1920s. But in a financial sense, the decade bore the seeds of its own destruction. The financial system was not structured to cope with the demands that were being placed on it. Although the Federal Reserve System had been instituted in 1913, it had not yet been tested by an overheated economy and a credit explosion—the sort that brought down the stock market in 1929. The period 1920–29 in the financial markets was characterized by a boom in both the market indices and new financial innovations, and a relaxed regulatory environment. Traditionally a recipe for growth, this period would eventually do more to turn the vision of wealth and hard work into a nightmare than any other combination of factors previously witnessed. The saga of financial markets and the dream begins during this period.

After the stock market crash of 1929 and the massive series of bank failures that followed, the American dream became retrenched but not forgotten. While the vision had not died, most of the folklore concerning attaining great wealth and unimpeded progress nevertheless underwent an agonizing public and governmental reappraisal. The Republicans, who had presided over this period of boom and bust, were inauspiciously ushered out of office and would not re-claim the presidency until 1952. Their fate in Congress was equally dismal. But within one year of the crash itself, new governmental programs were introduced seeking to rebuild the economy. Those programs, introduced slowly and with much compromise over the decades, were designed to keep the ideal alive while at the same time avoiding a return to the abuses of the past.

At this stage of the development of the economy and the markets, the visionary element entered. Market regulation in the form of the Banking Act of 1933 and the Securities Exchange Act of 1934, giving greater powers to the Federal Reserve and the newly formed Securities and Exchange Commission, sought to protect the public and financial institutions against past abuses by a tighter regulatory environment than had previously existed. The creation of the Federal Home Loan Bank Board, additions to the existing Farm Credit institutions, and the development of the Federal National Mortgage Association also helped create a patchwork of new financial institutions and agencies designed to stimulate the economy and allocate credit on a more even-handed basis than before. Although all of these institutions helped preserve and extend the financial structure, none of them could be attributed to a single visionary. No one architect was responsible for ensuring that the American dream would survive by proposing a new set of institutions and regulations.

Of all the various administrations that held the presidency between 1920 and 1989, the Roosevelt administration was responsible for passing most of the original regulatory and other legislative measures that have created the modern U.S. financial market structure. The models created have been used many times since to stimulate the economy in various ways, regardless of the political stance of the administration under which they were passed. But even within the ranks of the Democrats of that era, no one individual can be attributed with the conception of a master plan by which market regulation or the structure of federal agencies developed. American financial market development especially has evolved in what appears to be an ad hoc manner. When financial abuses or structural inadequacies put pressure on the markets and the economy, remedies usually followed quickly but were not in place to prevent the problems in the first place. Pragmatic politics usually won out over theory in most cases.

One particular example from the Hoover years and the early years of the first Roosevelt administration illustrates this point. After the market crash, Herbert Hoover reacted quickly by creating the Federal Home Loan Bank Board and the Reconstruction Finance Corporation. These institutions were designed to help prop up the savings and loan industry and provide federal assistance to banks and other businesses short of capital due to the Depression. Both organizations were successful and were continued during the New Deal years because they embodied the spirit of the reconstruction that would be necessary to stimulate the economy. As many of the other New Deal institutions that followed, they represented the guiding hand of government in the economy, which had not been seen previously. Many of these developments came at the same time as unpublished drafts of John Maynard Keynes's *General Theory of Employment, Interest, and Money*, subsequently to be published in 1936, were circulating in the academic community. On the surface, Keynes's ideas appeared to fit well into the legislative pattern of the New Deal. Had Roosevelt used Keynes's ideas as inspiration for his New Deal legislation?

Despite the close timing, the answer appears to have been no, at least in terms of immediate or direct influence. Roosevelt and Keynes had never met prior to this time and when they finally did, the outcome was less than satisfying for both parties. After their first meeting in May 1934, Roosevelt wrote to Felix Frankfurter that "I had a grand talk with Keynes and liked him immensely" but later remarked that Keynes had "left a whole rigamarole of figures. He must be a mathematician rather than a political economist." For his part, Keynes was also less than awed by Roosevelt. He said, with some regret, that he "supposed the President was more literate, economically speaking."[3] While Keynes may not have been the politician that Roosevelt had anticipated and Roosevelt not the economist Keynes had hoped for, it is unlikely that Keynes was unknown to Roosevelt's advisers, many of whom were former academics. But it does tend to destroy the direct personal link between them that would have suggested that one "master architect" was at work restructuring the American ideal.

Defining the American dream in twentieth-century financial terms remains a thorny problem. Simply attributing it to an Alger-like notion of hard work and good fortune is as vague as attributing the rise of northern Europe several centuries before to Max Weber's idea of a Protestant ethic. No one can doubt that the respective ideas played a role in developing industrialized capitalist democracies, but to leave institutional developments at their doorstep paints an incomplete picture. When the hand of the federal government is seen to influence U.S. financial markets and institutions, it usually does so for two reasons. The first is ideological: market mechanisms or practices, left to their own devices, tend to threaten the basic competitive principle on which the free-market economy is based. The second reason is also ideological and intrinsically practical. If established financial practice does not generally provide the greatest good for the greatest number, the entire structure is at risk—a potential liability no government would dare assume. The one-term presidency of Herbert Hoover remains the best example of this sort of liability.

The history of both the private markets and the public agencies during the post-Depression years gives ample evidence of the fact that many of the institutions that characterize U.S. finance were developed as a result of necessity rather than long-term planning. Modern commercial banking emerged from its original, wholesale nature in response to the changing needs of an increasingly consumer-oriented society. After the mid–1920s, banks that once loaned money primarily to commerce and industry found themselves in competition with investment banking houses eager to help companies raise capital in the markets. As a result banks began to seek new customers by expanding into the retail sector, previously the domain of credit companies and private lenders. After the investment banking industry became regulated following the crash, commercial banks were again able to fill a vacuum created by economic conditions and resume financing industry through new products created in the late 1930s. This cycle was repeated many times over the next 50 years.

Similar development occurred in the government-assisted agency market after the founding of the original farm credit agencies. Originally conceived as agencies to stimulate specific sectors of the economy and thereby avoid outright government intervention, their general models were later applied to the residential mortgage sector, higher-education loans, farm mortgages, and the thrift industry. While many of the actual agency functions became extremely complicated, the basic idea was simple. Government-assisted agencies were designed to intermediate between the private market for individual loans, of whatever nature, and the credit markets in order to ensure an even flow of credit to consumers regardless of economic or interest rate conditions. The investment community first eyed these agencies with some skepticism, but as time wore on their functions and the investment products created by them won acceptance, especially since most of them bore a form of government guarantee. It would be difficult to think of the modern residential mortgage market existing without the presence of the Federal National Mortgage Association or the Government National Mortgage Association.

Although it is traditional to think of the U.S. financial community in purely private terms, the development of investment banking, commercial banking, and the many products they have introduced over the years owes much more to political economy than even bankers would like to admit. Many standard financial concepts and products such as the prime rate, term loan, adjustable rate mortgage, and junk bond, to name but a few, came into existence only after legislation was passed allowing the concepts to become reality. What was previously a sparkle in their developers' eyes saw the light of day only when the legislative environment became favorable. In some cases, the initial euphoria accompanying them led to further problems as they became abused. When critical situations arose, legislation often came to the rescue to stabilize the financial environment.

But financial innovations cannot be understood as responses to legislation alone. Many financial products have histories longer than the period discussed here. Options for shares, financial futures, and variable, or adjustable rate, bonds have existed for years in concept. And before the 1970s, small markets as such did exist for them. But after the tumultuous financial upheaval of the 1970s, they became more integrated into mainstream financial practice. While legislation allowed many of these new markets to flourish, the products and concepts they employed had some proven track record in a previous life, whether in the United States or abroad.

U.S. financial markets and institutions have evolved in both regulated and relatively unregulated climates. While different sorts of markets and institutions have differing histories, the one common aspect they all share is a remarkable adherence to what has become known as the American dream. But as with all social and economic dreams, it should not be assumed that the assistance provided, or the wealth created, has been shared by all or that the financial functions have always performed admirably. As will be seen in the following chapters, mortgage assistance agencies and the farm credit institutions undeniably have facilitated mortgage lending between lending institution and borrower, but the latter still has to be able to afford that mortgage in the first place. And federal housing policy often bears the brunt of criticism for not providing enough housing for low-income groups or the elderly. It becomes apparent from the history of financial institutions and markets that they are the results of government policy but not its instruments. Accusing federal agencies or the financial markets and banking institutions of not providing the American dream to all on an equal basis is similar to executing the messenger for bad news. The history of the markets and their institutions remains the history of the messenger. While they contribute to policy in many cases, at the end of the day they do not create it.

During his term in office, Jimmy Carter perhaps came closest to giving the vision a more tangible policy orientation than any other U.S. President by declaring "war" on rising energy prices and dependence on foreign oil imports. He declared his energy program the "moral equivalent of war," borrowing the term from William James, whose essay of a similar title was published in 1910. If the country could divert its considerable power to a peaceful solution to the energy crisis in the same way as it had done previously in military matters, the energy problem could be defeated in a manner satisfactory to all. While the term was somewhat new, at least in political circles, it was not new in spirit. Franklin Roosevelt had done the same with the New Deal and Lyndon Johnson had embodied the notion in his Great Society programs.

William James would not have foreseen the impact his thoughts would have later in the twentieth century, especially when the moral equivalent had to be applied to economic institutions in order to achieve a higher end. He originally wrote: "I have no serious doubts that the ordinary prides and shames of social man . . . are capable of organizing such a moral equivalent. . . . It is but a question of time, of skillful propagandism, and of opinion-making men seizing historic opportunities."[4] As U.S history subsequently proved, there was indeed no shortage of politicians willing to seize the opportunity to rectify economic and financial problems. The methods chosen sometimes appeared haphazard but the basic ideal was maintained nevertheless: property, wealth, and savings would have to be preserved.

Such notions take the basic, hard-working vision of the nineteenth and early twentieth centuries one step higher onto another plane. At that level, it is better left to politics, rather than the more mundane workings of the markets to further define and protect the American dream. While no particular interpretation of recent U.S. history may be able to show adherence to the American dream in a satisfactory manner, the idea nevertheless provides a common ideological glue by which so many disparate financial practices have been brought together through one simple vision.

The role of the financial markets in facilitating the American dream coincides with the development of the government agencies that are twentieth-century creations. Thus, the history contained here begins in 1920, after the close of World War I. As the United States became more aware of the considerable power it could exert in international affairs, it also became aware, although slowly, that it could exert the same power at home in times of crisis. Financial history exhibits the same sort of crises that political and social history has displayed over the last 70 years. The manner in which the financial system and its regulators responded begins with the developments leading up to the crash of 1929.

NOTES

1. Alexis de Tocqueville, *Democracy in America*, vol. 1, translated by Henry Reeve (New York: Alfred Knopf, 1945), p. 254.

2. James Fenimore Cooper, *The American Democrat*, edited by George Dekker and L. Johnston (Baltimore: Penguin Books, 1969), p. 189.

3. Kenneth S. Davis, *FDR: The New Deal Years, 1933–1937* (New York: Random House, 1986), p. 320.

4. William James, *The Moral Equivalent of War and other Essays*, edited by John Roth (New York: Harper & Row, 1971), p. 14.

VISIONARY
CAPITALISM

1

Banking before and after the Crash

The development of the banking system in the United States in the twentieth century has been a long and often convoluted process. Since the turn of the century, events in the financial markets and numerous acts of Congress have created structural and functional changes designed either by intent or necessity, thereby giving the U.S. financial system a unique flavor. American banking has undergone its own evolution of a separation of financial powers that has divorced commercial banking, mortgage or thrift banking, and investment banking and helped create separate industries that nevertheless operate under the general rubric of banking. All of the historical changes have not actually expanded the universe of the banking industry itself but have created many more constellations within that universe that were not envisaged or apparent during the earlier part of the century.

The focus of twentieth-century banking developments rests solely on the activities of commercial banks in the earlier part of the century and continues up to the events that led to the stock market panic of 1929 and the ensuing banking legislation of the early 1930s. Those familiar with current banking developments and terminology will find that many of the practices of commercial banks during that period bear a remarkable resemblance to events occurring during the latter quarter of the century, perhaps testimony to the fact that the universe has not expanded but only come around full circle. This does not imply that earlier banking history will necessarily repeat itself: safety net legislation has sought to prevent that from happening, at least on a simple scale. But it does help underscore a point that is sometimes missing from technical or historical analyses of financial institutions. Over the years,

U.S. banking has contributed toward the same general goal as that of the earlier banking acts and New Deal legislation: in order to survive they were forced to participate in what has become known as the American dream. Legislatively and functionally, the commercial banks were obligated to limit their practices in the name of consumer or savers' protection. Rightly or wrongly, there were limited over time in the risks that they could take with depositors' funds to ensure that unforeseen financial developments did not destroy savings and forestall economic development at the same time.

On the face of it, commercial banks have always practiced their own particular form of banking, which has not changed much over time. In the twentieth century, they have accepted deposits and made loans, seeking to prudently match the aggregate maturity of their liabilities with those of their assets. Generally, this meant that loans made were usually of a short-term nature, in keeping with the short-term nature of their deposit bases. Unlike modern commercial banking, most of the loans made in the earlier part of the century were of a corporate or commercial nature; hence the name "commercial bank." But during World War I, these activities began to change and the assets booked became longer while the deposits remained short-term. This practice, often conducted through affiliate companies, changed the nature of commercial banking until the legislative flurry of the early 1930s. After that time, commercial banking was severely restricted and many new financial institutions developed, often prompted by legislation, that aided in the intermediation process if not directly competing with the banks themselves. Commercial banking did not change substantially after these events but returned to its original practices and began to seek new avenues of profit in the new regulatory environment.

A major difference between commercial banks operating in the earlier part of the century and those operating after World War II was retail, or consumer, business. Prior to the Depression, commercial banks served mainly commerce or industry by providing short-term loans for working capital purposes. The emphasis on consumer banking, making loans to individuals, did not play a major role in their overall profitability. Consumers' sources of credit were provided by merchants and credit unions rather than banks. Corporate loans were considered more secure because they tended to be self-liquidating, representing higher-rated credit risks than individuals.

This short-term emphasis could be traced back to the National Banking Act of 1864. That legislation sought to provide safety of depositors' funds by ensuring that banks kept their assets short term, in line with their short-term liabilities. At the same time, they were also restricted from operating in the securities markets either as underwriters or distributors of corporate securities. The vicissitudes of the marketplace were deemed too volatile for banks to be exposed to assets whose values could change suddenly. But during the period following the establishment of the Federal Reserve System in 1912, nevertheless, commercial banks entered the securities business.

Involvement in the underwriting and selling of corporate securities can be traced to the acquisition of a Wall Street investment banking house, N. W. Halsey & Company, by the New York-based National City Bank in 1916. This venture had a twofold purpose. First, it introduced National City to the increasingly profitable business of investment banking, which had long been the preserve of private investment banking institutions. Second, it also helped the bank extend itself to the retail sector by offering new issues of securities to the investing public, enabling it to become more oriented to the middle class rather than simply to the rich of the northeast part of the country. This new strategy of National City proved highly successful. Within ten years, it had become the largest distributor of securities to the public in the world.[1]

How the bank was able to complete such an acquisition in the face of the National Banking Act of 1864 is in itself a study in corporate organization and the exploitation of loopholes in the 1864 legislation. The actual purchase of Halsey was accomplished by the National City Company, an affiliate of the National City Bank. In general, security affiliates were state-chartered institutions, owned by the shareholders of the national banks, organized solely to circumvent the nineteenth-century legislation. The banks themselves could then lend money to those affiliates in order for them to engage in whatever sorts of business they deemed profitable.[2]

The term *securities business* used here refers to the underwriting and distribution of corporate bonds, not common stocks. During the period leading up to 1916, banks were most anxious to enter the corporate bond business as underwriters and sellers. They were already in a position to lend money to customers for the purchase of securities and this process was not necessarily risky as long as the value of the collateral, or securities themselves, was in excess of the loan required to finance them. And they were also active in the underwriting of U.S. government bonds as well as municipal bonds. The reason for the expansion into underwriting in the corporate bond realm had to do with the decline of short-term corporate loans as assets on banks' balance sheets.

After 1920, the amount of commercial loans as a percentage of total earning assets on the balance sheets of commercial banks began to decline. Loans declined from around 58 percent of earning assets to about 20 percent in 1936.[3] The increase in stock market activity and corporate securities led banks to concentrate more of their activities in the marketplace. The composition of the investing public and its activities in the securities markets bear witness to this trend. As the United States emerged from World War I as a creditor, rather than debtor, nation, activity in the securities markets increased with commercial banks integrally involved in the process.

In the decade prior to the stock market crash of 1929, activities in all sectors of the securities markets proceeded at an unprecedented pace. In 1925, the market value of New York Stock Exchange common stocks was some $27 billion. By 1929, the value had increased to almost $90 billion.[4] Equally important was the number of Americans holding securities investments. Prior to the war, an estimated 500,000 to 2 million individuals held some form of corporate equity investment. By 1929, the number had increased dramatically to between 10 and 20 million. Investors were paying for these shares with borrowed funds, or margin money. The common downpayment was between 10 and 25 percent, the rest being financed with loans from brokers. As one partner of a New York brokerage firm put it, "the public . . . were determined that every piece of paper should be worth tomorrow twice what it was today."[5]

The public's taste for common stock was not ill-founded. According to one estimate, in 1928 200 corporations controlled nearly half of the corporate wealth in the country.[6] Shares in these companies became the quickest way to make money, not to mention the scores of other new companies being founded and listed on the stock exchange every year. But investing in common stock was not necessarily an activity for the average working man. In 1922, 24 percent of the total national income was held by only 5 percent of the population; by 1929 it was held by some 26 percent. At the same time, the average hourly wage in 1922 was 48 cents per hour for a 44-hour working week. Seven years later, the hourly rate had jumped to 56 cents per hour for the same amount of time.[7] While the numbers appear somewhat meager by contemporary standards, they did nevertheless represent an improvement in the standard of living and compensation because consumer and wholesale prices remained at 1922 levels for most of the decade. However, it was the unprecedented increase in stock prices created by the expanding middle class that would eventually create the panic of 1929 and the ensuing banking crisis of the early 1930s.

While the rapid appreciation in share prices was accompanied by a general increase in the wealth of the average citizen, more demands for money were also felt for housing and consumer purchases as well. During the 1920s, the population grew by some 15 percent. Consequently, those items representing the latest in technology grew in popularity. For instance, in 1922, only 60,000 households had radios; by 1929, over ten million homes did. The same growth was found in telecommunications. In 1922, about 35 percent of U.S. households had telephones; this rose to 42 percent in 1929. The use of the phone also increased. In 1922, the Bell System logged about 37,000 phone calls. That number rose to over 61,000 calls by 1929. While the telephone recorded less dramatic growth than the radio, its use far outstripped installations. What the statistics cannot provide is the number of calls placed by investors to their brokers. But from the amount of securities transactions that took place over the intervening years, it is probably safe to say that both the telephone and the radio played no small part in engendering securities speculations.[8]

Until the 1920s, commercial bank assets were mostly found in commercial loans, U.S. government securities, real estate loans, and later in securities loans. Loans to individuals, or consumer loans, were not popular although the banks did make a concerted effort in the 1920s to lure more small retail depositors. Originally, retail banking meant lending to wealthy middle-class individuals and small merchants. Unsecured consumer loans were rare; when banks did offer them, more than one co-signer was required.[9] It was not until the banking crisis of 1933 and the intervention of a newly formed government agency that banks indirectly began to see increased profitability in lending to non-business retail clients.

In the ten-year period after the war, the number of banks in the country began to decline as a result of the economic crisis of 1920–21. Small banks especially were absorbed by larger ones and a general consolidation of the industry took place. Many of the small banks that either failed or merged were in the agricultural sector, a trend that was precipitated by the agricultural crisis of the same period. More will be said concerning this in Chapter 5.

Regrettably, the banks chose the road of lending to the small customer, which would prove to be the most risky. The margin money provided, fuelling customer purchases of stocks and bonds, was termed "call money." Technically, it meant that the amount of the loan could be called by the bank if the customer fell behind in his payments. In securities terms, this meant it would only be called if the market value of the collateral itself declined, eroding the equity portion of the investment. As securities prices began to rise, especially between 1922 and 1929, margin calls in general were not a problem to the investor since the market index rose threefold. But after October 1929, as prices began to plummet, calls became a very real problem since the market as a whole lost almost 80 percent of its value by 1932.

During this time, however, banks were expanding into other areas in order to enhance their profitability. During the same period, they were also expanding their base of operations by creating new branches. Under both the National Bank Consolidation Act of 1918 and the McFadden Act of 1927, commercial banks began to establish branches within their home states and cities in order to reach a greater number of individuals than they had before. These branches legally differed from affiliates in that they were considered part of the parent, offering the same services as the bank itself. The sole reason for their creation was to deliver banking services to a greater number of customers than the parent office could physically offer from a single location. The era of domestic bank expansion had begun in earnest.

The McFadden Act limited this branching to national banks that desired to "establish and operate new branches within the limits of the city, town, or village in which said association is situated if such establishment and operation are at the time permitted to State banks by the law of the State in question."[10] National banking associations were still limited to the authority of the state in which they were located. But another provision of the act (Section 7) allowed banks to expand their branches if they merged with another national or state banking association. All of the branches of the merged institution could be retained by the acquirer, thus allowing the expansion of the branch system by consolidation.

Expansion of banks across state lines was another matter. The National Banking Act of 1864 created the dual system of national and state banks and required all associations seeking a federal charter to apply to the Comptroller of the Currency. The original intent of the federal chartering system was to force state banks to refrain from issuing their own bank notes that were in many cases not interchangeable with each other, thus creating inefficiency in the national monetary system. In order to force banks to refrain from note issuing, Congress levied a stiff tax against such notes, eliminating some of their profits from loan-making. However, banks were still subject to state banking regulations even if they sought national charters, and most of the states prohibited ownership of their indigenous banks by out-of-state banking organizations. The McFadden Act formally prohibited banks from crossing state lines by expressly forbidding cross-border branching. This regulation, however, did not apply to branches established in foreign countries.[11]

Affiliate operations were not affected by much of this legislation since these spin-off operations were not branches in the literal sense. Their organizational structures and the loopholes that they used provided banks with great flexibility in offering ancillary banking services. The thrust into the securities business and bank expansion into the retail sector in general gave birth to a term that reappeared in the contemporary era of bank expansion after the 1980 passing of the Depository Institutions Deregulation and Monetary Control Act—the emergence of the "department store" bank, or "financial supermarket." This trend signaled a decided shift away from banking purely for businesses and illustrated banks' willingness to pursue the smaller saver/borrower business as a distinct profit center in addition to the more traditionally established lines of business. In this respect, banks were responding to a newly emerging trend: as the American middle class grew in size and importance, banks actively sought to provide it with enhanced services in more than one realm.

Securities affiliates were established by many national associations as state-chartered institutions. The stock of the affiliate was held by trustees who were also officers of the parent institution. Any profits made by the affiliate were paid to the parent, which distributed an agreed payout to shareholders. While this sort of arrangement was not unusual, the matter of funding the affiliate operations was more troublesome and would provide the undoing of many banks after the market crash of 1929. The parent institutions often funded the affiliates through loans that originally were not to exceed 10 percent of capital and surplus of the bank itself. A potential problem arose as banks created many affiliates and loaned the maximum to each.[12] In this manner, banks extended loans to themselves that were used to fund security market operations.

Affiliate operations and interlocking directorships were not new to banks only after National City's acquisition of Halsey in 1916. In 1913, the Pujo Committee investigating the creation of the Federal Reserve System heard testimony from George Baker, chairman of the board of First National Bank of New York, confirming that First National created affiliates in order to hold stock in other commercial banking institutions.[13] For example, as early as 1908 one of the major holdings of First National, through the First Security Company, was over 50 percent of the common stock of the Chase National Bank as well as substantial holdings in other New York and regional banks.

Perhaps the most flagrant example of the abuses of holding companies, affiliates, and interlocking directorships was to be found in the practices of Bernard Marcus and Saul Singer, both of whom controlled the Bank of the United States, located in New York City. A state-chartered bank, the Bank of the United States had 27 affiliates ranging from real estate and insurance to safe deposit companies. It had more than 400,000 depositors and almost $300 million worth of deposits when it was finally closed in 1930. The two senior officials used the affiliates to purchase stock in the parent bank, causing its market price to rise and inducing speculators to raise the price even further. They then attempted to sell stock they themselves had purchased at a profit in 1929, prior to the market rout. When further purchasers were not forthcoming they sold the stock back to the affiliates, lending them money to fund the purchases. After the October price fall, the investment had declined in value and they also lost, having loaned themselves the margin money. This, along with other abuses, was cited frequently in the congressional hearings that followed the market collapse and eventually led to the securities and banking regulations of 1933–34.

Despite circumventing banking laws and flying in the face of congressional committees, banks were obviously able to proceed with their inroads into the bond business without much official intervention. Prior to the market crash, they were underwriters of many different types of bonds, from Treasury and municipal obligations to corporate bonds and issues of foreign governments. During the 1920s, a new trend emerged as U.S. corporations began to shift the emphasis and nature of their own borrowings. With the relative stability and prosperity that followed the war, many companies began to refund their debt by converting short-term loans and facilities into longer-term bond borrowings to ensure a fixed cost of funds for the long term. This shift would naturally deprive banks of their traditional business of extending short-term loans unless they were willing and able to participate in this new emphasis on bond borrowing. Since they had already had years of experience in underwriting and selling Treasury and municipal securities, the penetration into the corporate sector was not new to them. But the new corporate emphasis, when coupled with the previous experience, especially in the foreign bond sector, did present one particular problem that would be addressed formally in the Securities Act of 1933. Since disclosure was not uniform, many prospectuses accompanying new issues contained only bare-bones information that often did not fully inform the investor of the various credit risks attached to some borrowers. Banks themselves, through their own research departments, often provided investors with their own analysis of the creditworthiness of the underwritings. This practice would come under attack with the banking and securities acts of 1933. In such a manner, banks were also led into the underwriting and selling of corporate equities. In their rush to expand, they would commit oversights that drew much official criticism before the securities business was eventually divorced from commercial banking.

PRE-CRASH ACTIVITIES IN THE EQUITY MARKET

The major difference between bond and equity investment is the matter of investor risk. Equities, according to modern portfolio analysis, are considered more risky investments than bonds on two counts. First, in the event of liquidation of a company bondholders, as creditors, are compensated before equity holders. Second, bonds are considered more stable in market terms and will only vacillate in price given a change in the interest rate environment. The same general view held in the period preceding the market crash of 1929. The only way that banks could have entered the equity business in any meaningful manner was by proclaiming that the equity of certain companies was a safe investment for the investor to hold—as safe in some cases as holding bonds.

In 1927, both the optimism of some bankers and the legal environment permitted affiliate companies to begin underwriting common stocks. Charles Mitchell, who assumed the presidency of National City in 1921, announced that security salesmen of the bank's affiliates would begin offering common stocks to the investing public. One of his basic assumptions was that certain stocks could be classified as sound investments and that the country's prosperity rested on solid foundations.[14] But his optimism was not entirely self-centered. By that date, the public was feverishly buying stock and this new service could be viewed merely as acquiescence to public demand.

The McFadden Act of 1927 and pronouncements of the Comptroller of the Currency also aided in the process to no small degree. The act legally enabled national banks to engage in the investment banking business, but only for bonds. It also officially recognized the security affiliates and gave the Comptroller the power to rule on the types of securities the affiliates could underwrite. The affiliates were given free rein to engage in equity business by the Comptroller. Beginning in 1927, the banks found themselves in both the bond and equity business.

The underwriting function, when coupled with the distribution function, gave commercial banks a strong profit motive for underwriting equities. As with bonds, the originator of an underwriting deal, or lead manager, was able to maximize its profits by reaping a larger fee than simply an underwriter or seller alone because it participated in the full underwriting/selling fee. Ordinary underwriters or members of the selling group took a smaller portion of the total fee because of their less risky position.

Underwriters of securities were exposed to any market movements while the security remained unsold. This risk exposure was limited not only to the amount of fees built into the discount the bank paid for the securities. If the market price of the security fell 5 percent while it was still in underwriting and the underwriting fees were 3 percent, the bank would stand to lose all of its profit margin plus 2 percent in addition if the securities were sold at that lower price. While the underwriting business was potentially profitable, it did nevertheless add an element of market risk to banks' more traditional risks.

During most of the 1920s, most of the banks' activities remained in underwriting bonds rather than common stocks. National City was the leader; in the period 1921–29, it participated in or originated one-fifth of all bonds issued in the country as well as about one-fifth of all U.S. corporate bond issues.[15] While the inroads made by the larger, money center banks seemed substantial there are strong arguments for claiming that this did not substantially increase their risks. Prior to World War I, much capital was provided to companies by banks in the form of term loans rather than bonds. Under those circumstances, the asset remained on the books of the bank and could not be sold to investors. Thus, the new form of business could not be said to be entirely alien to banks since they did have close relationships with these borrowers in the past, although in a different manner of lending.

In market terms, the debt/equity ratios of U.S. companies prior to and immediately following the stock market crash were relatively conservative. For instance, in the period 1927–30 total sources of funds to U.S. companies was some $7.3 billion. Of this amount, $2.4 billion was raised through debt offerings, $2.1 billion through common and preferred offerings, and the remaining $2.8 billion from retained earnings.[16] Corporate bond yields were also relatively low in the two years prior to the crash. Long-term (ten-year) prime corporate yields were approximately 4.20 percent in both years, a decline of almost 1 percent since the beginning of the decade.[17] After the market collapse, yields moved even lower, establishing a downward trend that lasted until the close of World War II.

One of the compelling factors banks cited as a chief reason for expanding into both the corporate bond market and the equity market was interest in all sorts of corporate securities by their customers. Speculation in equities and margin trading became widespread prior to October 1929, and as a result, the market capitalization of all securities listed on the New York Stock

Exchange reached an historic high. The Exchange itself estimates the total market value to have reached $90 billion by 1929.[18]

While consumer demand may have been the engine that fueled the stock market rise, it was the commercial banks that provided the liquidity in the form of margin loans so that investor buying fever could be satiated. As U.S. industry began to rely more on the capital markets for financing and less on term loans from banks, capital market activity increased, with more securities being offered to the public as a result. And since the banks had spent most of the 1920s reorienting their businesses toward the consumer sector, they were doubling their exposure to the process by underwriting these securities and then lending money to investors to purchase them.

During the period 1922–28, loans on securities by banks increased from 18 percent of total loans made at the beginning of the period to about 28 percent prior to the market crash. At the same time, total loans and investments of banks increased by 40 percent, or $15 billion.[19] Deposits increased at the same time and the reserve balances of Federal Reserve member banks also increased. By 1928, a policy of firmer credit by the Federal Reserve had resulted in a slowing of bank credit but did not halt the speculation in the securities markets as many corporations, or nonbank lenders, continued to make loans to brokers in order to continue market activities.

The stockmarket speculation of the period was aided in no small part by the easing of interest rates and a general level of postwar prosperity not witnessed before. Central to the market crash and the reasons that banks became so integrally involved was the behavior of individual savers and speculators whose attitudes toward the accumulation of wealth had changed in the period following the war. It was in this period that the American dream became more defined and placed severe strain on the institutional framework of U.S. banking and the securities markets.

THE DEVELOPMENT OF THE AMERICAN DREAM

The vision of the United States as the land of opportunity can be found in the investment and expenditure patterns of the population during the postwar years, from 1920 until the stock market crash nine years later. Over that period, explosive growth was found in several sectors of the economy, which can be traced to the desire on the part of the populace to further their standard of living, expand educational opportunities, and accumulate private wealth.

The distribution of income in the United States in this period was distinctly skewed in favor of the wealthier classes, as mentioned earlier. Between 1922 and 1929 5 percent of the total population received about 14 percent of the total income, a percentage that would not begin to fall substantially until after World War II.[20] It was this group that the banks began actively to court with their emphasis on retail banking after the first war ended. The rest of the population earned more modestly, although their wages did continue to rise. In 1922, the average wage of employees in all sectors was $1,067, rising to $1,405 by 1929.

On the face of it, the average compensation appears to have progressed at a conservative rate, although the rise in hourly rates increased at a total rate of 25 percent over the period. However, one compensating factor was the inflation rate. Over this period, the wholesale price index dropped by about 1 percent while the consumer price index gained only slightly over 1 percent. Considering that prices remained stable for such a long period, the modest gain in wages nevertheless helped trigger a consumer boom.

By 1929, the population stood at about 61 million persons, a gain of some 8 million over the 1920 census. This postwar boom in the population was accompanied by a greater dissemination of news, financial and otherwise, than was previously the case. In addition to the rise in the number of households owning radios, the number of broadcasters also increased dramatically. In 1922, only thirty AM radio stations were operating in the country and manufacturers produced 100,000 sets. By 1929, over 600 stations were operating and the industry produced almost four and a half million sets annually.

Higher education also witnessed dramatic growth within this period. Between 1920 and 1930, the number of degrees awarded by U.S. colleges and universities almost tripled, with 53,516 degrees granted in 1920 as compared with 139,752 in 1930. This growth represented the highest rate in the history of U.S. higher education until that time. While the financing of tertiary education remained mostly a private matter until after World War II when the government began its subsidized student loan programs, education quickly became equated with the general notion of prosperity and advancement.

Another area that underwent rapid growth was residential housing and mortgage debt. This one sector, perhaps more than any other, represented the epitomy of the American dream. Total new housing starts stood at 247,000 in 1920 and peaked at 937,000 units in 1925 before slipping back to 753,000 in 1928. After the crash, the number of units dwindled and reached a postwar low in 1933 of only 93,000 units. The amount of residential nonfarm mortgage debt also increased, from $9.35 billion in 1920 to $29.5 billion in 1929. Perhaps the most fundamental part of the American dream, housing was the one tangible asset that Americans accumulated at the fastest growth rate during this prosperous decade.

Consumer debt for items other than housing also rose at a brisk rate although the structure of that debt was somewhat different from that in the latter part of the century. After the economic slowdown of 1920–21, consumer debt stood at $3 billion in 1922, rising to $7.1 billion in 1929. As will be seen in Chapter 4, much of this credit was supplied by merchants and small savings institutions rather than commercial banks per se. It was not until the government partially guaranteed some forms of consumer loans in the early and mid–1930s that commercial banks began turning their attention to the nonmerchant class of consumers. The largest increase in debt during this period, other than for home purchases, was used for the purchase of securities.

New York Stock Exchange (NYSE) volume and performance figures for the decade amply illustrate the public penchant for securities. In 1920, the Exchange witnessed a turnover of some 227 million shares. By 1929, that figure had risen to a record 1.13 billion, a figure that would not be seen again until 1963. Bond volume actually recorded a decline, falling from a nominal $3.9 billion in 1920 to slightly under $3 billion by 1929. Much of this decline can be attributed to the fall in popularity of new U.S. Treasury bonds offered while corporate bonds, municipals, and foreign bonds all recorded strong gains. Corporate and foreign issues yielded about three-quarters of 1 percent to 1 percent higher than comparable maturities of Treasury bonds and this spread proved alluring to investors. It should be noted that this sort of spread still prevailed in the 1980s; however, as nominal coupon rates were much lower in the 1920s, they represented a much greater yield advantage to investors.

Market performance, as measured by the Standard & Poor's index of common stocks (using 1941–43 as a base of 10), jumped from 8.4 in 1922 to slightly over 26 by 1929. After the market setback in October of that year, the index began to slide and touched 6.9 in 1933 before beginning to recover thereafter. However, it was not until 1954 that the index was able to match its showing in 1929, and much of this speculative buying was financed by margin buying. Broker loans totalled $1.8 billion in 1922, half of which was provided by New York City commercial banks. The balance was provided by other commercial banks and nonbank lenders. By 1928, the total figure had reached $6.4 billion, of which only one-quarter was provided by New York City banks and less than 14 percent by outside banks. More than half, or $3.9 billion, was provided by nonbank lenders, including corporations that entered the market as eager lenders seeking a return on their funds as competitors of commercial banking institutions.

Prior to the banking and securities acts that were to follow several years later, margin loans were made at the discretion of the broker involved in the transaction. It was not until 1934 that the Federal Reserve uniformly imposed its own margin requirements on the investment community. When first imposed, margin requirements were a standard 65 percent of the market value of the security involved. Before the market fall, much smaller margin requirements were in force and it was possible for an investor to buy or sell short a common stock for as little as 10 percent of the current market value. When the crash occurred, margin calls were not met in many cases and brokers were forced to liquidate the securities involved in order to recoup some of the losses incurred by customers unable to find the necessary liquidity. The U.S. financial markets had witnessed the first results of the high degree of personal leverage on the part of investors.

In the quest for greater accumulation of wealth and a higher standard of living, both the public and the commercial banks helped set the stage for the Depression that was to follow the market crash. However, even the bleak prospects caused by the Depression would not alter the American dream. This particular vision needed an architect if it was to continue to be the stimulus for increasing industrialization and productivity. Part and parcel of the design of this new superstructure would be institutional safeguards against both the causes of the market crash and the subsequent deleterious effects on the banking system. Financial institutions would remain the cornerstone of the new financial order but would not be allowed to penetrate and dominate the financial markets as they had in the past.

The new structure that emerged over the next decade sought to employ the markets to provide assistance to the institutions that would in turn continue to help finance both commercial and retail needs. A "wall of separation" was deemed necessary as the preliminary part of this superstructure in order to divide underwriters and sellers of securities from the commercial banks, which were normally expected to act in a prudent fiduciary manner. The market crash paved the way for the congressional reaction that was to substantially alter the face of the U.S. financial system. Each of the abuses committed by banks in the prior decade on behalf of investors and speculators would be addressed by legislation designed to construct a safety net under the financial system.

The crisis of the 1920s was laid at the door of the banks because they had been able to exploit loopholes in a patchwork of legislation in order to expand their asset and profit bases. The public outcry that followed was largely based on reports in the news media revealing interlocking directorships, bank loans to directors, and the extensive interbank holdings of holding companies. The American dream had been seriously fractured in that immeasurable savings had been lost and the prosperity of the postwar years had all but evaporated. The immediate response would be new legislation that was radically different from anything then experienced in U.S. history.

THE NEED FOR THE WALL

In the wake of the stock market carsh, all of the activities of commercial banks in the securities markets came under intense scrutiny by Congress. Many of the activities originally questioned by the Pujo Committee of 1913 again became topics of debate because it became painfully obvious that the U.S. financial system had been damaged by the activities of banks, corporations, and individuals in search of profit in the markets with the use of borrowed or imprudently loaned money. But it was not only investors and speculators who had lost money in the market debacle. Because of the loans made by commercial banks to the market, either directly or indirectly, massive banking failures occurred, forcing the closure of hundreds of institutions and destroying much of the savings accumulated during the previous decade by those who had never invested in a security.

The banking crisis of the 1930s underscored the fraility of the U.S. banking system. Although the most popular generalization concerning U.S. banking in the 1920s was that the country was "overbanked," the term itself is perhaps too nebulous to explain fully the rather peculiar nature of banking that led to the crisis. Commercial banking up until that time was highly balkanized; that is, it was conducted along relatively fragmented geographical lines. The prohibitions against interstate banking and bank expansion generally led to the creation of many small institutions that remained local in nature. At the same time, the widespread use of the holding company, created to hold more than one bank stock, laid the groundwork for a domino effect if one of the component institutions began to weaken or eventually failed. Meanwhile, the widespread use of interlocking directorships illustrated that directors of one institution were borrowing money from another in order to speculate in the equity market, in many cases bidding up the share price of one institution with money borrowed from another. When the system began to crash down around these abuses it became apparent that further controls were needed, both in the banking sector and in the financial markets, if public confidence was ever to be restored.

The legislative response came early in the decade with the passage of the banking and securities acts. Both types of legislation sought to prevent further abuses and provide a modicum of investor protection at the same time. By the time that both sets of laws were enacted it was already too late to prevent the financial crisis, but both attempted to restore the system to public confidence and pave the way for future economic growth despite previous structural inadequacies. However, one former problem would not be legislated away: the balkanization of the U.S. banking system would remain intact although many of the institutions that were swept away in the tidalwave of 1929–30 would not reappear. The new system emerged in a rationalized form, with more specific restraints on the banks and the markets, but the banking industry would still be severely limited by legal and geographical constraints.

The stock market's precipitous decline was not initially viewed as a crash per se but as more of a temporary setback. Although the market index declined by 19 percent between 1929 and 1930, it was between 1930 and 1931 that the full effects of heavy leverage by investors began to take its toll as the market declined another 35 percent. By 1932, it would again decline by almost 50 percent from its 1931 level and the Depression had set in. But the initial response in 1929 was still sanguine, if somewhat guarded.

The day after the market's initial drop, a *New York Times* headline proclaimed "Wall Street optimistic after stormy day; clerical work may force holiday tomorrow."[21] Even as the market continued to fall on subsequent trading days, much of the blame for investor panic was attributed to a backlog in both the tickertape and the back rooms of brokerage firms rather than as a fundamental loss of investor confidence in a highly inflated market. Even President Hoover proclaimed the system as fundamentally sound, although this claim was in keeping with his basic position that the fall in values was a loss of public confidence and that it was the business of government to rebuild it by consensus rather than direct political action. This faith in the role of the market economy was not misplaced; rather, it only helped to underscore the fact that the banking system and the markets had never witnessed such a precipitous drop in values and that no one was quite sure of how to rebuild the tottering system.

The market crash was difficult to measure simply by gauging the decline in the market averages or indices alone. The impact on individual stock values in some cases was extremely pronounced and extended into the early years of the 1930s. The two most active stocks on October 28 and 29, 1929, were General Motors (GM) and Cities Service. General Motors closed on October 29 at a price of $40 per share, down $14 ½ from its opening the day before. Cities Service closed at $22 ½ down $23 ¾ from its opening the day before. More important than the drop in market price was the decline in price/earnings (P/E) ratios. The automaker suffered a drop in P/E from 17 to 6 times earnings in 1929, while the oil company fell from a ratio of 69 to 20 times earnings. This slide continued into 1930 as well. The low P/E for GM in that year was 10, while Cities Service fell to nine times earnings. The commercial banks fared little better. National City Bank of New York registered a high P/E of 120 in 1929, falling to 37 after the crash. By 1932, as the nationwide banking crisis deepened, it dropped to 8, where it remained until 1933. Chase National dropped from 62 to 29 in 1929 and fell further to 5 by 1931, where it remained through 1932.[22]

The extraordinarily high price/earnings ratios of many listed stocks gave credence to the fact that the market had witnessed a phenomenal increase in value, whether on an earnings or absolute price basis. Price/earnings ratios of as high as 150 times were not uncommon for smaller listed companies; even some of the larger firms had ratios between 75 and 100 times. But it was the banking and financial industries that were the hardest hit by the fall in the market. As of September 1, 1929, the value of all stocks in the financial industry on the NYSE was slightly in excess of $2 billion. By July 1, 1932, the value of those institutions that survived had fallen to about $364 million.[23]

Equally troublesome were the prices of bonds that had been underwritten by the banks in the post–1920 period. Foreign bonds especially came under severe downward price pressure as it became apparent that many of these issues of foreign governments had little or no chance of meeting their interest or principal repayments in the current international economic climate. Issues of Bolivia, Peru, Poland, Uruguay, and Yugoslavia all underwent down-gradings by the rating agencies and suffered steep price declines, in many cases falling from around par to less than 20 percent of par. Other issues of northern European borrowers fared much better and sometimes even rose to a premium as yields for all issues tumbled in the marketplace. But it was the rapid decline of the Eastern European and Latin American issues that would play a large part in the enactment of the Securities Act of 1933 because both investors and analysts claimed that the banks originally underwriting these issues had not taken due diligence in fully disclosing the financial conditions in and of the countries involved at the time of original flotations.

The period from 1920 to the market crash would have been recorded as a decade of bank failures and suspensions even if the market crash had never occurred. Between 1921 and 1928, a total of 5,053 banks in the country suspended operations. But between 1929 and 1933, the toll the market crash took on the banks was even more staggering. In 1929, some 659 banks were suspended and the number of failures began to rise dramatically. By 1933, the annual toll had reached 4,000, bringing the five-year total to 9,755, or 14,808 since 1921.[24] During a period of relative prosperity the smaller banks especially had been weakened by the agricultural crisis of the earlier part of the decade as well as by the encroachments of national banks seeking to expand their branches, subsidiaries, and asset bases. Deposits at these sus-pended banks remained in the $100 million–$200 million range per annum until 1929, when the amount involved touched $1.69 billion. In 1930, the deposits amounted to $837 million, of which almost $300 million was attrib-uted to the closure of the Bank of the United States, the New York State-chartered bank operated by Marcus and Singer. But it was 1933 that wit-nessed the largest amount of total deposits suspended—$3.6 billion.[25]

The continuing banking crisis culminated in the banking holiday imposed by President Franklin Roosevelt shortly after he took office in 1933. The policies of Herbert Hoover had proved inadequate in dealing with the fail-ures. Although Hoover had formed many commissions and study groups to investigate the growing crisis and had made suggestions for universal Federal Reserve membership of commercial banks, he never introduced legislation or pressed for any fundamental changes in the banking structure. Although many of his recommendations did in fact recognize the extent and causes of the crisis, most of his ideas were unrealized when he left office in 1933.

Hoover's central theme was that the crisis was one of confidence and that a full public disclosure of the extent of the crisis would only lead to further panic and loss of confidence. However, the saving public had already dem-onstrated its loss of confidence in the banking system. Depositors of all sorts had begun to withdraw their money from commercial banks and the United States began to experience capital flight, or the export of gold. Obviously, the assumption was that money outside a bank was safer than money within one. Both the withdrawals and the hoarding presented serious problems for both the Federal Reserve and the Treasury and directly led to the passing of the President's Proclamation of March 1933 and the Emergency Bank Act of 1933, passed several days later. The Emergency Act empowered the President to declare a national bank "holiday" in order to prevent further hoarding and capital flight. The legislation was read and passed with great speed in Congress, with most of the terms dictated by the executive branch.

Declaring a bank holiday enabled the executive branch, through the Treasury and the Comptroller of the Currency, to prevent widespread withdrawals of funds from banks and the further exporting of gold. Banks were, however, able to conduct business for customers in order to maintain a basic day-to-day financial existence. The several proclamations that established the banking holidays were designed to accomplish two objectives: first, to restore solvency and close banks that did not meet minimum standards; and second, to prevent further panic. One important lesson was learned from the public's behavior during this period of crisis. While both national banks and state-chartered banks that were members of the Federal Reserve suffered withdrawals, postal savings deposits were actually increasing. Since President Taft initiated the postal savings system in 1910, the full faith and credit of the United States had been pledged to those types of deposits. Between 1931 and 1933, these deposits had increased from approximately $350 million to over $1 billion.[26] This public reaction would play an important role in helping to establish the Federal Deposit Insurance Corporation in the Banking Act of June 1933.

During the same period of the early Roosevelt administration, Congress was holding hearings on the causes of the stock market crash and the banking crisis. The Senate Banking Committee in particular interviewed various members of the financial community to gain a better picture of the machinations of financial institutions before and after the crash. This committee became known as the Pecora committee, named after its chief counsel, Ferdinand Pecora. One of the central witnesses before the committee was Charles Mitchell, president of National City Bank. The committee probed into Mitchell's personal finances as well as National City's banking behavior in the call money market in the period following the crash. As a result of his testimony, Mitchell was forced to step down as president at the urging of his board of directors and President Roosevelt himself. His testimony, as well as that of many others, helped to inflame public opinion against the bankers and the investment community and would lead directly to the radical proposals of the Banking Act of June, later in the year. Banking and bankers had slipped to perhaps a new low in public esteem. Even the chroniclers of Citibank's history admit that "National City touched the low point of its corporate existence" with Mitchell's resignation.[27]

In both his inaugural address and his proclamation the new President exhibited a direct grasp of the banking problems and, unlike Hoover, a stern determination to meet them head on. In his first "fireside chat," broadcast over the radio on March 12, 1933, Roosevelt addressed the public for the first time concerning his proclamation of the first banking holiday and the extension that immediately followed it. In part, he stated,

Remember that the essential accomplishment of the new legislation [Emergency Banking Act] is that it makes it possible for banks more readily to convert their assets into cash than was the case before. . . . This currency is not fiat currency. It is issued only on adequate security, and every good bank has an abundance of such security.[28]

This remark presaged the major legislation proposed by Senator Carter Glass that would be passed in Congress three months later. Converting assets into cash and adequate security would come to mean no more loans to security affiliates to engender stock market speculation—loans that, if called, may not be forthcoming because of the market's decline. All of the imprudent actions of the 1920s, leading to the market's precipitous fall, the banking crisis that ensued, and revelations of the Pecora committee, had set the stage for new legislation designed to keep commercial banks out of the securities business.

THE WALL APPEARS

During the early 1930s, Senator Carter Glass had been busy attempting to fashion legislation designed to prohibit abusive banking practices by restructuring the banking industry. However, proposals he made in the last months of the Hoover administration were not acted upon, as Hoover himself concentrated on short-term relief measures to deal with the banking crisis rather than undertake legislation designed to root out the cause of the problem. After Roosevelt took office in March 1933, Glass reintroduced legislation originally introduced in the previous congress to reorganize the U.S. banking industry. Within three months, compromises had been ironed out concerning some of the bill's provisions and the Glass-Steagall proposals became the Banking Act of 1933, universally known as the Glass-Steagall Act.

The new legislation had three focal points as its centerpiece and was aimed at restructuring the commercial banking system. The first was changes in the banking structure of the country, including the Federal Reserve System which had proved somewhat inadequate in handling the crisis. Second, the act provided for the creation of the Federal Deposit Insurance Corporation (FDIC), designed to insure deposits at commercial banks. Third was the separation of commercial banking and investment banking so that depositors' funds could no longer be loaned to stock market investors or used to finance securities underwritings. All three proposals originally met fierce opposition but the objections crumbled in the wake of widespread public discontent with bankers in general.

In the first area of the banking structure, the Banking Act made several changes in practices relating to bank branches and also strengthened provisions of the Federal Reserve Act. National banks were allowed to have branches on a state-wide or city-wide basis depending on their size (as measured by their capital), subject to the regulations of state banking authorities. The capital of newly established national banks was also raised from the previous standard and the officers of the banks were subject to removal from office if the Comptroller of the Currency or the Federal Reserve deemed that they were in violation of banking law or sound banking practices. Equally, banks could no longer make loans to their own executives, a measure designed to prevent further stock market speculation in bank stocks by directors.

This latter prohibition was reflective of the public mood against bank executives. Public opinion was solidly against bankers in general and that portion of the legislation met with almost no resistance at all. Several years after the passing of the act, public officials still berated bankers at all levels for their role in the crises of 1929 and the early 1930s. Perhaps the best known of them was William O. Douglas, one of the first members of the Securities Exchange Commission. He later became its chairman, and later still an associate justice of the Supreme Court. In a speech delivered at the University of Chicago in October 1936, Douglas attributed the chaos of the earlier part of the decade and the Depression to

financial termites . . . those who practice the art of predatory or high finance. They destroy the legitimate function of finance and become a common enemy of investors and business. . . . [T]hey have been present with such frequency that the importance of dealing with them directly and forthrightly cannot be denied.[29]

With such virulent metaphors in abundance it is not difficult to see why the Banking Act was passed so quickly. Those measures that it was not designed to deal with quickly found their expression and remedy in the two acts soon to follow.

The legislation also consolidated some of the powers and functions of the Federal Reserve. The twelve district Fed banks were no longer permitted to engage in open-market operations (the buying and selling of Treasury bills to affect the money supply) by themselves but now were to engage in these operations on a system-wide basis. The Fed was also given the power to limit the amount of interest paid on time deposits and eliminate the payment of interest paid on demand deposits. Banks were now put on a level playing field in an attempt to dissuade them from competing for funds by raising their deposit rates. This regulation would remain in effect until 1980, when Congress passed the Depository Institutions Deregulation and Monetary Control Act which effectively deregulated U.S. interest rates.

The Federal Deposit Insurance Corporation (FDIC) was also established by the Banking Act with two express purposes. First, it enabled the corporation to purchase, hold, and liquidate the assets of national banks that closed because of insolvency. Second, it insured the deposits of savers at those institutions. The FDIC was originally invested with capital of $450 million with which to pay insurance if the need arose. When the plan became effective after July 1, 1934, deposits of up to $10,000 were insured in this manner. Revenues of the FDIC were to be paid into the corporation by member banking institutions, which were to pay a premium so that the corporation had adequate funds. Originally, the premium paid was one-quarter of 1 percent of a bank's total deposits.

Of these two parts of the Banking Act, the creation of the FDIC was the more radical. The restructuring of the banking industry was not particularly new and can be viewed as a restatement of banking laws already on the books. But it was the third portion of the act that would have the most serious consequences for the commercial and investment banking communities since it was that portion that created the "wall of separation."

Banks were prohibited from holding stock of any other corporation, underwriting any issue of securities, or purchasing and selling corporate securities for their own accounts. The only exception to the prohibitions enabled banks to act as transfer agents for securities. The term "securities" as used in the original act requires some clarification. It was meant to include corporate securities only—shares or bonds. Obligations of the U.S. government and its various agencies that were already established at the time were exempt, as were municipal bonds. The activities of affiliate companies were also severely curtailed. Loans made to affiliates were to be secured by collateral in excess of 20 percent over the value of the loan itself. The old days of stock market abuse through securities affiliates were over, as was the once profitable business of underwriting corporate bonds (including foreign bonds) and stocks. Banks would have to revert to areas of business that fell within traditional accepted commercial banking practice.

Even with the passage of the Banking Act, legislation continued at a brisk pace to deal with other stock market matters that could not be legally addressed by banking legislation. The first issue concerned investor protection through adequate public disclosure of new securities issues. The second came shortly thereafter with the passage of legislation designed to regulate the financial markets themselves.

Investor protection against the lack of adequate public disclosure of the financial affairs of some new securities issuers had been a concern since the stock market crash, when some foreign bonds and many stocks fared poorly in the secondary market as their financial conditions became better known to the investing public. Prior to 1933, disclosure of a securities issuer's condition was left primarily to the states, some of which had "blue sky" laws dating back to the prewar years. However, if a state did not require a uniform vetting of a security seller's position, the investor was left at the mercy of the underwriting agent, whose obligation was no more than a moral one to inform the investor of its clients' financial health. In the case of many foreign bonds, especially those of some Latin American countries, underwriters' disclosure was scant at best and totally lacking at worst. Because of this lack of uniformity, the Securities Act of 1933 was passed to address the problem on a national level.

The provisions of this legislation were quite simple and stirred up opposition only among the Wall Street community. All new securities to be sold to the public were required to be filed, or registered, with the Federal Trade Commission. The purpose of the registration statement was to record the financial position of the seller so that its financial condition was known to the investing public. Each new issue also required a prospectus to accompany it, divulging the same information as the registration statement, so that potential buyers could read the information for themselves. There was a list of exempt securities that did not, and do not, require filing; the exempt list includes securties of the U.S. Treasury, agency securities, and municipals. Thus registration was limited to corporate stocks and bonds and bonds of foreign issuers, the same sort of eligibility found in the restrictions of the Glass-Steagall Act.

Initially, the process met resistance from the investment community, mostly because of the extra paperwork it created when a new security was issued. The Act imposed civil liabilities on directors of companies who knowingly filed false information in order to mislead the public and laid the onus for starting the litigation on the purchaser who felt that he had been misled. Criminal penalties were also included if a statement was deemed to be deliberately misleading or "materially untrue."

Although the Securities Act dealt mainly with problems affecting the issue of new securities, it also contained provisions designed to prevent fraudulent transactions in all securities, and was specifically designed to cover secondary market transactions as well. In this respect, misleading or fraudulent circulars distributed interstate in order to promote outstanding issues were also subject to the same sort of penalties. However, a year later Congress passed the Securities Exchange Act, creating the Securities and Exchange Commission, which would have ultimate jurisdiction in dealing with this latter provision as well as all security-related sales to the general public.

On June 6, 1934, the Securities Exchange Act was passed. As one of its first interpreters noted, "What has been heretofore evolution has become revolution."[30] This act, the most far-reaching piece of securities legislation ever produced in the country, developed controls over the trading of securities, the amount of margin credit that could be created in buying or selling securities, and the continual sale of new and secondary market securities to the investing public. In order to oversee these new regulations, it created the Securities and Exchange Commission (SEC) and invested it with power to regulate all aspects of the securities business except one—

the amount of credit created by margin trading. That area was left to the Federal Reserve Board since it entailed more of a banking/credit function than did securities trading itself.

The SEC was originally composed of five commissioners appointed by the President; no more than three of them could come from the same political party. One of the five was designated as chairman. All members were to hold this new position as their only vocation and were paid for their services. Perhaps most importantly, none of them was allowed to engage in any stock market trading while he sat as commissioner. President Roosevelt's choice for the first chairman was to prove highly controversial. When he appointed Joseph P. Kennedy, a banker, to the post, a public outcry followed because of Kennedy's previous dealings in the market, especially prior to and during the crash. But Kennedy's tenure proved to be very short-lived; he resigned from the SEC a year after being appointed. During that time, he helped organize the commission's structure and helped sell the new concept to the investment community with which he was on very close terms. Kennedy was succeeded by James Landis, later to become dean of Harvard Law School.

The legislation required all stock exchanges intending to deal with the public to become registered as national securities exchanges and exempted only those that were small if they could prove that registration itself was more cumbersome than their actual or perceived liabilities to the public in the event of fraud or misconduct. It also specifically defined the activities and roles of brokers, dealers, and other members of the exchanges, set specific prohibitions against manipulation of securities prices, required registration for new securities, defined a "marginable" security, and laid out the civil and criminal penalties for willful misrepresentation and fraud. The one area that the SEC had no powers within was the commodity futures markets, as those arenas did not trade negotiable securities as such. Regulatory power over those exchanges would be vested in the Commodity Futures Trading Commission.

While the SEC had been given far-reaching power in overseeing the securities industry and the exchanges, it would take several more years of organization and monitoring before the commission would become fully operational and accepted by the investment banking/brokerage community. And during that period, other financial crises would occur that would put pressure on the newly formed body and challenge its role in the marketplace. Nevertheless, the stock market crash of 1929 had proved a watershed in U.S. financial history. Never again would financial institutions be permitted to engage in practices that would dampen the American dream by putting their depositors' savings at risk in the markets. Dealings in those markets would subsequently be subject to a much greater degree of scrutiny than before. As a result, share and bond prices came to reflect a true rather than inflated value of a company's financial position and prospects. The American work and savings ethic was safer in 1934 than in previous years although further refinements would be needed in the years to come. Banks and the securities markets were now much more tame than in the past, but the continuing battle for new business and profitability would again put pressure on all sectors of the financial community and regulatory legislation and would continue to redefine the financial side of the American dream.

NOTES

1. For a description of National City's strategy and the events preceding it see Harold B. van Cleveland and Thomas Huertas, *Citibank, 1812–1970* (Cambridge, MA: Harvard University Press, 1985), pp. 72–88.

2. An excellent description of the legal background and organization of security affiliates can be found in W. Nelson Peach, *The Security Affiliates of National Banks* (Baltimore: Johns Hopkins University Press, 1941).

3. Peach, *Security Affiliates*, pp. 22–23.

4. New York Stock Exchange, *Marketplace: A Brief History of the New York Stock Exchange* (New York: New York Stock Exchange, 1982).

5. Ibid.

6. Ibid.

7. See U.S. Department of Commerce, *Historical Statistics of the United States: Colonial Times to 1970* (Washington, DC, U.S. Department of Commerce, 1975), Part 1.

8. Ibid., Part 2.

9. National City was one example. In its drive to become a "financial department store," it began to offer unsecured retail loans to individuals to provide an unfilled source of consumer demand as well as to help offset the loanshark problem in New York City. The rate on these loans was 6 percent discounted, while the interest paid on small depositors' funds was 3 percent. See van Cleveland and Huertas, *Citibank*, pp. 119–22.

10. Cited in Herman Krooss, ed., *Documentary History of Banking and Currency in the United States*, vol. 4 (New York: Chelsea House Publishers, 1969), p. 2649.

11. Overseas branches of commercial banks were governed by an agreement between the parent commercial bank and the Federal Reserve, allowing the bank to form a branch abroad. After the Edge Act was passed, allowing international banking subsidiaries to operate across state lines for the express purpose of engaging in international banking, these new facilities became known as Edge Act and Agreement corporations.

12. For a more detailed explanation of this process see Peach, *Security Affiliates*, p. 53.

13. At that particular hearing, the question was put to Baker as to whether he believed there was a "money trust" in the United States, composed of a small coterie of influential men who, by virtue of interlocking directorships, held a disproportionate influence over the U.S. monetary system. Baker's reply was negative; he did not believe there was. But he did admit on additional questioning that concentration of banking in the hands of the few, while not dangerous, had "gone about far enough." See Krooss, *Documentary*, vol. 3, p. 2125.

14. See Peach, *Security Affiliates*, p. 106.

15. van Cleveland and Huertas, *Citibank*, p. 141.

16. John Ciccolo, "Changing Balance Sheet Relationships in the U.S. Manufacturing Sector, 1926–77," in Benjamin Friedman, ed., *The Changing Roles of Debt and Equity in Financing U.S. Capital Formation* (Chicago: University of Chicago Press, 1982), p. 69.

17. See Sidney Homer, *A History of Interest Rates* (New Brunswick: Rutgers University Press, 1963), p. 350.

18. New York Stock Exchange, *Marketplace: A Brief History of the New York Stock Exchange*.

19. Federal Reserve Board, *Annual Report*, 1929.

20. U.S. Department of Commerce, *Historical Statistics of the United States: Colonial Times to 1970* (Washington, DC: U.S. Department of Commerce, 1975), Parts 1 and 2.

21. New York Stock Exchange, *Marketplace: A Brief History of the New York Stock Exchange*.

22. See Barrie Wigmore, *The Crash and Its Aftermath: A History of Securities Markets in the United States, 1929–1933* (Westport, CT: Greenwood Press, 1985), chapter 1 and Tables A.1–A.5.

23. Wigmore, *The Crash*, pp. 640–43.

24. Federal Reserve, *Bulletin*, September 1937, p. 31.

25. Ibid.

26. J. F. T. O'Connor, *The Banking Crisis and Recovery Under the Roosevelt Administration* (Chicago: Callaghan & Co., 1938), p. 24.

27. van Cleveland and Huertas, *Citibank*, p. 188.

28. Krooss, *Documentary*, vol. 4, p. 2710.

29. William O. Douglas, *Democracy and Finance* (New Haven: Kennikat Press, 1969), p. 8.

30. Charles H. Meyer, *The Securities Exchange Act of 1934 Analyzed and Explained* (New York: Francis Emory Fitch, 1934), p. 11.

2

The Capital Markets since the Crash

After the 1929 crash, the financial markets dove into a tailspin from which they did not fully recover until the years following World War II. During those years of recovery, the winds of change prompted by the Securities Exchange Act of 1934 were given further impetus by a panoply of new regulations designed to ensure that another crash did not take place, at least not by repeating the abuses of the boom years of the 1920s. Now that commercial bankers were effectively precluded from dealing in the securities markets, most of the changes affected a virtual oligopoly of smaller institutions, the investment banks, and brokers. These smaller, less well-capitalized organizations were left with the daunting task of adjusting to a growing economy while attempting to reinstill public confidence in the securities markets.

From the post-crash period until the major bull market of the Reagan years, political developments played a major role in determining investor attitudes. While politics in general have always played a central role in helping to create booms as well as busts in the markets, as will be seen later in Chapter 8, a major issue having a pronounced effect has been the capital gains tax. Since the Sixteenth Amendment to the Constitution was passed in 1913 the United States has levied an income tax on all wage earners, both individuals and corporations. Embodied in the tax has been a continuing controversy over the tax treatment of capital gains and losses—those sources of revenue and loss that are incurred outside an individual's normal course of business. More often than not, that treatment has been set at a different rate on the tax scale than ordinary income after certain adjustments have been made. While these differing rates have produced both proponents and detractors over the years, one indisputable fact surrounds the controversy: the rate of taxation has had an undeniable effect on investor attitudes toward the marketplace and the accumulation of wealth through investments rather than through "ordinary" work.

Income tax has been an inescapable fact of life since that time although attitudes toward the capital gains element continue to vary along ideological lines.[1] On the one side are those who prefer capital gains to be taxed at the ordinary income tax rate, with no special treatment made for those who use money to make more money. The crux of this argument is the idea of fairness. Those in a position to make gains in the market should not be treated any differently from those less wealthy. The opposing and equally powerful argument simply states that gains made in the market ultimately provide a source of revenue for government because the reinvestment of those gains creates more value that helps fill the public coffers. Between these two admittedly oversimplified positions is a range of arguments that are more detailed. But the fact remains that the markets have benefited greatly from periods in which capital gains (and losses) have been treated preferentially rather than at ordinary rates unless those ordinary rates themselves were deemed low enough to spur further investment.

Originally, the income tax made no distinction between income earned and income realized from the sale of property of whatever kind. This effectively meant that any gains from stock market transactions during and immediately following World War I were taxed at ordinary rates, which were quite high. In most cases, individuals with the highest per capita incomes have capital gains as the largest percentage of their annual income. Prior to the boom years of the 1920s, the maximum tax rate was as high as 70 percent on all sorts of income, earned or unearned. But before that rate could be judged to have had a deleterious effect on the market, the first beneficial treatment of capital gains came into effect—coinciding with the public's appetite for securities investments.

The stock market boom of the 1920s owed much of its impetus to a subsequent change in the original capital gains treatment. In 1922, Congress placed a limit of 12.5 percent on the tax on capital assets held for more than two years. At the same time, a top rate of 70 percent still existed on the highest level of earned income. Capital losses were treated in the same manner: in 1924 Congress limited the amount of capital losses an individual could deduct to 12.5 percent. Corporations were treated differently. Their capital gains were fully taxable at the ordinary rate until 1942, although losses were fully deductible and remained so until 1932.[2]

The 1920s investment boom can be attributed to both the change in the tax and the general growth in economic prosperity. While the public per se did not have extensive experience in the stock markets, it was more familiar with bonds and, as seen in Chapter 1, this is where the early part of the boom began. The favorite investment of the war years had been the Liberty bond, issued by the government. While hardly as intricate or risky as a corporate bond, the extensive holdings of the bonds whetted the public's appetite for fixed income securities. It was this familiarity that the commercial banks built on when forging into the corporate bond business after World War I. But with the massive defaults witnessed after 1929, this flirtation with fixed income securities would come to a quick end, especially when foreign bonds were involved. Because of the crash and the Depression, securities quickly fell out of public favor. The other casualty, as seen in Chapter 1, was the banking community as a whole.

The securities business also suffered serious setbacks after the crash and fared almost as poorly as the commercial banking community. In the immediate post–1929 years, almost 2,000 securities houses failed due to defaults on margin loans and capital losses on trading positions. What is not generally known about the securities houses is the fact that many, but not all, were also deposit takers from wealthy individuals. Many of the deposits taken in were loaned through the call money market; thus, when these institutions failed they also created serious losses among their depositors. Rather than be classified as a commercial bank, those houses that did take deposits were better known as private banks. Very few of these institutions remain in existence today.

After the crash and the ensuing Pecora hearings, the investment community was vastly changed from the free-wheeling days after the war. The quick passage of the Banking Act and the two Securities Acts proved that the public and Congress were in a state of fury with banks, brokers, and everything that smacked of the securities business. And the psychological rebound was not that quick in coming: it was not until 1968 that the volume on the New York Stock Exchange exceeded the volume transacted on October 29, 1929. Obviously the markets played a pivotal role in raising capital and trading in the 30-year interval, but public confidence was slow in returning.

POST-CRASH DEVELOPMENTS

After 1934, the securities business was solely in the hands of securities houses while the commercial banks went a different way in search of new business and profits. The legislation of the first 100 days of the Roosevelt presidency had created a new climate in which the surviving firms would have to compete. The exchanges that these houses traded on were now registered with the SEC. The amount of margin money that could be loaned was subject to Federal Reserve requirements, not distributed solely at the broker's or banker's discretion. Furthermore, in 1934 Congress also changed the nature of the capital gains tax by narrowing the number of exclusions. The new regulation exempted only property held by the taxpayer for sale to customers in the ordinary course of business. The two-year holding period was also removed for the first time. Preferential treatment began after one year, when only 80 percent of the gain would be taxable. Thereafter, a sliding scale was introduced so that assets held over ten years would be taxed at only 30 percent of the gain incurred. One major purpose of these revisions was to take away from professional traders and speculators their formal right to deduct trading losses in full as ordinary losses.[3]

The 1930s were to prove as unfriendly to the securities houses as the 1920s had proved friendly. With the demise of Caldwell & Co., a Nashville firm founded in 1917, and the near demise of Kidder, Peabody & Co. (before being aided by J. P. Morgan & Co.), the markets lost some of their major traders and position-takers as well as underwriters. After the 1934 legislation was passed, many institutions were forced to decide whether to become an investment bank or to remain in the commercial banking business. During this period, many of the modern investment banking houses in existence today were born, among them the First Boston Corporation and Morgan Stanley & Co. Many others were also founded and later merged with other firms, one of the most notable being Blyth & Co., which named Charles Mitchell, the former chairman of National City Company, as its new chairman.[4]

While the securities industry was undergoing structural changes, it was also cleaning itself up to meet the new challenges ahead and regain public confidence. The Securities Exchange Act had provided new regulations for the conduct of business on the exchanges, but the over-the-counter market was still left unregulated, technically because it did not meet the definition of an exchange per se. Under the aegis of the Investment Bankers Association (IBA), significant progress was made during the five years following the legislative flurry of 1934 to construct a self-regulating body that would oversee activities in that particular marketplace. The result was the National Association of Securities Dealers (NASD), formally created in 1939.

NASD was formed in close consultation with the Roosevelt administration. It brought the over-the-counter market into line with the regulations laid down by the SEC Act of 1934 and all of the securities firms quickly joined. Coupled with the earlier regulations, it effectively made the securities business perhaps the most tightly regulated in the country. What had once been a free-wheeling industry had undergone an almost complete metamorphosis. Most securities houses had little choice but to acquiesce to the new environment. Both government and public sentiment demanded it.

During the period prior to the beginning of World War II, the investment banking business slowed considerably from the flurry of activity experienced before the Depression. As public sentiment shifted away from stocks, most of the new issue activity came in the bond markets for corporate offerings. But even there, underwriting profits fell as the volume of new issues slowed to a trickle of former levels. New corporate issues amounted to $330 million in 1933 and increased to $4.4 billion in 1936, but dropped to $2.2 billion in 1937. At the same time, over 70 percent of these issues were refundings, new issues used to refinance existing issues sold several years prior.[5] As a result, negotiated underwriting fees fell and the investment banks suffered a loss of revenues and return on their capital. While the larger firms fared better than the smaller, the years prior to 1940 were lean ones nevertheless.

Because of the fall in new corporate offerings, many securities houses attempted to increase their brokerage services to the public. The years between 1933 and 1937 witnessed an upturn in stock market activities before the market crisis of 1937 and brokerage commissions became one way of ensuring many firms' survival. Curiously, this trend was a repeat of events that had occurred about 15 years before, when commercial banks, also suffering from a structural change in their basic business, decided to court the small investor and saver by entering the retail business for loans and bonds. But in the 1930s, the securities houses had an established precedent for emphasizing brokerage. The retail brokerage business was viewed as a complement to other investment banking activities. In order to combine as many functions as possible under one roof, the brokerage function was viewed as necessary, especially when performed alongside the dealing and underwriting functions.

During the discussions preceding the passing of the SEC Act, or Fletcher-Rayburn Bill, investment bankers insisted on being able to keep the two functions under one roof, arguing that they did not represent a conflict of interests. Detractors claimed that acting as a broker/dealer and underwriter could harm client interests by enabling underwriters or dealers to foist securities on clients in which they had a vested interest. If a securities house sold its inventory of underwritten securities, or securities in which it made a market but that were unsold at the time, to investors it was effectively dumping unwanted investments into others' portfolios. One of Roosevelt's later advisers claimed that this combined function had played a critical role in the 1929 crash. Some of Wall Street's largest failures, he claimed, were houses with perfectly solvent brokerage accounts. Their failures came about when the positions that they had accumulated in inventory collapsed in the market debacle, bringing down otherwise solvent brokerage accounts with them.[6]

The investment bankers retaliated with an argument that, after much discussion, finally emerged victorious. The argument stated that separating the functions would make it economically unviable for some firms to continue in business if the divorce was officially mandated. Originally, their arguments fell on the same side as those of commercial bankers who had lost depositors' funds through imprudent lending. The same had happened to the private bankers'/brokers' clients on a smaller scale. But no deposit taker, regardless of its size or nature, would be able to commit depositors' funds to security market lending. Diversification would now have to take on a fiduciary definition if the brokerage/securities business was to survive without being able to count investors' monies as capital.

The years following the SEC Act were not prosperous ones for the stock exchanges any more than they were for the bond markets. The criticisms of William O. Douglas, among others, that the exchanges were nothing more than "private clubs" finally forced the New York Stock Exchange to reorganize itself in 1938. It reorganized its governing structure and named its first full-time president, William McChesney Martin, in the same year. But turnover continued to suffer throughout the decade. In 1939, total turnover amounted to slightly more than 260 million shares, down from over 800 million in 1930. Despite the fact that many firms were attempting to continue emphasizing retail brokerage services, the entire industry had fallen on hard times that would not improve until after World War II.

Federal regulation of the securities industry was not confined to the 1934 legislation and the creation of the NASD. Several other additional regulations added in the late 1930s also put limitations on the securities industry. The Public Utility Holding Company Act of 1935 extended regulation of the public utilities industry to the SEC. All utilities were required to register with the SEC, which was charged with regulating new financings, and the utilities dealt with the investment banking community in a manner different from the past. Perhaps the most notable investment banking practice to arise from this act was the matter of "competitive bidding" for new utility financings, requiring the companies to put out a new financing for bid and to accept the best underwriter's price.

In 1939, the Trust Indenture Act was passed. This new law required all issuers of publicly issued bonds to file a trust indenture with the SEC and name a trustee responsible for ensuring that all parts of the bond indenture were carried out to the letter. Most trustees were commercial banks, carrying out these functions through their trust departments. But the individual trustees were not to be members of the bond-issuing company or one of its investment bankers.

A year later, in 1940, the Investment Company Act was passed, requiring investment companies to file a statement with the SEC to the effect that they were indeed publicly held companies in the business of investing other people's money. Their activities, especially their relationships with investment bankers, were closely supervised so that the abuses occurring in the mutual fund business in the 1920s would not be repeated. Title II of the Act contained the Investment Advisers Act, requiring investment advisers to register with the SEC as well. This particular part of the law regulated the activities of advisers and prohibited them from engaging in specific practices deemed inimitable to the good of the investing public. By covering investment companies and advisers, the act sought to control those who ere effectively part of the securities business but not acting as underwriters or broker/dealers. In Wall Street parlance, those on the "buy side" of the business were now regulated as much as those on the "sell side."

All of the legislation passed did little to alter the structure of the investment banking houses, although it did severely limit their activities by law. The host of new regulations also served to limit the entry of new firms into the business. The success of the industry, free of commercial banking competition, now hinged on its ability to adapt to new changes in the financial and economic environment. The lean years that preceded World War II only helped to curtail the entry of new houses. Being capital-intensive by nature, new start-up operations would be few while those already established would seek to consolidate their operations. The pyramid structure of the industry, as viewed through its ad hoc syndicate formations for new underwritings, has not changed substantially over time and still persists today.[7] But even the outbreak of World War II and a revival of the economy did not necessarily improve conditions in the stock and bond markets. As an industry, Wall Street continued to suffer from the competition of the war effort and continued public skepticism.

WAR AND POSTWAR DEVELOPMENTS TO 1960

Despite the new regulated environment, the stock and bond markets did not recover from the traumatic post-crash years immediately. Public offerings of bonds were crowded out of the marketplace by the government's various war financings, which were distributed by investment bankers in a manner reminiscent of the Liberty bond financings during World War I. The general mobilization turned the public's mind from investments to the war effort. The New York Stock Exchange, long a bastion of male dominance, came to rely on women employees to help in its backroom efforts, replacing its male employees who had joined the military services. Even during the war years, sentiment had not swung full circle in favor of the markets and their major participants; murmurs of investment monopoly and antitrust were still in the air.

Ironically, it would be at least another ten years before the backlash of the early 1930s finally began to subside, illustrating that the public concern with the causes of the crash was far from short-lived. The securities industry was still under the regulator's microscope and would again be charged with collusion and unfair practices. In this second stage of post-crash examination, the practices of investment bankers would again be subject to scrutiny in order to determine whether enough had been done by the new regulatory environment to ensure against a new "money trust'—this time centered on providing long-term rather than short-term credit, as originally had been the focus of the Pujo and Pecora hearings.

New York Stock Exchange volume reflected the falling interest in investments by the public, especially in the period following 1937. That year's turnover was 324 million shares and the Standard & Poor's stock price index stood at 87.5 (1926 = 100). By 1940, volume had decreased to 208 million and the index slid to 83.7. But in 1941, the market hit a low of 69.5, the lowest since 1931, and volume dwindled to 171 million. A year later, the market hit its lowest turnover since before World War I, trading only 126 million shares before beginning an upward spiral thereafter.[8]

Both the primary and secondary markets felt the brunt of continuing investor disenchantment and the onset of war. The level of new issues remained at a low ebb as the Treasury began its own war financings. Those new stock offerings that made their way to market were integrally involved in the war effort. For the most part, new listings on the New York Stock Exchange were those of manufacturing companies such as American Car and Foundry. Manufacturers of synthetics and medicines also prospered during the war. Pfizer, the manufacturer of penicillin, was first listed in 1944.

The war years did, however, witness a resurgence in the amount of capital gains registered by investors. During the 1930s, losses rather than gains dominated income tax returns until 1942. Beginning in 1943, money was again being made in the market. In that year, gains exceeded losses for the first time since 1936 and continued in an upward spiral thereafter. Analyzed by income groups, those in the net income bracket of $5,000–$25,000 reported the largest aggregate capital gains until 1946. But when measured by capital gains as a percentage of net income, those in the higher income brackets ($300,000 and higher) recorded gains as a higher percentage than those in the lower brackets.[9]

In the corporate bond market, borrowers took advantage of relatively low levels of interest rates to refinance issues that had originally appeared in the 1930s. This activity did not help many of the smaller investment banking firms because the refinancings were done through the houses that had syndicated the borrowings originally. However, a trend began to emerge during the later war years, lasting to the mid–1960s, that would give impetus to the market as a whole. Beginning in 1945, the quality of corporate bonds issued was higher than it had been in the prewar years. The quality of new issues, as measured by the rating agencies' designations as well as the subsequent default rate of older long-term issues, was markedly higher in the postwar period than in the period 1900–43.[10]

The shift in bond quality can be attributed to the new disclosure rules as required by the Securities Act. In Chapter 1, the high number of defaults on foreign bonds was mentioned as one factor that disturbed both investors and regulators in the years 1930 through 1933. Under the new regulations, foreign bonds, issued either by government or corporate entities, were technically classified as corporate issues, and as such had to be registered with the SEC. Domestic bonds, issued by municipalities or the newly created government agencies, were exempt from the registration process. Once the capital-raising process began in full swing after the war years, the disclosure would help keep marginal borrowers from borrowing for working capital purposes. As a result, the default rate began to fall from the earlier part of the century.

In 1942, a major change became effective in the capital gains tax that would remain in place for the next 35 years. The holding period for determining a short- as opposed to a long-term gain was shortened to six months from one year or more. The taxable amount of gain was assessed by deducting any losses from gains, determining the holding period, and calculating the amount of tax due. This change allowed investors to save a substantial amount on taxes paid and gave the markets some impetus while they were still lingering under the cloud of the crash. While the actual level of taxes paid would change as the tax code was modified over the next 35 years, the period was nevertheless remarkable for the consistency in treatment of gains via the holding period.

Nevertheless, the drop in new-issues activity and the slow turnover on the stock exchanges cut into the profit margins of the securities houses. War had helped put the economy back on its feet but the investment banking and securities community did not participate to the extent that they had in the years following World War I. But another challenge was looming that would again attack the very heart of the new issues business and the way that Wall Street was organized. This new challenge was an odd combination of prior regulatory precedents, historical banking relationships, and allegations of price fixing that again put the securities industry on the defensive.

During the immediate postwar years, the Justice Department assembled a case against the investment banking community that attacked the way in which the new-issues market was organized. In the *U.S. v. Henry S. Morgan et al.*, the government alleged that over the years, 17 investment banks had colluded to fix prices in the new-issues market by effectively precluding other members of their own industry from competing for new-issues business. They were charged specifically with price fixing in violation of the Sherman Act.

The Justice Department's case took almost two and a half years to present and was not finished until 1953. During that period, almost every aspect of the new-issues process was exhaustively examined and discussed. At the core of the prosecution's case was the allegation that the traditional negotiated bid process was uncompetitive because many investment banks enjoyed long-standing relationships with the issuers of securities, some predating the enactment of the securities acts, which precluded other issuing houses from competing in the bidding process. Because of these relationships, new-issues pricings violated the provisions of the antitrust laws, effectively leading to a monopoly in the new-issues business.[11]

At the heart of the case was the matter of competitive bidding, an underwriting and syndication technique that had been mandated by Congress for public utilities. Many critics of the traditional negotiated bid method of underwriting maintained that this process should become standard practice, regardless of the business of the issuer of securities. As the prosecution attempted to show, many investment banking houses eschewed the competitive bid method as unprofitable and disliked it because it would upset their traditional relationships with securities issuers by allowing other small investment banks to compete on a level playing field of sorts.[12]

After lengthy prosecution evidence, it became apparent that the government had not made its case and *U.S. v. Henry S. Morgan* was dismissed for lack of sufficient evidence, despite the fact that it became one of the lengthiest and most documented cases in U.S. jurisprudence up until that time. Much of the prosecution's case rested on proving general banking relationships that dated back to the earlier part of the century and could not be adequately sustained for lack of more specific evidence. By 1953, the investment banking community emerged victorious, but only after considerable time and expense.

The result of the case was that the securities business, or more specifically, the new-issues business had been exonerated of price fixing and had emerged from the proceedings with a clean bill of health in the public's eyes, something it had not enjoyed in more than 20 years. The old "money trust" arguments subsided as it became evident that the investment banking business had a pyramidal structure by necessity rather than collusion. As capital financings grew in the years following the war, it became obvious, as it had during the litigation proceedings, that a securities house and client had a special relationship, developed over time in ad hoc fashion. How well an investment banker handled a new issue had a distinct impact on the client's ability to raise more capital in the future and could directly affect the cost of capital. If competition for its own sake upset that balance, it could alter the future financing plans of many companies and indeed have a deleterious impact on capital expansion and economic growth.

Despite the apparent victory of the investment bankers, many of the developments prompted by the SEC Act of 1934 began to change the securities business. Although competitive bidding did not become the standard method of underwriting unless mandated by law, its presence in certain sectors of the market plus lower returns on negotiated underwritings eventually led to a structural change in the way that many firms handled business. The erosion of underwriting margins, only a small proportion of total securities industry profits in general, led more than one originating house into permanent retail operations, seeking to capture profits through secondary market turnover rather than from originations.[13]

Stock market turnover was slow in regaining momentum immediately after the war because of the increase in margin requirements imposed by the Federal Reserve in 1945. In order to protect against speculation, which would hinder the war effort and have potentially inflationary consequences, the central bank raised the margin requirements from 50 to 75 percent. This reduced the amount of short-term trading that normally occurs in margin accounts and led to lower turnover. The margin level was raised again in January 1946 to 100 percent, effectively requiring all purchases and short sales to be paid for in cash. It remained at that level for over a year, although by 1949 it was lowered again to 50 percent. It was not until 1958 that the level again reached its postwar high of 90 percent.

The 1950s were a period of relative quiet in the markets. On the investment banking side, new-issue volume remained low. Corporate security issues remained in the range of $7 billion to $13 billion per year. State and municipal issues were in the range of $4 billion to $9 billion per year. The syndicate system remained in much the same form as it had during the 1940s, with some new wrinkles in the dynamics of syndicate behavior.[14] But the underwriting business remained essentially an oligopoly within an oligopoly. The houses that had been used to doing the most deals remained those that did the most in the period up to 1960. In an extensive study of the investment banking business published in 1963, the SEC estimated that about 5 percent of the industry's firms grossed 60 percent of the income generated by the securities business as a whole.[15] Because of the expertise required to originate and trade securities, as well as the capital-intensive nature of those activities, the major firms retained their hold on the business.

On the secondary market side, exchange volume remained within the same relative growth ranges as the new-issues side. Average daily volume on the New York Stock Exchange grew from slightly under two million shares per day in 1950 to about two and a half million in 1955, and reached three million shares by 1960. In terms of annual volume, the growth was about the same, growing from about 500 million shares per annum in 1950 to slightly less than 1 billion shares by 1960. While the industry continued to grow at a moderate pace, trading volume did not match that set in the boom years of the 1920s, despite the fact that many securities houses began to reorient themselves toward the smaller retail investor. The situation would not change substantially until the market boom that developed later in the 1960s. While the period from 1970 was crucial to the development of all the U.S. markets, mainly because of new financial product developments based on changing international financial conditions and inflation, the period to 1960 was one of consolidation from the traumas that had beset the markets and the securities industry following the crash.

DEVELOPMENTS FROM 1960 TO 1987

Only with the passing of time and renewed optimism in the course of the economy did the markets again begin to flourish. The long period of gradual decline in interest rates and increase in stock market and new-issues activity did not begin until the mid–1960s. The long bull market in bonds can be traced from 1920, when yields to maturity began to fall, but it was only after the 1929 crash that a true downward trend set in. Yields on long (20-year) corporate and Treasury bonds did not reach their 1929 levels again until 1960. Similarly, although the stock market was active, volume turnover did not reach its pre-crash levels until 1968, in the Johnson administration.

Several periods were crucial to the later surge in stock market activity, both in the secondary and primary markets. After 1955, a year of record stock market returns, the secondary market again witnessed strong growth in the middle years of the 1960s. Investor returns between 1962 and 1967 were the highest since the Korean War years. These returns were measured on a real rate-of-return basis as well as on a weighted basis.[16] Returns on equity investment outstripped returns on fixed income instruments, which did not yield much when calculated on a real (after inflation) basis. As a result, stock prices began to increase.

Beginning in 1964, stock market value and volume grew substantially in every year. A two-year correction followed in 1970–71 before the market again grew, slowing briefly in 1981, a year more significant for the credit markets than the stock markets. The prolonged bull market also helped to change the face of the investing public. In 1965, an estimated 20 million individuals owned shares directly rather than owning an interest in them through an intermediary. As the market indices grew each year, the number of shareholders also increased so that by 1970 the number had risen to over 30 million.[17] While exchange turnover was dominated by institutional investors, who have normally accounted for 50 to 75 percent of volume in any given year on average, the bull market of the mid–1960s nevertheless attracted many individuals to the market for the first time and, in aggregate, more certainly than at any time since the boom years of the 1920s.

The increased general interest in the markets helped create new regulations concerning investor protection. Until 1970, the idea of investor "insurance" for securities accounts had never reached fruition as FDIC and FSLIC insurance had three decades earlier. In 1970, the Securities Investor Protection Corporation (SIPC) was finally established as a government-sponsored private corporation to ensure brokerage accounts against loss if the firm at which they were held became illiquid. During the bull market of the 1960s, some securities firms became overextended and went into bankruptcy, leaving their account holders with heavy losses. SIPC insurance guaranteed the accounts up to a certain dollar maximum so that faith in securities trading would be maintained even if the brokerage house became insolvent. While SIPC did not guarantee the market value of securities against loss, it did provide protection against the securities house becoming bankrupt. The individual who held his own securities would not be affected by the new guarantee; only securities held by the trading firm for the investor were covered in such a manner. But it was apparent that the idea of insurance, originally extended to depositors in 1934, would eventually have to be extended to securities investors in such a manner if securities investing was to be encouraged rather than left to the vicissitudes of the rapidly expanding marketplace.

The New York Stock Exchange also initiated several innovations in response to this rapidly changing environment. In 1970, public ownership of member firms was approved so that securities houses could themselves "go public" and raise additional capital to meet the challenges of the expanding market. In 1971, Merrill Lynch became the first member organization of the Exchange to become listed on the Exchange itself. Also in 1971, the NYSE itself became incorporated. A year later its first salaried chairman, James Needham, took office. But by 1973, the bull market had come to an abrupt halt and the market retreated. While turnover continued to grow, the market indices slid back to their levels of ten years prior and did not advance substantially until the latter part of the decade.

The first postwar bull market was fueled by a general economic expansion and by the emergence of new types of listed companies that engendered intense investor interest. During this period, the modern conglomerate emerged as a highly aggressive company taking over others, often in quite different lines of business, in order to hedge its activities against an economic downturn. The targets of these newly emerging aggressive companies became the subject of intense takeover speculation and the market indices rose accordingly. Another type was the "concept" company, one that sold a new financial concept as the basis of its operations. Often, these latter types were more marketing firms than providers of goods or traditional services. Between the two general categories, all aggressive firms selling new or different products became known in Wall Street parlance as "go-go" companies of the decade.

Despite the layers of investor protection that had been added over the years, one of these concept companies in particular eventually did more to tarnish the image that the securities industry had acquired since 1953 than any other single event to date. The ramifications of the activities of this company helped to put a serious damper on the market's advance and renewed individual investor fears over the feasibility of equity investments and the brokers that recommended them. While the securities industry had substantially improved its former reputation and accepted additional regulations, there were still cracks in the pavement on the road to the American dream.

Beginning in the early 1960s, a small California firm, the Equity Funding Corporation, had been selling an insurance cum mutual fund concept that found many willing investors in the strong stock market. The concept that was sold was a British one that had never been seen before in the United States on a large scale. The idea of equity funding involved investors purchasing a combination of life insurance and a mutual fund investment from the company or one of its subsidiaries. The investor bought the mutual fund shares which in turn funded the life insurance policy. The idea was simple: at the end of a decade the life insurance was paid in full while the mutual fund would be worth more than the original purchase price in an assumed strong market.

Building on this concept, the company began to expand rapidly and recorded some of the most impressive earnings growth of the decade. Its shares soared from $6 in 1964 to over $90 by the end of the decade. More importantly, it was held by many well-known institutional investors in the country as well as by a host of small investors. But its status as a growth concept company came to an abrupt halt in 1973 when it was revealed that most of the earnings were bogus and that it had engaged in numerous illegal practices.[18] The Equity Funding scandal became the largest financial fraud in U.S. history. After its affairs were settled in the courts, investors lost approximately $300 million on its stock. Court records revealed that its fraudulent books were overlooked by the firm's auditors, investment bankers, SEC regulators, and most securities analysts. The day trading in the stock was halted, a short-term panic struck the stock market, and the Dow Jones average lost about 3 percent of its value.

As a result of the scandal, the Watergate affair, and the recession caused by oil price rises, the markets retreated and the number of small shareholders declined. From a peak of over 30 million in 1970, individual shareholders again declined to 25 million in 1975 and did not reach the 30 million level again until 1980.[19] During this period of individual shareholder decline, trading was dominated by institutional investors, many of whom were foreign. As will be seen in more detail in Chapter 7, many international investors were preoccupied with an extraneous factor that did not have much impact on the domestic investor, whether institutional or individual. With the breakdown of the Bretton Woods system of fixed parity exchange rates, the floating value of the dollar became a crucial factor in investment decisions. Faced with both stock market volatility and dollar volatility, many international investors eschewed U.S. equity investments, thereby adding to the market's general decline until early in the next decade.

While the stock market is often assumed to be a surrogate for new-issues activity, a new trend has developed since about 1960 that cannot clearly be seen through a discussion of the stock market alone. Despite several bull markets and a gradual rise in interest rates, much new-issues activity was centered in the bond market rather than the equity market, especially for corporate issues. When combined with a similar rise in debt financing by the Treasury, federal agencies, and municipalities, the period witnessed a debt explosion that was unprecedented in American history. Consequently, the balance sheets of U.S. corporations began to change structurally as debt/equity ratios changed to reflect the new penchant for bond financings.

While the stock market was strong during the latter 1960s, the debt/equity ratios of the typical U.S. manufacturing firm remained essentially the same as they had been during the 1940s and 1950s: that is, about 25 percent debt to 75 percent equity. However, when the market began to slow, the ratios began to rise in favor of debt and by 1974, the ratio was almost even at about 50 percent for each.[20] Ironically, as interest rates rose even more in the early and mid–1980s, the ratios grew higher. Debt had begun to find a greater favor in investors' eyes as well as being seen as an alternative to equity financing.

The reason for the surge in popularity of bonds can be attributed to three factors. First, as already mentioned, the equity markets were not performing particularly well and returns to investors were down from previous periods. Second, given the poor state of the new-issues market, debt financing became perhaps the only alternative, while the tax deductibility of interest remained the major allure for corporate borrowings. Third, and most important, was the matter of real rates of interest. Although the real cost of borrowing was higher after 1970 than it had been at any time since the Depression, it was still relatively low when compared with the implied cost of equity suggested by the levels of price/earning ratios investors had attached to equity investments.[21]

The growth in the markets in the mid- to late 1960s, continuing through most of the next decade, was found mostly in the bond markets. During the period 1968 to 1977, the value of corporate equities in the market actually remained the same. In 1968, equities were valued at slightly more than $1 trillion; by 1977, their value was only $5 billion more. During the same period, corporate debt more than doubled, and U.S. Treasury debt and municipal debt also almost doubled. Mortgage debt, discussed in Chapter 4, made great market inroads after the introduction of Ginnie Mae in 1968 and Freddie Mac in 1970 and also doubled in the amount outstanding by 1977.[22]

The supply side alone does not adequately explain why debt rose in popularity. On the demand side was the appetite of institutional investors, the major investors in securities, for investments that were relatively conservative in value. After the bear market of the early 1970s and the Equity Funding scandal, that conservatism became even more pronounced. Fixed-income instruments did not bear the same perceived risk as equities, especially in volatile market conditions. The stock exchanges were quick to recognize this and in 1975 the New York Stock Exchange restructured its previously fixed commission schedule to be more flexible. As of May 1 of that year, the fixed commission schedule that member firms charged their customers was abandoned in favor of negotiable commissions. Effectively this meant that large, institutional clients were able to negotiate the commissions that they paid to securities houses for the purchase and sale of large amounts of shares. While the effects on the exchanges were not immediate, this was an implicit acknowledgement that transactions costs for equities would have to be lowered, given the shift in preference for bonds that was quickly developing.[23]

Changing market conditions, plus tighter regulations on certain types of investors, had both direct and indirect effects on the markets in the latter half of the 1970s. One important piece of legislation that would affect the equity market in particular was the Employee Retirement Income Security Act (ERISA), passed in 1974. This was the broadest piece of legislation aimed at the pension fund industry ever passed by Congress. It was designed to curtail certain abuses in that industry which had put some pension funds under a cloud, imperiling their retirees. ERISA specifically spelled out the rights of individuals to join their company's pension funds and the manner in which vesting was to be obtained. It also created the Pension Benefit Guaranty Corporation (Penny Benny), a federally sponsored insurance plan, similar in design to the FDIC or FSLIC, to provide insurance for employee pension benefits in the event an employer was unable to do so. While most of this legislation was necessary to clean up an industry that had been loosely regulated, the parts of ERISA that would influence the markets had to do with investment management behavior and the eventual development of new security products.

The ERISA also applied a uniform federal "prudent man" rule of investing to pension fund managers as the Investment Advisers Act had originally intended in 1939. However, since that time, prudence as such had been subject to state definition rather than a more uniform federal definition. Advisers who acted imprudently, by buying securities inappropriate to their clients' risk thresholds, could be subject to litigation for mismanaging their clients' money. This ordinarily meant that pension funds would be forced to invest only in investment grade securities: those with quality ratings of BBB or higher by Standard & Poors or another rating agency's standards. While this sort of regulation appeared appropriate, it constricted many pension funds by forcing them to invest in high-quality securities bearing relatively low returns. The riskier investments, which would be expected to yield a higher return, might be excluded because of their lack of a high-quality rating; this would in turn cut down on the potential returns of the fund or any investor similarly constrained.

One of the other major effects of ERISA was to allow individuals to construct their own personal pension plans, better known as Individual Retirement Accounts (IRAs). These could be created if the individual was not covered by a pension plan at work. Individuals could set aside a certain amount of funds each year in investments that would not be taxed until the plan was liquidated at retirement, when the gains accrued would theoretically be taxed at a lower rate of income tax than would be in force while the contributor was still earning a salary. As well as extending benefits to those who might not be otherwise covered by a pension, IRAs also help to remove some pressure from people who might otherwise have to rely solely on social security benefits in their later years.

These new forms of retirement accounts prompted the investment community to create new types of financial instruments that were tailored to some extent to meet the requisites and objectives of the individual, as well as institutional investors whose objectives may have been the same in a broad sense. Some of these new products will be discussed further in Chapter 7. Shortly after the introduction of IRAs, money market mutual funds were introduced on a large scale. These new types of mutual fund investment allowed investors to obtain market rates of interest on a mutual fund investment that could be purchased for a small amount of money, in contrast to the average round lot on Treasury bills or commercial paper—amounts that were often out of reach of the small investor. Money market funds became a favorite of IRA investors because they allowed individuals to keep abreast of market rates of interest. They became but one example of the investment community's marketing response to the new possibilities opened up by IRAs. Zero coupon bonds would be another example, although they were not introduced until the early part of the next decade.

In most cases, much of the financial innovation that took place in the mid–1970s, continuing well into the 1980s, surrounded fixed-income investments rather than common stock. The asset distribution of two of the largest institutional investors in the country, life insurance companies and pension funds, reflected the change in sentiment. Between 1973 and 1983, the assets of life insurance companies increased from $252 billion to almost $655 billion, an increase of 259 percent. During the same period, insurance company holdings of common stocks increased from $26 billion to $65 billion, an increase of 250 percent. Corporate bond holdings increased at the same rate, from $92 billion to $232 billion, registering a 252 percent gain. But U.S. government securities gained over 690 percent and real estate holdings increased by over 292 percent. While equities increased with the average rate of asset growth overall, the rates of growth witnessed in the prior decade slowed considerably. Between 1960 and 1972, equities jumped from only 4 percent of life insurance company holdings to over 11 percent, for a growth rate of 540 percent.[24] While equity holdings had grown with the insurance companies themselves, their rate of growth was overtaken by other investments deemed to be more secure.

The asset mix of private, non-insured pension funds also registered a change, although not quite as pronounced as those of the life companies. Between 1960 and 1972, equities rose from 43 percent of assets to 74 percent, while corporate bonds fell from 41 percent to 18 percent. But between 1973 and 1982, equities dropped back to 59 percent of holdings while corporate bonds remained about the same. The drop in equities was compensated for by a rise in the holdings of Treasury bonds and mortgage agency bonds, which had grown in popularity since the introduction of Ginnie Mae in 1968 and Freddie Mac in the years immediately following.[25] While equities were still a sizable percentage of total pension fund portfolios, their popularity nevertheless declined in favor of Treasury and agency bonds. As the yield spread narrowed between corporate issues and Treasury or agency issues during this period, investors opted for the relative safety of the latter in light of the uncertainty caused by oil price rises and the regime of floating exchange rates caused by the collapse of the Bretton Woods system in 1971–72.

As will be seen in Chapter 7, after 1973 the new listed options market began to experience increased activity as investors began either to hedge or speculate using calls and, to a much lesser extent, puts. As hedging and speculative activity increased, the options market initially thrived because as market volatility increased, floor trading thrived on widely fluctuating prices. However, what was good for the options market was not necessarily good for the stock market; some of that intense activity in the derivative instruments only helped to detract from equity investments. While the Dow Jones Average rebounded in the mid–1970s from its earlier lows and maintained essentially the same level until 1979, the market was not able to make any real gains in adjusted terms.

In 1977 and 1978, two subtle changes in the capital gains tax proved to be harbingers for the future. In 1977, the holding period for a long-term gain was changed from six months to nine months. In 1978, the holding period was extended to one year or more. In order for an asset to be taxed at the preferential rate, it had to be held for a longer period of time than was previously the case. Since 1942, a gain was considered long term if the asset had been held for a minimum of six months. However, the change in the holding period did not change the manner in which the gains were treated. Assets held for less than the minimum period were still taxed at the investor's ordinary tax rate. Long-term gains taxes were still confined to 50 percent of the profit (less losses), as they had been since 1942. The change in the holding period proved to be a major factor in market volatility in the next decade, as investor reaction became more short term. Rather than hold a security longer to take advantage of the capital gains tax, investors were more apt to sell assets if a profit could be realized regardless of the time it was held.

The late 1970s was a period of general market uncertainty due to increasing oil prices and rising interest rates. On the New York Stock Exchange, volume continued to grow and the general indices rose above their 1975 levels, the low point of the decade. However, volume grew faster than the indices as the stock markets in general gave a vote of "no confidence" to the policies of the Carter administration. In inflation-adjusted terms, the growth in the indices was minimal until the Republican victory in the presidential election of 1980. But by 1980, recession had set in and it was not until 1982 that the market took on a much more positive tone. This trend resulted in the largest bull market on record, lasting until the market collapse of 1987. Later in 1984, the bond markets would also join in the general economic euphoria and register price gains that were unprecedented in scope.

The stock market's rise began in late 1982. The Reagan administration's early emphasis on supply-side economics and a reduction in the capital gains tax in 1982 from 30 percent to 20 percent of gains held for more than one year provided the early impetus. Equally important was the speculative fever engendered by the wave of mergers and acquisitions that began about a year later, aided to a large extent by the availability of credit supplied by the newly emerging junk bond market. This trend made many companies the target of both friendly and hostile suitors willing to pay premiums over stock market value for their shares. As a result, the market indices more than doubled their values between 1982 and 1987. In 1982, the New York Stock Exchange recorded its first 100 million-share day and by the middle of the decade turnover had reached an average of about 150 million shares per day. This increased share volume was in sharp contrast to 1978, when the record for trading was 65 million shares.

Beginning in 1984, the bond markets also began their meteoric rise. The monetary policies of the Federal Reserve, led by Paul Volcker, began to lead to a reduction in the inflation rate and, in some cases, negative growth in the money supply. The markets responded by bidding up prices and returning yields to levels that had not been seen since 1979. In early 1984, yields on 30-year Treasury bonds stood at about 14 percent, the historic high yield for long-term Treasury securities. In May 1986, yields had fallen to 7.25 percent for a newly issued long-term Treasury. The new yield levels suggested that investors had registered a gain of over 80 percent on a bond bought only two years before, excluding interest from the calculation. Bond investors were able to register gains normally reserved for investors in stocks.

The fall in interest rates also proved a boon for the investment banking industry as many companies began to refinance bonds issued earlier with higher coupons. The same time period thus became the period of the largest number of bond calls in the history of the markets. As old issues were retired, new ones replaced them with lower coupons and the investment banking industry benefited by reaping a record amount of underwriting commissions. When this fee income was combined with the commissions collected from brokerage, investment banks recorded their best profits in over two decades. Unlike the period following the passage of the Securities Exchange Act of 1934, these refinancings were accompanied by a general public euphoria for equities as well. These two factors combined to establish the greatest uninterrupted bull market in U.S. financial history.

In addition to new-issues activity and record secondary market turnover, the securities industry also benefited from the wave of mergers and acquisitions that become prevalent after the drop in interest rates. Structuring and financing these deals through new offerings was not the only way in which investment banks profited. Many also began to engage in merchant banking activities for their clients, whether those clients were the target of a takeover or the acquiring firm itself. In many cases, the larger investment banks also bought a portion of the deal for their own books with the intention of realizing a short-term or medium-term profit. Ordinarily, this sort of position-taking without the intent of immediately selling equities on to the public was outside the range of normal investment banking practice. Additionally, some of the houses also loaned money for takeovers, using their own capital for which they charged interest as a commercial bank would ordinarily have done. Much of the takeover boom was financed by commercial banks, but in this case, investment banks began to compete in a limited fashion with the commercial banks, a phenomenon not seen since the pre-crash days of the 1920s.

The Reagan years, however, could not be characterized as a silver lining without a cloud. The federal budget deficit had grown to about $240 billion by 1986 and the merchandise trade deficit continued to grow to about $150 billion, aided by a strong dollar that consistently made imports inexpensive and exports expensive. The export situation especially led to a pronounced crisis in the agricultural sector as farm exports fell, forcing a credit crisis in the Farm Credit System, as outlined in Chapter 5. Both the stock and bond markets reacted negatively, as expected, to the lack of progress in reducing the two deficits but continued to register overall gains despite them. But speculative fever could not be reduced by negative economic developments, as investors continued to take advantage of markets that had been essentially moribund for such a long period.

The Tax Reform Act of 1986 provided some disincentive to the markets by abolishing preferential rates for capital gains and disallowing the tax deduction on most forms of consumer interest (the latter phased in over a three-year period). The act also limited the amount of margin interest that could be deducted against investment gains. It was the abolition of the preferential capital gains tax, and with it the holding period, that led directly to increased stock market volatility, resulting in the temporary collapse in October 1987. As long as the holding period was no longer of consequence, investors were apt to buy and sell in a shorter time framework than was previously the case. However, the abolition of the capital gains tax was accompanied by lower individual tax rates and an increasingly simplified tax scale that benefited individual taxpayers perhaps more than any tax reform of the twentieth century. At the same time, many corporate tax loopholes were abolished and the corporate tax rate rose to compensate for the revenues lost from individuals. But the capital gains tax, based on preferential holding periods, had been a cherished item since its introduction 60 years prior and its abolition was suspected of triggering short-term trading activity set on taking profits without regard for time. This increasing short sightedness, plus persistent fears of the effect of the trade deficit and its impact on the dollar and interest rates, led directly to the largest market drop in history after five years of unabated growth.

THE "MARKET BREAK" OF OCTOBER 1987

Although it is usual to think of the financial markets in separate terms, they all nevertheless function as one general marketplace in economic terms. While the capital markets are usually lumped together in one category as places in which capital is initially raised and subsequently traded, they fulfill the same general purpose. The derivative markets, or hedging markets, however, are based on instruments that can be used singly or in combination to help the investor hedge the risk of capital markets instruments in order to protect investments from capital loss. When they do not behave in similar fashion, however, the economy is at risk. The magnitude of that risk depends to a great degree on the extent to which they act separately, especially under conditions of economic uncertainty.

Beginning on October 13, 1987, the stock markets began to lose value, culminating in the precipitous market drop of October 19. During that one-week period, the Dow Jones Industrial Average lost 769 points, representing 31 percent of its value. On October 19 alone, the drop was 22 percent of the index, representing the largest market drop in history in such a short period of time. The extraordinary bull market that had begun almost six years before came abruptly to an end, evoking memories of and comparisons with the 1929 crash. But the 1987 events led to neither crash nor depression and the market again reached its pre-October levels two years later. While many conditions surrounding the 1929 crash appeared to have resurfaced, many of the safety precautions built into the Glass-Steagall Act and the Securities Exchange Act 53 years earlier ensured against a financial and economic collapse.

The idea of all the markets acting as one was originally embodied in a study by a presidential task force released three months after the collapse which examined the market mechanisms and events that led to the massive sell-off.[26] This idea meant that the intermarket mechanisms, or linkages, that ordinarily connect the markets failed to hold up to widespread selling pressure, only exacerbating the situation. While the report of that particular commission and others made recommendations designed to prevent further chaos, most tended to ignore the strengths of the market system which acted as a prop to prevent even further price declines and the eventual collapse of the financial system.

On the surface, the period leading up to October 19 bore a great resemblance to the events prior to the autumn of 1929. The market indices in both cases were at an historic high and a great deal of equity investment was due to margin trading. Interest rates were relatively low in both cases. After the high inflation of the earlier part of the decade, the yield curve was again in a positive slope in 1987 and long-term Treasury bonds yielded about 7.5 percent to 8 percent in the months preceding the turmoil. Gross national product was strong, if not robust, proceeding at about 3.9 percent in real terms; after-tax corporate profits were up sharply from the previous year; and unemployment was at the 5.5 percent level. Superficially, it would appear that a precipitous decline was not justified.

Most of the fears triggering the markets' decline centered around interest rates. After recovering from a prolonged bout of high short-term interest rates, the markets focused on any signal that would again lead to higher rates in the future. A major concern was the size of the merchandise trade deficit, running at about $150 billion per annum. As the deficit continued to rise, concern set in over international interest rate levels, especially those in West Germany and Japan. In order to weaken the dollar and stem the rise of imports, it was feared that those two trading partners would raise their domestic interest rates in order to lower the value of the dollar versus the yen and the deutschemark. If those rates rose, the assumption was that U.S. interest rates would also rise, putting an abrupt end to the bull markets in both stocks and bonds.

Adding to the markets' short-term nervousness was a potential tax change aimed at the expanding corporate takeover market. Many of the large take-overs had been financed through the use of junk bonds (see Chapter 7). These high-yielding instruments were issued to provide the financing for the purchase of target companies. Since its inception several years earlier, the junk bond market had been predicated to a large extent on the tax deductibility of interest payments. The House Ways and Means Committee was studying the possibility of reducing the deduction so that the merger trend would not rely to a very large extent on the cash flow benefits engendered by the deduction. Although the Committee did not succeed in abolishing the deduction, the fear of the potential ramifications of a vote in favor of abolition forced many investors and speculators to sell shares in potential takeover targets.

Interest rate fears and tax fears were further exacerbated by the cross-relationships between equities on the one hand and options and futures trading on the other. Those using options to speculate rather than shares forced a selling spree in the options market, which in turn put further selling pressure on the shares those options represented. Program traders, those who invested in a combination of equities, options, and stock index futures using simulated models, also had automatic orders to sell that were triggered by a price movement in any one of the instruments they happened to be using at the time. In addition to the more traditional investors who reacted to short-term economic factors, these traders also received sell signals as the market began to decline, thereby adding still more pressure to an already weakening market.

The results in the stock markets were dramatic. The presidential task force estimated that over $1 trillion was wiped off the value of traded equities as a result. The amount of real losses (as opposed to paper losses) was obviously less, but the impact on investor confidence was significant. The steady growth in the market indices and investor holdings, prompted by the earlier fall in interest rates and the cut in the capital gains rate earlier in the decade, had come to an end, at least temporarily. Over 60 percent of U.S. stocks were assumed to be in the hands of individual investors at the height of the market, not including indirect holdings through mutual funds and pension funds.[27] Even if a loss of confidence was not measured in investor attitudes toward the stock market, any negative reaction, as reflected in consumer behavior and spending, could have far-reaching results. Consumption in 1986 accounted for about 65 percent of the GNP. While this was less than the 75 percent registered in 1929, households had considerably more debt in 1986, with interest payments accounting for about 10 percent of disposable income as opposed to 2 percent in 1929.[28]

Immediately after the market's fall, the Federal Reserve sought to calm investor fears concerning financial institutions by adding liquidity to the banking system. Interest rates fell dramatically, especially those on Treasury bills, as investors bought short-term instruments with the proceeds of stock liquidations. Within a day, the major market indices of many foreign stock markets, especially London and Tokyo, also dropped substantially. "Black Monday" was not just a U.S. phenomenon and the drop in the other major markets underscored the linkages that had been established in the new deregulated international financial environment.

After it became apparent that the financial system had withstood the shock of the market collapse, the focus shifted to those institutions and mechanisms that had contributed to the precipitous price rout. While the banking system had survived the shock without any serious repercussions, public confidence had again been shaken as it had in 1929–30. However, in this case the factors were not a *cause célèbre* as they had been after the first crash. At the heart of Black Monday were causes that would be examined by regulators and industry professionals as well as by congressional committees similar to the Pecora committee, whose findings earlier in the century had paved the way for the original banking and securities markets regulations.

The problems that the market collapse underlined were mainly structural in nature. Although on a general level they are ordinarily expected to operate as one, actual market mechanics and trading techniques had become so sophisticated that even a small ripple in one could have repercussions in the others because of sophisticated arbitrage techniques. Thus, pressures in the stock markets were equally felt in the options markets and stock index futures markets; the reverse was true as well. Operating in tandem, these pressures were difficult to withstand in the stock market alone because U.S. capital markets at the time did not have built-in safeguards against precipitous price movements. For instance, if a price fall or rise occurred in one of the commodity futures markets, the amount of price movement was constrained by a predetermined fluctuation known as a "limit movement." These commodity futures limits were designed to protect both investors and floor brokers against a rapidly moving market that could force illiquidity on their participants by causing margin calls. While this source of price movement protection was common in the futures markets, it had never been introduced into the stock or options markets, where such same-day price fluctuations were much less common.

On October 19, when just such a price movement was witnessed, the market had no structural way of limiting trading and prices continued to fall throughout the day as a result. The floor traders responsible for making market quotations among themselves in listed stocks (specialists) were also caught by the surge of selling and forced to continually mark down prices. One of the major criticisms of the stock exchanges was that specialists simply marked down prices to discourage further selling, thereby adding to the losses. Almost immediately, specialists were accused of having too little capital to deal with the number of shares that were being traded. That accusation had not been heard since the market's short-term drop on the day President Kennedy was assassinated; it would be echoed by several presidential commissions in the ensuing months.

The over-the-counter market shared the same problem and was beset with sell orders and a general lack of liquidity. Market makers were reluctant to accept liquidation orders and prices fell in about the same proportion as they had on the exchanges. Many small market-making firms eventually closed their doors and the prices of many unlisted stocks remained at depressed levels even after exchange-listed shares began to rebound in the following months. Generally less efficient and less liquid than the exchanges, the over-the-counter market suffered more than others and displayed a greater lack of investor confidence than its auction market counterparts.

Although the markets involved reacted in the same manner, general regulations surrounding them did nothing to stabilize prices in the very short term. Despite the fact that the SEC is the federal regulator for the stock and options markets, the two trading arenas are otherwise totally separate. In the first instance, exchanges are self-regulating bodies and as such are not able to act in tandem unless specifically designated to do so by federal law. The futures exchanges are even less able to do so because they are regulated by the Commodity Futures Trading Commission (CFTC) but otherwise are equally self-regulating. The linkages that were established between the markets by arbitrageurs and others were functional; at a structural level there was little that could be done initially to stabilize prices because they all came under the same sort of investor pressure.

The remedies that were suggested to prevent further precipitous price falls were mainly mechanical in nature. The presidential task force's conclusions were the first to be made after the "market break," as the price drop became known, and focused on the lack of coordination between the various exchanges. The principal recommendation of this group was that a market "circuit breaker" be put into effect that would prevent the stock market from falling without an intervening stabilization period.[29] Although not suggesting the level of limits to be established by such a device, the recommendation was that this preventative measure, among others, should be implemented and monitored by a single regulatory agency. Of all the regulatory agencies that were involved in the financial markets, the report concluded that "the weight of evidence suggests that the Federal Reserve is well qualified to fill the role of intermarket agency."

Following the general recommendations of the task force, President Reagan created the Working Group on Financial Markets on March 18, 1988. The purpose of this group was to suggest specific measures to deal with problems underscored by the task force. This group consisted of Alan Greenspan, chairman of the Federal Reserve; David Ruder, chairman of the SEC; Wendy Gramm, chairman of the CFTC; and Glenn Gould, Undersecretary of the Treasury for Finance. After two months of study and deliberation, the committee produced its interim report, which first introduced the idea of limit movements, or a "circuit breaker," for use by the New York Stock Exchange.

Following the "one market" concept, the major recommendation was that "all U.S. markets for equity and equity-related products—stocks, individual stock options, stock index options, and futures—halt trading for one hour if the Dow Jones Industrial Average declines 250 points from its previous day's closing level." If the Dow continued to fall to 400 points below that original opening level, a closing of two hours would be enforced.[30] While these limits would not help ensure against further market declines, they would nevertheless allow the markets to catch their collective breaths momentarily in order to perform their back room operations in a more orderly fashion than had been the case in October 1987. Both the original crash of 1929 and the "market break" had one factor in common: both caused an enormous backlog of orders that created much chaos and incalculable losses, thereby leading to an erosion in investor confidence that in itself is difficult to quantify.

Although circuit breaker mechanisms were adopted for use they did not have an immediate test. The market indices again matched their 1987 levels two years later in September 1989, never having fallen substantially since the market break. Investor confidence returned more quickly than it had after the original crash. The second price fall indicated that sufficient safety net legislation could indeed prevent a serious ripple effect in the banking sector, preventing panic and the loss of savings that such panic could cause. But perhaps more importantly, the market break proved that the American dream of accumulating wealth through investment could be kept intact through a series of regulations adopted over time. While protecting the public from speculative fever in a period of general financial deregulation, especially in the banking sector, that deregulation itself often engendered fever by creating an environment that encouraged savers and investors to seek out the highest rate of return even on such simple investment vehicles as time deposits and money market mutual funds. While it appears that the financial markets have come under increasing control, the banking sector has in fact come under less control—not necessarily on the federal level but on the practical level, where the saver is concerned. Deregulation has meant greater opportunities for the bank customer, who has come to equate bank products with those in the markets on a much closer level than at any time since the 1920s. The evolution of banking since 1934 is the subject of the next chapter.

NOTES

1. Although the ideological lines had been drawn on this topic years prior to the passage of the income tax itself, the final interpretation was left, in the early years, to the U.S. Supreme Court. In a 1920 decision, *Eisner v. Macomber*, the Court ruled that the income included any gain made from either capital or labor. Later, in 1921, the Court ruled in *Merchant's Loan and Trust Company v. Smietanka* that income, according to the Sixteenth Amendment, included a gain from the sale of one item as well as the sale from many items in the course of doing business. In all cases, income was meant to mean that economic benefit that accrued to an individual only after a transaction had taken place, not merely after a valuation of a person's holdings.

2. For a full description of the changes in capital gains treatment until 1950 see Lawrence Seltzer, *The Nature and Tax Treatment of Capital Gains and Losses* (New York: National Bureau of Economic Research, 1951).

3. Ibid., p. 21.

4. For a further description of the post–1934 development of the newly structured investment banking community see Vincent P. Carosso, *Investment Banking in America: A History* (Cambridge, MA: Harvard University Press, 1970), especially Chapter 17.

5. Ibid., p. 393.

6. Ibid., p. 378.

7. S. L. Hayes, A. M. Spence, and D. Van Praag Marks, *Competition in the Investment Banking Industry* (Cambridge, MA: Harvard University Press, 1983), p. 23.

8. New York Stock Exchange, *Yearbook*, 1947 (New York: New York Stock Exchange).

9. Seltzer, *Nature*, p. 367ff.

10. The default rate on corporate bonds issued from 1945 to 1965 was less than 0.1 percent of the volume outstanding, as compared with a rate of 1.7 percent for those issued between 1900 and 1943. Similarly, the spread between the yield on corporate offerings and the U.S. Treasury benchmark rates was lower in the postwar period than in the prewar period, illustrating the lower perceived investor risk involved. See Thomas R. Atkinson, *Trends in Corporate Bond Quality* (New York: National Bureau of Economic Research, 1967), p. 3.

11. For a detailed treatment of these proceedings see Carosso, *Investment Banking*, especially Chapter 21.

12. Ibid.

13. Hayes, Spence, and Marks, *Competition*, p. 24.

14. Ibid., p. 27.

15. Carosso, *Investment Banking*, p. 505.

16. For a general measurement of the return on both common stocks and bonds see Lawrence Fisher and James Lorie, *A Half Century of Returns on Stocks and Bonds: Rates of Return on Investments in Common Stocks and on U.S. Treasury Securities, 1926–1976* (Chicago: University of Chicago Press, 1977), especially p. 75.

17. New York Stock Exchange, *Fact Book*, (New York: New York Stock Exchange, 1988), p. 61.

18. A comprehensive account of the Equity Funding fraud, including a chronological account plus various documents of the court-appointed trustee involved in settling the case, can be found in Lee Seidler, F. Andrews, and Marc Epstein, *The Equity Funding Papers: The Anatomy of a Fraud* (New York: Wiley, 1977).

19. New York Stock Exchange, *Fact Book*, 1988, p. 61.

20. New York Stock Exchange, *Supply and Demand for Equity Capital* (New York, 1975).

21. See Fisher and Lorie, *A Half Century*, p. 109.

22. See Vincent Massaro, *The Equity Market: Corporate Practices and Issues* (New York: The Conference Board, 1979), especially Chapter 1.

23. The abolition of fixed-rate commissions also gave rise to the discount broker, a member firm that charged lower commissions than an ordinary broker, or "wire house," did to clients regardless of the size of their order. In return for the lesser charges, the discount brokers did not provide investment advice or research, but merely supplied barebones brokerage services.

24. American Council of Life Insurance, *Life Insurance Fact Book*, 1984.

25. Federal Reserve System, *Flow of Funds Accounts, Assets & Liabilities Outstanding 1959–1982* (Washington, DC: Federal Reserve System).

26. Nicholas F. Brady et al., *Report of the Presidential Task Force on Market Mechanisms, January 1988*. Other members of this commission included James Cotting, Robert Kirby, John Opel, Howard Stein, and Robert Glauber. The report, submitted to President Reagan, was originally published on January 8, 1988.

27. Ibid., Chapter 1.

28. Ibid., pp. viii–8.

29. The other conclusions of the task force suggested that market clearing systems should be unified to reduce risk, that further information systems should be developed to monitor transactions in related markets, and that margin requirements should be consistent to reduce financial risk. See Brady et al., *Report*, p. 69.

30. *Interim Report of the Working Group on Financial Markets* (Washington, DC: U.S. Government Printing Office, May 1988), p. 4.

3

Commercial Banking since 1934

In the years following the regulatory legislation of 1933–34, the banking industry and the securities houses underwent a rebuilding period. In addition to finding themselves out of the securities business, commercial bankers also had to rebuild the public confidence that had been lost following the massive bank failures of the prior decade and the early 1930s, when over 14,000 institutions failed. Commercial banks now were in much the same position as they had been prior to the expansion of the 1920s; their survival would now depend on performing more traditional banking services that did not involve securities or securities-related business. The development of commercial banking between 1934 and 1980 hinged on finding new avenues of profitability that were not restricted by the Glass-Steagall Act and subsequent regulatory legislation.

The Glass-Steagall Act was not the only legislation constricting commercial banks. The McFadden Act of 1927 also proved a barrier to expansion outside the home states of banks. While originally interpreted to allow banks to underwrite securities, this act prohibited commercial banks from branching outside their state of domicile, in keeping with the spirit of the National Banking Act of 1864. The only way that banks had been able to operate across state lines was through subsidiaries, enabling them to operate in other states by serving only international customers. The Edge Act of 1919 allowed them to create subsidiary companies, owned by bank holding companies, that were legally allowed to perform banking services with foreign persons or entities outside their home states if local regulations were favorable. These operations became known as Edge Act corporations and were able to engage in foreign financial operations in addition to commercial banking per se. The combination of these two pieces of legislation plus the strictures imposed by the Glass-Steagall Act were to give U.S. banking a distinct character that was to last until 1980.

In the wake of the Roosevelt era legislation, banks were both restrained on one hand and given exclusive powers on the other. Although unable to engage in securities underwriting, they were still able to underwrite and trade Treasury securities and municipal securities; these areas were to prove quite profitable in the years ahead. While restricted on the amount of interest that could be paid on deposits by Federal Reserve Regulation Q, they nevertheless had the exclusive right to offer transaction, or checking, accounts. And while having to rely on deposits for funding, they were greatly aided by the newly created FDIC insurance. Although it took away many of the functions banks had assumed during the 1920s, the Glass-Steagall Act nevertheless helped restore public confidence by providing insurance for deposits at both commercial banks and savings and loan associations, the latter being insured by the FSLIC.

The challenges that banks faced after 1934 were manifold. Limited by regulations, they nevertheless had to expand in order to meet the demands for money created by an expanding economy. Unable to cross state lines, their natural route was expansion through merger. As the population grew, they were also faced with the challenge of offering new products in order to increase their profitability. Compounding their difficulties, thrift institutions had an advantage over commercial banks that would last until 1980: Regulation Q allowed them to offer marginally more interest than the banks in order to preserve their hold on mortgage lending, ensuring some stability in the mortgage market. In order for the commercial banks to grow, they would have to compete in a universe that was severely limited.

During the post-crash period, the interest rate environment proved conducive to depository institutions as a whole. Interest rates, both short and long term, remained relatively low on both a real and nominal basis until the 1970s. Depositors were therefore not inclined to withdraw funds from the banks to search for higher yields in comparable sorts of investments or savings vehicles. However, when interest rates did begin to rise, all depository institutions would come under pressure since they were not able to compete effectively with market rates and new products that were not limited by Federal Reserve regulations. As will be seen later in this chapter, the new financial environment created by inflation in the 1970s and early to mid–1980s ushered in a new period for commercial banking that was unprecedented in scope. In order to adjust to the new environment, bank activity would eventually be deregulated to preserve the integrity and viability of the financial system as a whole. That deregulation also increased pressures to dismantle the Glass-Steagall Act and allow banks again to compete with the investment banks and securities houses, which had enjoyed a virtual monopoly in the corporate securities markets since 1934.

Despite the encumbrances that burdened banks from 1934 to 1980, the modern money center bank nevertheless emerged and U.S. institutions reached the top of the banking totem pole, or "league tables," among all depository institutions on an international scale when measured on a total asset basis. During this period, two external models were crucial to the development of the modern commercial banks. The first was the organization of the Canadian banking system, which had fared much better during the Depression years than its U.S. counterpart. This success was due to the nationwide branching system enjoyed by Canadian banks, not constrained by a domestic version of the McFadden Act. The second model was the dominance and profitability of the "universal banks," traditionally West German or Swiss institutions able to offer both commercial and investment banking services under one roof. Both models were the envy of U.S. commercial bankers over the years who could only look wistfully at the stability and profitability of institutions not constrained by government regulations.

THE POST-CRASH YEARS TO 1946

Immediately after the crash, nationwide bank deposits began to drop. By 1933, they had reached a low of $38.6 billion, the lowest figure in almost two decades. But after the passage of the banking laws, they immediately began to rise again. The most noteworthy factor in the subsequent increase was the insurance protection offered by the newly created FDIC. As confidence in the banking system returned the number of deposits grew and by 1935 the amount totalled $48.9 billion.[1] On a nationwide basis, there were fewer banks in existence than in the heyday of the 1920s, but those that had survived found themselves in a more liquid, and less risky, position than when securities formed an integral part of their businesses.

As confidence returned, the banks found themselves in the peculiar position of having increased deposits while at the same time experiencing soft loan demand, especially from their traditional corporate customers. Not being able to book loans, they sought out safer but lower returning assets in the form of U.S. Treasury securities. In 1930, the total of all banks' loans and investments was some $56.6 billion. Of that amount, $38 billion was booked as loans, while the balance of $18.6 billion was booked as investments. By 1935, the mix had changed dramatically. Of a total of $45.7 billion, $20.3 billion was in loans and the balance in investments.[2] This was not to prove a temporary phenomenon; investments would outnumber loans until 1955, when the percentages again began to favor the latter for reasons that will be discussed later in this chapter.

The return on U.S. Treasury securities was not particularly attractive, however. Treasury bills yielded only about 15 basis points in 1935, or 0.15 of 1 percent. Treasury bonds yielded about 25 times that number, but this amounted only to about a 4 percent return. The heavy reliance on Treasuries also added to bank reserves and most large banks were awash with funds that would lead to a decline in activity in the federal funds market. New types of loans, and customers, would be crucial to banks' profitability in the years to come. Because of this pressure to find new avenues of profit, the American dream again arose after being so severely hampered by the crash and the Depression.

In response, the banks turned to two avenues, both representing unchartered ground. The first trend was a new emphasis on wholesale banking, or lending to companies, again bringing banks into conflict with the bond market. The second was a new emphasis on retail, or individual, banking—actively seeking out the small borrower whose consumption would prove to be the cornerstone of the economy. The importance of both would be underlined by the instability of international banking, a traditional profit center, which declined due to the increasing risk of war during the 1930s.

Bankers may well have been confused by the risks involved in wholesale, or corporate, lending, especially when the economic outlook was uncertain at best. Forced to divest their holdings in other companies in 1933–34, they now found themselves in an equally risky position of having to lend to companies fighting off the results of the Depression. In 1934, Chase National Bank of New York liquidated the Chase Securities Corporation and with it one of its prized holdings, the American Express Company. Similarly, National City Bank of New York liquidated the City Company, its prized securities affiliate. In the years immediately following, they turned to the corporate sector, seeking borrowers of funds. National City, as one example, sought out firms that had decent prospects for growth but somewhat limited access to the bond markets. As a result, it established a relationship with the United Parcel Service, among others, and loaned it significant amounts in the years following. While good relationships were established during this period, the prospects of finding a borrower that had a decent track record were not always so easy. "It is almost impossible to lend money to anybody from whom you have a reasonable chance of getting it back," remarked the chairman of National City in 1934.[3]

One answer for the large banks was the development of the term loan, a loan made to a corporate customer for a period of more than one year. Ostensibly, loans of this type of maturity looked suspiciously like a corporate bond rather than a more traditional short-term commercial bank working capital loan. Nevertheless, both Chase and National City began making loans of this nature to customers. In order not to run afoul of the newly established securities authorities, term loans needed the blessing of both bank examiners and the SEC to be marketed effectively. Both gave approval in 1934 and the term loan began its life as a limited but necessary tool of the commercial banker.[4]

On the back of the development of the term loan was a new tool for pricing loans, developed by Chase and the major money center banks. Since Treasury bill rates were so low, the banks decided to price loans to their best customers at a basis point spread over the Treasury bill rate. This would have the effect of increasing the banks' returns over the small Treasury bill returns while at the same time providing corporate customers with a source of funds that was cheaper than borrowing in the bond markets, especially if the new registration costs were included in the cost. This new rate became known as the prime rate of interest; the rate banks charged their prime, or best, customers.[5]

Prime lending was not without its critics. There were those who felt that lending to blue-chip companies diverted banks from their primary mission of helping put the country back on its feet by lending to small businesses. One of these critics was Jesse Jones, chairman of the Reconstruction Finance Corporation (RFC), an agency created in 1930 during the Hoover administration. The RFC was dedicated to stimulating the economy by providing governmental assistance to financial institutions and smaller businesses. One of the measures used to aid financial institutions was the purchase by the RFC of preferred stock issued by banks for the occasion. When many of the same banks confined their lending to blue-chip companies rather than the small business enterprise, Jones was highly critical because he felt the brunt of the Depression was being borne by small businesses that had to borrow directly from the RFC rather than from banks.[6]

But it was in the realm of retail banking that the greatest inroads would be made, setting the trend for the future. As seen in Chapter 1, some progress had been made in this area in the early 1920s, when the concept of "financial department store" was first bandied about in banking circles. But the trends of the 1920s, which envisaged selling securities to the retail investor, and the divestitures of 1934 put an end to that portion of commercial bank logic. In its place, retail banking of the modern era would be ushered in, at rates of interest on loans far exceeding those that could be earned by lending to companies.

The bank that was most responsible for introducing retail banking was the California-based Bank of America, the fourth largest bank in the country in the 1930s. Beginning in 1929, Bank of America established a personal loan department. The strategy behind such a move was evident. Consumers had been accustomed to paying as much as 30 percent for personal or consumer loans through finance companies. Bank of America set its rates at 13 percent and immediately began to feel the effects through heightened loan demand. The default rate was low, proving that individual customers were not the poor credit risks they had previously been considered. The bank's default rate on such loans was only 0.11 of 1 percent.[7]

Early in its experiment with retail loans, Bank of America also loaned money for home improvements and the purchase of electrical appliances through the auspices of the Federal Housing Act of 1934. Following quickly on the heels of success in this area, it also extended itself into automobile loans, again coming into competition with finance companies. Another area the bank explored successfully was that of buying accounts receivable from companies needing working capital. These sorts of loans extended the retail concept into the small business area and Bank of America became one of the few institutions that drew praise rather than criticism from Jesse Jones, both at the time and in later years.

Much of the success of personal loans was due to the great migration of people to California, which continued to enjoy a growth in population and expansion of its industries. But much of it was also attributed to the bank's founder, A. P. Giannini, under whose aegis the retail business originally grew. "Banks must develop new lines which, while different, are just as sound as the old. It does not take much of a credit man to say 'No' to a borrower but it does take time, labor and understanding to find a basis on which a loan can be made," Giannini was quoted as saying as late as 1938, some nine years after entering the retail loan business.[8]

The war years temporarily altered the new thrust into wholesale and retail banking. Banks geared themselves for the war effort and their asset mix reflected this trend. While deposits continued to increase, assets became more concentrated in Treasury securities, especially bonds. Between 1940 and 1945, loans and investments increased from $54.1 billion to $140.2 billion. By 1945, investments accounted for $110 billion of the total, outnumbering loans by a large margin.[9] But despite the growth in deposits, consumer loans still accounted for a high proportion of actual loans made. The installment loans and other forms of consumer credit created in the last decade now became a problem to the federal government even before the American entry into the war. In August 1941, President Roosevelt made a proclamation concerning the extension of consumer credit. The board of governors of the Federal Reserve was charged with limiting the amount of consumer credit that could be created, given the booming economy and the need for funds to finance the war effort. As a result, the amount of credit that could be extended by banks for the purchase of consumer durables, the maturity, and the minimum periodic payments for such purchases was to be limited by the Federal Reserve, eventually embodied in Regulation W. These restrictions on the amount of consumer loans that could be made forced banks to concentrate most of their activities on helping to sell Treasury securities to help finance the war effort. While the efforts would prove profitable, as they had during World War I, most credit allocation was geared toward aiding the government rather than the consumer or the small business. At the same time, however, it was necessary to control the amount of interest on Treasury securities so that the costs of borrowing would not spiral.

During the war, Treasury yields were controlled by the Federal Reserve in order to make returns attractive, especially to banks. This was known as the official "pegging" of Treasury yields. Treasury bill yields and long-term bond yields were kept in a sharp, positive slope, with the short maturities yielding three-eighths of 1 percent while the long bonds yielded 2.5 percent. The slope was maintained by the Federal Reserve district banks when they announced in 1942 that they would purchase all Treasury bills offered at three-eighths of one percent. Later in the same year, the Federal Reserve Open Market Committee instructed the district banks to replace such purchases with sales of a similar amount of Treasury bills with the same maturity at the same yield if requested by the sellers before maturity.[10] This pegging had the effect of making yields predictable and stable, ensuring the holder a rate of return that would not vacillate as much as it would under normal market conditions.

Managing interest rates on Treasury securities could not occur without monetary consequences, however. While commercial bank deposits increased, so also did the money supply; by 1945 the total money supply equalled almost half the gross national product.[11] Prices continued in an upward spiral, making the control of consumer credit, rationing, and price controls all the more necessary. The pegging of Treasury securities continued into the next decade, as did certain forms of credit control.

The war years also saw the rise of women as a more important element in commercial banking operations. As in the stock exchanges, women were employed in more important positions than was previously the case, as many male workers were serving in the armed forces. When the male employees returned from service, many were given additional management responsibilities reflecting leadership qualities that had been acquired in the military services. This increased pool of managerial talent also played a central role in bank development after 1950 as the banks entered a new era of growth and expansion, both domestically and internationally.

EXPANSION AND GROWTH, 1946–70

After the end of the war, the economy expanded and banks contributed by increasing their loans to both businesses and individuals. Price controls were lifted in late 1946 and prices began a steep rise across the board. The Treasury paid off a substantial amount of its outstanding debt and the banks naturally benefited, having been a major holder of government securities. The result was a shift in bank assets from government bonds to newly created loans, especially to business. Term loans and installment credit loans again increased and both types became a major source of revenue for the banks. But before the economy could be free of the effects of the war effort, the Korean War broke out and many of the same restrictions that had prevailed during the global conflict were again used to finance the new war effort.

Within months of the outbreak of war, wage and price controls were adopted, credit controls were again established, and income taxes were raised to help fund the Treasury. A Voluntary Credit Restraint program was established and banks were asked to make loans only for "productive" purposes that would not diminish the war effort. The pegging of Treasury securities continued but only to 1951, when it was abolished. Thereafter, interest rates began to rise in line with price inflation. The steady growth in the economy plus the higher tax rates helped increase the demand for credit, and business loans continued to grow on banks' balance sheets. Term lending especially prospered during the war as many small businesses used loans to finance mergers and acquisitions. The bond markets were still deemed too expensive and, in some cases, restrictive for small and medium-sized businesses, and the banks profited as a result.

After the cessation of hostilities, the banks sought out merger partners in order to cope with the new business environment. Still constricted by the McFadden Act and a panoply of state banking laws, in many cases they sought out other institutions as suitable marriage partners rather than open *de novo* operations. Many of the mergers were between the large money center banks and more specialized wholesale or retail banks whose activities would complement those of the more specialized buyer. In 1954, Chemical Bank merged with the Corn Exchange Bank, a retail institution that would add diversity to Chemical's primarily wholesale operation. The following year, National City merged with First National Bank of New York, a wholesale institution with less than 10 percent of National City's total assets. The result was the First National City Bank of New York. In 1955, the largest of the mergers occurred when the Chase National Bank merged with the Bank of Manhattan Company, another smaller retail bank. The result made Chase Manhattan the country's second largest banking institution after Bank of America.

This period of merger was confined primarily to intra-city mergers unless state banking laws allowed for more ambitious expansion. New York State's Stephens Act of 1934 was but one example of state legislation confining the institutions.[12] For the first time since the 1920s, banks were faced with demographic problems caused by the movement of the population to the suburbs: they began to experience a slower growth rate in their deposits than had previously been the case. Adding to this problem was the shift in their assets from investments to loans. As mentioned earlier, beginning in 1955 loans outnumbered investments as a proportion of assets for the first time in decades. In order to compete with regional banks in other parts of the country, the money center banks needed to actively seek new sources of funds if they were to continue growing.

The response to this new problem was threefold. First, banks sought to expand beyond their original domiciles, whether they were a city or region within a state. Second, they needed to develop new instruments for short-term funding that did not violate Regulation Q. Third, they would eventually seek out overseas markets where Federal Reserve regulations did not apply.

In this latter case, this also meant seeking out foreign rather than domestic customers and assuming any additional risks that this sort of lending entailed.

Intrastate banking was given a fillip by the Bank Holding Company Act of 1956. This legislation gave the Federal Reserve greater powers to oversee holding companies than it had received under the 1933 Banking Act. If a holding company controlled 25 percent of the voting stock of two or more banks, it was required to register with the Fed. Upon doing so, it would be required to divest itself of any interests not related to banking and apply to the Fed before acquiring more than 5 percent of another bank. Having registered with the central bank, it would then have to submit itself to regulation and periodic examinations. In short, a bank holding company was to be exclusively in the banking business, subject to the appropriate regulations.

While the new legislation appeared airtight, bankers found a loophole in it worth exploiting. For instance, First National City interpreted the act to mean that intrastate banking mergers would be tolerated, state banking laws such as the Stephens Act notwithstanding. Almost immediately, it sought to merge with the County Trust of Westchester County, a retail bank serving the suburban area. Both New York State and the Fed demurred at first but by 1960 the handwriting was on the wall. The New York State Legislature passed the Omnibus Banking Act, allowing New York City banks to merge with those in Nassau and Westchester counties.[13]

The slow process of gaining both Fed and state banking commission approval did not help alleviate the funding crisis that the banks quickly found themselves in. As the population continued to migrate toward the suburbs, banks found that the structure of their lending presented a problem. Term loans especially caused some concern because, unlike shorter working capital loans, they were not self-liquidating in short periods of time. Equally, the commercial paper market was developing quickly, enabling larger companies to borrow at market rates of interest, avoiding bank intermediary charges for loans. New sources of funds would be needed if the banks were to continue their growth.

This growing need plus the banks' expansion into intrastate branches were the two main themes of commercial banking in the 1960s. One major source of funding for operations began to develop in the late 1950s with the birth of the eurodollar market. In 1957, most money center banks, as well as their European counterparts, began to rely on external dollars as a source of deposits in addition to those booked in the United States. These deposits proved increasingly valuable over time because they enabled banks to avoid Federal Reserve regulations.

A eurodollar is a dollar deposited in a banking institution outside the territorial United States. The market as such originated when non-American holders of dollars deposited them in European banks rather than in U.S. banks within the United States. Interest was paid in dollars and ordinarily was loaned to borrowers also located outside the country. Originally, the institutions accepting these funds were foreign, booking most of the deposits in London. Shortly thereafter, U.S. bank branches in London and other select foreign money centers also began accepting offshore dollar deposits. The U.S. banks' motives for doing so were simple: such deposits were free of Federal Reserve requirements and Regulation Q interest rate ceilings.

The regulatory climate in 1957 underscored the importance of this new source of funds. Regulation Q prohibited banks from paying interest on demand deposits and limited interest to 1 percent for time deposits of less than 90 days.[14] This proved to be a disincentive for the use by major corporations of commercial banks for some of their working capital balances. The banks consequently felt a liquidity squeeze. But in the new euromarket, interest could be paid free of Regulation Q ceilings and banks had the advantage of not having to create reserves against the deposits. The rigidities of regulation helped create a new market that would grow over the next 25 years to total more than $800 billion. At the same time, the new market helped to solidify London's reputation as the major international financial center. British banking regulations did not apply to these dollar deposits since they were treated as external funds and therefore had no impact on British domestic monetary policy.

A major step was taken to correct the funding problem domestically with the introduction of the negotiable certificate of deposit (CD). In order to again attract corporate funds that were being sold more profitably in the marketplace, a new wrinkle was added to the traditional large-denomination time deposit. In 1961, First National City Bank devised the negotiable CD, a time deposit that investors could sell in the secondary market without penalty if liquidity was needed. First National City arranged for the Discount Corporation of New York, an established money market dealer, to make a secondary market in these new instruments.[15] While the new instrument took several years to gain acceptance, a major funding hurdle had nevertheless been cleared.

The introduction and subsequent success of the CD added a new dimension to bank funding. In order to attract funds through CDs, banks were now required to pay a market rate for these instruments although reserve requirements still applied. This effectively raised the cost of funds to the banks, which until this time had been accustomed to enjoying the benefits of Regulation Q protection on the amount of interest paid for customer deposits. While ceilings still applied to CDs, the Federal Reserve was more lenient concerning the amount of interest paid on CDs; as a result the cost of funds for banks began to rise. Banks began to recapture funds, but the old pattern of doing so through low-yielding deposits had passed. Through the use of eurodollars and CDs, a new era of competitive banking had been ushered in, although the full consequences would not be felt for at least another decade.

Ten years after the original holding company legislation, another holding company act was passed that helped set the tone for further expansion of services. In 1966, the Bank Holding Company Act was amended to further define competition among banks. One provision of this amendment gave the Fed the ability to approve acquisitions through holding companies that might reduce competition among banks as long as the public benefit outweighed the disadvantages. At the same time, single bank holding companies were exempt from Fed registration. This loophole immediately gave rise to the reorganization of many banks into single holding companies. Banks immediately reorganized so that their holding companies held the stock of only the core bank central to their businesses. Other subsidiary operations were organized to enable banks to enter related financial services such as leasing and mortgage originations. With one stroke of the pen, banks immediately reorganized in order to spread their activities beyond the scope of the McFadden Act through subsidiary operations.

Congress was quick to react to the oversight in the 1966 amendment. In 1970, it passed further amendments to the 1966 legislation in the Bank Holding Company Act of 1970. Registration on single bank holding companies was imposed and any company that held bank stock was required to register, regardless of the amount of stock it held in a bank. Furthermore, the new amendment applied a test of future public benefits to expansion. Acquisitions were expected to provide benefits to the public that would outweigh potential disadvantages such as concentration of financial resources or unfair competition. If a bank holding company could prove that its expansion offered advantages to the public, the new service would be allowed. If the expansion was deemed inequitable or uncompetitive, it would not be allowed to proceed.

One of the nonbank services that holding companies provided was credit card facilities. This was an area of potential profit that had been inaugurated by the Western Union Company, which had been issuing cards to select customers since World War I. The concept was launched on a nationwide basis by the Diners Club in 1950, soon followed by the American Express Company in 1958. Banks, however, were slow to enter the business because of their limited access to a wide customer base and because of funding problems. Equally, credit card facilities required administrative skills that many banks did not possess in the late 1950s or early 1960s. Early experiments with credit cards had failed and many of those pilot projects that were attempted were subsequently sold to finance companies.

As nonbank activities, credit cards needed sources of funding other than deposits as well as a wide customer base. The first successful card, known as BankAmericard, was launched by Bank of America in 1963. Through its extensive California branch network, the bank was able to reach more potential customers through marketing than any other U.S. bank. The card proved to be profitable after several years of operation. It became so profitable that it was franchised to other banks shortly thereafter and became known by its generic name, the Visa card. In 1965, MasterCard was introduced by a consortium of other banks. All of these new card operations were bank holding company ventures.

The source of funding for credit cards was commercial paper issued by the bank holding company. Obviously, these new ventures required a non-deposit source of funding and the short-term market nature of commercial paper was ideally suited for funding customer purchases using cards. Commercial paper issued by holding companies was exempt from Federal Reserve interest rate ceilings and the holding companies could borrow as much as was needed in the marketplace to fund card operations. The availability of credit did not prove to be a problem for such ventures as it had a decade prior, when demographic shifts in the population brought the banks under severe pressure. In this case, banks were able to respond to the branching restrictions imposed by the McFadden Act by offering services on a nation-wide basis that were still within the realm of consumer credit, without all of the regulatory and financial baggage required by merger with, or acquisition of, another bank.

Credit card operations were one, but not the only, example of bank expansion through a holding company. Other examples, all subject to Federal Reserve review, were leasing operations, insurance agencies, data processing agencies, and mortgage lending, to name just a few. Many subsidiary operations were started *de novo* while others were acquired from existing specialized companies. The narrow geographical constraints of existing banking laws were compensated for by offering financial services on a nationwide basis. These services also helped to diversify banking operations, thereby enabling the banks to free themselves from the risk of being exposed to only their local economic environments. The same motive also led them to expand their international operations as well.

During the 1960s, the euromarket grew in size and importance and the banks were quick to recognize the profitability involved in lending dollars and other currencies to U.S. corporations as well as foreigners. For instance, in 1964, the estimated net size of the eurodollar market was about $9 billion. By 1968 the figure had almost tripled to $25 billion, and by 1970 it had almost tripled again to about $65 billion.[16] As international trade continued to grow and dollars became the accepted "universal" currency for many transactions, more offshore deposits were created. Those deposits found their way into loans made by both domestic and foreign banks eager to lend at rates that were not subject to Federal Reserve control. U.S. banks were able to lend the funds to domestic American companies for use either at home or abroad. What made this business so profitable was the nature of the rate of interest charged. Eurodollar lending was done on a floating, or adjustable, basis at a spread over the eurodollar rate. In such a manner, banks were able to make term loans at rates that floated, rather than having to fix them at a specific rate for the term and risk suffering a yield curve change after the loan had been created. They were thus able to ensure that the revenues from a loan exceeded those paid on eurodollar deposits, regardless of interest rate levels. This pricing method, common for European banks, was something of an innovation for U.S. banks and would lead them to aggressively pursue this market into the later 1970s and early 1980s.

Eurodollar lending served the corporation rather than the individual and complemented the banks' expansion into consumer finance on the domestic front. By 1970, banks had become much more diversified than they had been only ten years before. They entered the new decade ready to expand their lending operations worldwide. Their new-found diversity was still protected from serious competition because a large part of their prosperity hinged on Regulation Q protection; interest rates on deposits were still dictated by the Fed. Although banks were forced to pay more for funds if they originated from issuing CDs, taking eurodollar deposits, or issuing commercial paper, the large deposit bases attributable to customers' savings provided a captive, and cheap, source of funds. In the following decade, the winds of change began to blow, leading to nothing less than a revolution in U.S. banking as extensive as that created by the original 1933 legislation.

THE WINDS OF CHANGE IN THE 1970s

The 1970s were a decade of momentous change in the financial markets that severely affected banks' cost of funds as well as the revenues derived from lending. Other profit centers, such as foreign exchange dealings, also came under increased pressure and forced banks to make structural changes in the way they dealt in currencies in response to new international events. New financial products were introduced that effectively competed for savers' funds and later created disintermediation on a large scale, challenging banks' role as safe depositories of money. By the end of the decade, the financial environment was ripe for new regulatory change in order to protect the integrity and viability of the system.

In 1970, the economy was in the midst of a recession and at mid-year the Penn Central Railroad failed. Commercial lending had declined due to the economic environment and pressure was mounting on the dollar in the foreign exchange markets. Pressure on the dollar was compounded by persistent rumors in the markets that the dollar would eventually need to be devalued by somehow altering its convertibility into gold. In August 1971, President Nixon officially cut the convertibility and set into motion events that effectively put an end to the Bretten Woods system of fixed parities, which had been instituted after World War II. The immediate result was an increase in the price of gold and a depreciation of the dollar against the other major currencies.

During this period of currency turmoil, interest rates rebounded from the low levels experienced in 1970 and began to rise. Between 1969 and 1970, both short-term and long-term interest rates had fallen dramatically, with short rates accounting for the most marked decline. Rates on Treasury bills and commercial paper had fallen about 3 percent while long bonds had fallen about 1.38 percent. In the last quarter of 1972, rates again began to rise despite wage and price controls instituted by President Nixon. The prime rate also began to climb, from 4.75 percent in early 1972 to 6 percent by the end of the year.

The Arab-Israeli war of October 1973 led to the oil embargo of the United States by the Arab oil exporters, lasting until the spring of 1974. During that period, inflation had begun to rise and would exceed 12 percent by the end of that year. The prime rate also climbed to 12 percent. The increasing inflation rate and the rise in interest rates was to affect banks in two ways. First, it prompted most of them to increase their international operations so that they could recycle much of the oil money deposited by the producing nations by lending it to those in need of cash because of increased oil imports. This was usually done through foreign branches rather than by the domestic banks themselves. Second, the rise in rates also signaled the birth of a new instrument that began to effectively compete with bank deposits for savers' funds—the money market mutual fund. Both developments had a profound impact on commercial banking although the effects were not immediately felt.

Money market mutual funds were introduced in the early 1970s by mutual fund companies. The funds were organized in much the same way as common stock mutual funds, in that the investor bought shares in the fund which in turn had invested in a pool of money market instruments. The funds had the advantage of being invested in a spectrum of instruments that offered the investor a market rate of interest. A fund invested in commercial paper, for instance, returned near the aggregate yield of the pool. In late 1974, that rate was about 9 percent. At the same time, banks were still limited by Regulation Q and were offering 5.5 percent on time deposits. The advantage for investors was obvious. For relatively small amounts of money, they could receive a market rate of interest higher than a bank could legally offer.[17] If interest rates rose, the yield on the fund would also rise, enabling the investor to keep abreast of rising interest rates and inflation. The fund also offered liquidity to the investor; it could be sold at any time if cash was needed.

The general rise in interest rates was accompanied by a rise in short-term and medium-term borrowings during the same period. The amount of bank loans increased from $191.7 billion in 1970 to $494.1 billion by the end of 1974. Commercial paper borrowings also increased from $33 billion to $51.7 billion. Loans had replaced investments securities as a large portion of overall assets. Loans accounted for around 70 percent of assets by 1974, dramatically reversing the percentages of the post war years.[18]

The reasons for this increase in borrowing can be attributed to the stock markets' poor performance plus the tax deductibility of interest payments. When the Dow Jones Industrials fell below 600 during the 1970–71 recession, many companies were forced to the debt markets and to banks to raise funds rather than sell new equity. As a result, the balance sheets of many U.S. companies became more heavily ladened with debt. While the banks were positioned to be one of the major beneficiaries of this trend, funding again became a problem as it had in the prior decade.

In the early stages of development, money market mutual funds attracted investors by offering market rates of interest and liquidity. The latter feature especially had a significant impact on banks' cost of funds. In 1974, two-thirds of the total assets of the funds were invested in domestic bank CDs. During the period 1974–78, the total assets of the funds ranged between $5–7 billion, meaning that CDs accounted for about $3–4 billion of the total. But after 1978, the funds began to grow, reaching $30 billion in 1979 and $200 billion by 1981. As interest rates rose, making the funds more popular, the CD element began to decline as a percentage of the total to about 25 percent by 1981. However, the exponential rise in the total also meant that outstanding CDs rose to $50 billion.[19] As a result, banks' cost of funds began to rise. By purchasing shares of a fund, investors sent a clear signal to banks that higher interest rates and liquidity were preferable to the regulated rates offered by traditional time deposits. In order to keep abreast, banks were thus forced to pay a higher rate for smaller depositors using a new, institutional intermediary.

Although these new funds were not insured in the traditional manner by the FDIC, the safety element did not dissuade investors from placing money in them. Two banking failures, one domestic and the other international, helped to underscore the fragility of some banks under the new economic climate. In 1974, the Franklin National Bank of New York and the Bankhaus I.D. Herstatt of Cologne, West Germany, closed their doors. Both had become victims of the new foreign exchange environment and recorded heavy losses in the foreign exchange market. Franklin's loss was slightly less than $40 million while Herstatt's was approximately $100 million. Franklin's problem was one of funding. As rumors spread of its foreign exchange losses it was unable to raise CDs to fund itself on a short-term basis and eventually had to be assisted by the Fed. The FDIC subsequently sold its assets to the European-American Banking Corporation. Herstatt's problems spilled over into its U.S. correspondent banks, notably Chase Manhattan, as creditors sought redress for their lost or frozen assets from Chase.[20] While both failures were resolved in the same year, it became apparent that the banking system was again under pressure as the domestic and international financial environment changed rapidly.

Higher costs of funding and the continuing search for profitable loans caused many U.S. banks to increase their foreign loans and their activities in the euromarket. After the initial rise in the price of oil and the subsequent increases imposed by the OPEC cartel, the demand for hard currencies, especially the U.S. dollar, became more pronounced as many countries began borrowing for balance-of-payments and other trade-related purposes. As mentioned earlier, U.S. banks were recipients of many of the dollar surpluses deposited in the eurobanking system by OPEC and other nations running trade surpluses. The recycling of these funds, to those nations and their government-sponsored enterprises in need of money, was a source of potential profit, especially when domestic loan demand was periodically soft. The debt explosion that was rapidly developing domestically had an international dimension that the banks were quick to exploit.

After almost four decades of development, the term loan again moved to the forefront of banking. Many sovereign borrowers sought loans in the range of 5–10 years to maturity in order to offset the consequences of increased oil imports. Others used the same source of funds to borrow against oil revenues to expand their domestic economies. In both cases, term loans proved to be a faster alternative than the international bond markets, in which medium-term lending was the rule rather than the exception. But in many cases, the bond markets were closed to countries that did not have the highest credit rating. Bank loans became the major source of external funds for countries that had a greater need for capital than their own domestic markets could provide.

U.S. banks, and those from the other major industrialized countries, were quick to fill the vacuum and supply funds that were being deposited in greater and greater amounts by the oil-rich producers. Between 1970 and 1977, the number of international bank credits increased from $4.7 billion to $41.6 billion per year. While borrowers from all geographical areas borrowed heavily during this period, those in the developing, non-OPEC countries borrowed the most, their loans rising from $446 million to $20.8 billion.[21] The profit margin on these loans was the obvious motive for engaging in this sort of lending because the revenues were derived from two sources. First, the spread was fixed over the London eurodollar offered rate (LIBOR) or over the domestic prime rate. It was not uncommon for spreads to exceed 1.5 to 2 percent over the appropriate rate, which was itself adjusted periodically. Second, the amount of the loan was normally syndicated among the banks themselves rather than loaned by one institution. When the banks arranged a syndicate, they also charged an underwriting fee to the borrower, similar to the fees charged by investment banks for bond issues. Combining these two charges, banks were able to post heavy profits for the loans as long as the borrower was able to service the debt.

Syndication meant that any one bank's exposure to the borrower was limited. For instance, in a loan of $100 million syndicated to 50 banks, any one bank's exposure was limited to only $2 million, assuming that all parties participated equally. Given the adjustable, or floating, nature of these loans, many banks that ordinarily did not lend to international borrowers were able to participate. In addition to the money center banks that actively pursued such loans, many regional U.S. banks were invited to participate as well. As a result, the category of international lender extended far beyond the large banks to many whose ordinary business was otherwise domestic. Many of these lenders did not list the origin of the loans on their balance sheets because they were only a fractional part of their overall loan portfolios. Through such syndication methods, the international lending explosion reached down through the ranks of all banks to affect even the smaller institutions.

Another new product appeared in the 1970s that intruded on banks' traditional preserves: the negotiable order of withdrawal (NOW) account, a checking account that paid interest. As interest rates began to rise, this new product was actively offered by banks and thrift institutions. After their appearance, the regulatory authorities gave their implicit blessing to them by allowing them to be offered. But a suit brought in a federal court challenged the regulatory authorities of the various types of depository institutions (the Fed, the Federal Home Loan Bank Board, and the National Credit Union Administration) to allow such accounts without congressional approval. In April 1979, the court ruled that the regulators had indeed exceeded their authority and gave Congress until January 1, 1980, to pass legislation allowing NOW accounts. Congress responded by passing the Consumer Checking Account Equity Act, which permitted the regulatory agencies to authorize the accounts. By the time the legislation passed, NOW accounts had been offered for almost eight years.

The major factor affecting commercial banks in the 1970s was inflation and higher interest rates. As the decade came to a close, U.S. inflation stood at an historic twentieth-century high and interest rates reflected this. Inflation, as measured by the consumer price index, had steadily climbed since 1972 and stood near 13 percent by the end of the decade. The federal funds rate was close to 14 percent, the discount rate was over 12 percent, and the (90-day) Treasury bill rate stood at 12 percent. The yield curve had become negatively sloped, with long-term Treasury bonds yielding slightly more than 10 percent. At the same time, the maximum rate of interest paid on 90-day deposits at commercial banks was still only 5.5 percent. Money market mutual funds had attracted over $30 billion in assets and would attract an astonishing $35 billion more within the next year. Perhaps most importantly, the real rate of return was negative on all interest-bearing instruments, with the exception of commercial paper.

The latter part of the 1970s produced two political events that significantly shaped the deregulatory legislation to be passed in 1980 and again in 1982. The first was the election of Jimmy Carter as President in 1977; the second was the appointment of Paul Volcker as chairman of the Federal Reserve Board in 1979. One of Carter's campaign promises in 1977 was to balance the U.S. budget. At least partial adherence to that same idea two years later led to the imposition of short-lived credit controls in an attempt to bring down interest rates and inflation. Volcker's leadership at the Fed signaled a change in the way interest rates and the money supply were viewed when dealing with the same problems.

The 1970s proved to be a watershed decade in U.S. financial history. The American dream was under attack through inflation and low rates of return, but consumer spending and outstanding mortgage debt continued to climb nevertheless. Installment credit increased by over 60 percent between 1976 and the end of 1979 and outstanding mortgages increased by slightly less than 50 percent.[22] The recession of 1974–75 gave way to a period of growth fueled by consumer spending that produced increases in the monetary aggregates. The Fed, under the aegis of William Miller, had been slow to react to these new developments, preferring to allow only gradual increases in the federal funds rate as an antidote to the rise in the money supply. By the autumn of 1979 it became apparent that more drastic action was needed in order to cope with the problem.

Banks were the chief beneficiaries of the boom in consumer spending. Consequently, they were the major targets of the Fed's new shift in monetary policy, which was announced in October 1979. On October 6, Paul Volcker announced a change in the method by which the Fed would attempt to slow monetary growth. The new emphasis would focus on the level of member banks' reserves in attempting to come to grips with money expansion. The gradual policies of the previous Fed would be abandoned. The discount rate, standing at 11 percent at the time, was increased one full point to 12 percent. The federal funds rate would be allowed to rise or fall more dramatically than in the past, when fractional changes were customary. Finally, although reserve requirements were to remain unchanged, a special reserve requirement of 8 percent was to be imposed on certain types of large-denomination deposit accounts in addition to their ordinary reserve requirements. The immediate impact was predictable and far reaching. All the financial markets experienced significant price falls only a week and a half short of the fiftieth anniversary of the 1929 crash.

In the wake of the Fed announcement, the cost of funds began to rise. In some cases, the costs exceeded the amount that banks could charge on loans because of state usury ceilings. The precipitous rise in interest rates also aided the money market mutual funds, which witnessed the largest net rise in amounts outstanding in their brief history. Equally important was the disquiet the rate rise caused among banks. The new reserve requirements meant that banks would have to create more reserves at the Federal Reserve Bank that would earn no interest. Thus many member banks opted to leave the Fed system voluntarily rather than suffer opportunity losses on the additional required reserves. Defections from the central bank's ambit, combined with the disintermediation caused by the money market funds, created more turmoil in the markets that only legislation would be able to subdue.

THE DECADE OF CHANGE

All of the factors contributing to monetary turbulence produced political events that substantially changed the American financial landscape. This new environment was characterized by deregulation on the one hand and increased powers for the Federal Reserve on the other. In this case, there was no single event such as war that could rally the banks and the markets on the side of the federal government. Previous experiments with pegging interest rates no longer served the financial system because it had become too complex for any one series of regulations or practices to remedy. In quiet periods, new bank products such as NOW accounts, providing interest on checking accounts, could possibly have been assimilated into the financial system more easily than they were in the late 1970s. By 1980 these products, plus money market funds, were creating difficulties for the Fed as it tried to come to grips with money supply growth. The immediate response from the Fed was a redefinition of money supply. For the Carter administration the response was a return to a time-tested method of controlling credit— imposing restraints.

Early in 1980, the Fed announced new money supply measures designed to take into account the new liquid instruments that had been created over the last decade. The new measures broke down the traditional M–1 into two categories, M–1A and M–1B.[23] By doing so, the Fed was attempting to further divide M–1 into more specific liquidity measures so that it could better track money growth that might have gone undetected using the old measures. The new categories at first created some confusion in the financial markets and were eventually discarded several years later when the new products were included in the more customary M–1, M–2, and M–3. However, one byproduct of the new system outlived the transitory numbers. The two measures of M–1 were announced by the Fed every Friday and the banks and credit markets anxiously awaited these numbers every week. Positioning by banks and dealers in anticipation of the announcements tended to make the credit markets extremely volatile since most remembered the Fed's original special reserve requirements, also announced on a Friday, and the chaos they had created as interest rates began to rise the next business day. Traditional "Fed watching" took on an even more urgent tone with these Friday announcements.

The new method employed by the Fed would take several years to be felt in the monetary aggregates. However, an administration program was launched at the same time that attempted to come to grips with high interest rates. By the end of the first quarter of 1980, the prime rate stood at 20 percent and Treasury bill yields exceeded 14 percent. In March, President Carter announced a program of credit restraints that was intended to reduce borrowing and inflation. The restraints were coupled with a reduction in federal spending, ostensibly designed to balance the 1981 budget. The combination of the two produced the desired effect but was, unfortunately, short-lived.

The budget-balancing program attempted to trim federal spending by $14 billion for the fiscal year 1981. In the previous year, the Congressional Budget Office estimated that expenditure cuts of at least $25 billion would be required to lower the inflation rate by as little as 1 percent.[24] However, the cuts produced a slowdown in the economy that coincided with, or triggered, a recession that was to last until 1982. But the inflation rate was not substantially affected. Interest rates did drop temporarily, however, because of the credit restraint program adopted at the same time.

In March 1980, the Credit Control Act was invoked. This piece of legislation was a vestige of the Nixon administration and evoked memories of similar measures used during the postwar period. The Federal Reserve was authorized to "regulate and control any or all extensions of credit." This included licensing credit transactions or persons involved in credit use, setting limits on the terms of loans made, or prohibitions on certain types of credit extensions.[25] Banks were encouraged to hold loan growth to a specific percentage of those already on the books to all types of customers.

Consumer credit was also a target of the program. Special reserve requirements were leveled against increases in consumer credit; additional reserve requirements were instituted against deposits; and a surcharge was attached to borrowings from the discount window of the Fed. As a total package, the program was comprehensive. Consumers in particular began to retrench out of bewilderment, if nothing else, at the scope of the program, which was aimed at most consumer purchases.

Whether the credit restraint program coincided with or caused the recession is a moot point for present purposes, but a slowdown in economic activity nevertheless occurred. Inflation fell several percentage points and interest rates declined. However, the program was to be short-lived. It was dismantled by the summer of 1980 and interest rates again began an inexorable rise. The program was at odds with the policies of the Fed, which at the same time was attempting to defend the dollar from falling on the foreign exchange markets. One method of holding the dollar firm was to let interest rates rise, which would make the currency and dollar-denominated assets appealing to foreign investors, who would then bid up its value. By the end of 1980, the results of the program had become apparent: growth had declined while inflation and interest rates rose, producing what popularly became known as "stagflation."

Banks were seriously affected by these measures since loan demand declined and investors flocked to money market mutual funds as a hedge against inflation. The funds themselves had been included in the restraint program since banks were required to deposit reserves of 15 percent over their previous outstanding levels at the beginning of March. But once the program was dismantled, their growth again resumed an upward trend.

All of these pressures on commercial banks led to a continuous withdrawal of banks from the Federal Reserve. Between 1975 and 1980, 365 federally chartered banks withdrew from the Fed, opting simply to remain state-chartered institutions.[26] The reason for these defections had to do with the banks' reserves. The Fed had more stringent requirements concerning legal reserves of commercial banks than did the states in general. In central banking parlance, legal reserves could be held only as cash, earning no interest at the Fed. Many states allowed commercial banks to hold those reserves in interest-bearing securities such as Treasury bills or municipal notes. The financial temptation for many banks was too great to allow them to continue earning no return on those reserves. As a result, the Federal Reserve's grip was loosened rather than tightened.

While the banks' position was understandable, the Fed was nevertheless losing control of many institutions in a time of financial crisis. As a result, legislation was needed to strengthen the central bank's grip on the banking system while at the same time allowing banks more freedom for maneuver in order to prevent further disintermediation. The economic climate had become too volatile to allow the marketplace to solve these problems on its own. The legislative solution came in March 1980 with the passage of the Depository Institutions Deregulation and Monetary Control Act, known either by its acronym DIDMCA or simply as the Monetary Control Act. This legislation was the culmination of more than a decade of pressure for financial reform from within the banking community and the Fed.

The Monetary Control Act was the most comprehensive piece of banking legislation since the Banking Act of 1933. As its full name implies, it had two sides: a deregulation side and a monetary control side. On the deregulation side, it phased out interest rate ceilings on deposits paid by banking institutions. Rather than eliminate Regulation Q ceilings with one stroke of the pen, it planned for an orderly phasing out of ceilings by no later than March 31, 1986. The process was placed in the hands of the Depository Institutions Deregulation Committee, a body also created by the act.[27] At the same time, it eliminated state usury laws limiting the amount of interest that could be charged on home mortgage loans, business loans, and agricultural loans, as well as any state restrictions limiting the amount of interest paid on deposits.[28]

Federal deposit insurance was also included in the legislation. Insurance was increased to $100,000 from the $40,000 previously in force. Also under the umbrella of this act was the Consumer Checking Account Equity Act of 1980, mentioned earlier, which allowed all depository institutions to offer interest-paying checking accounts.[29] Savings institutions were given greater latitude than had previously been the case. Thrifts were now able to offer credit card facilities, make a certain proportion of their loans to consumers, and invest in commercial loans and corporate bonds. While limitations were placed on the percentage of total assets that thrifts could invest in these new areas, they had nevertheless been given the right to encroach upon some of the traditional preserves of commercial banks.

These changes, affecting all depository institutions, were accompanied by stricter monetary control. In order to prevent the defection of other commercial banks, the Fed was given the power to set uniform reserve requirements for *all* depository institutions, and not just federally chartered commercial banks. This eliminated much of the incentive for banks to withdraw in favor of state banking regulations that mandated lower legal reserve requirements. At the same time, the Fed's services normally performed only for member banks were extended to all depository institutions, including access to the discount window for borrowed reserves. While many of these measures were welcomed by the banking community, the gradual approach adopted, especially concerning the phasing out of Regulation Q and the absence of other key questions such as interstate banking, made DIDMCA less comprehensive than the banking community had hoped. However, these other issues were not dead but in a temporary holding pattern.

While DIDMCA broadened the power of thrift institutions, apparently at the expense of commercial banks, the thrift industry still required more assistance than the legislation had given it. During the late 1970s and early 1980s, the industry as a whole had been losing money. By the end of 1981, FSLIC-insured savings institutions' profits had fallen by 7 percent from the previous year.[30] The thrifts were suffering from a problem that had confronted commercial banking in the 1930s and 1940s: being mainly local institutions, they served a narrow geographical area and had limited sources of funding other than deposits. When real estate loans went bad, losses had to be absorbed and little could be done to expand their asset bases. High interest rates and alternative forms of savings also helped to disintermediate them as well as commercial banks; as a result, the entire industry was under severe pressure. Their plight also put pressure on the mortgage market and while DIDMCA had put in place measures to help ensure their future viability, their immediate prospects were not good. Thus, another piece of legislation was passed in 1982 that was aimed at all banking institutions, with the thrift crisis especially in mind.

In October 1982, President Reagan signed into law the Depository Institutions Act of 1982, also known as the Garn-St. Germain Act. This piece of legislation was as revolutionary as the DIDMCA in that it addressed itself to interstate banking mergers without overriding the provisions of the McFadden Act. It also provided for new accounts for depository institutions so that they could counter the effect of money market funds by offering higher rates of interest on certain types of accounts, and further extended the types of assets that thrifts could invest in. However, the Garn-St. Germain Bill did not address itself directly to the housing market, preferring to leave the role of agencies in the mortgage markets to their own time-proven devices. By strengthening the savings and loans (S & Ls) it was hoped that the mortgage market would receive the assistance needed without direct governmental intervention.

A new deposit account was also created that immediately boosted the ability of depository institutions to compete for funds with the money market funds. A money market deposit account (MMDA) was created that allowed banks to immediately remove interest rate ceilings and pay a market rate of interest. These accounts required a minimum balance and offered limited checking privileges. The major attraction of these accounts, as with other bank accounts, was that they were guaranteed by deposit insurance. In the year after the accounts were authorized, the amount of money market mutual funds in the hands of small investors declined by almost $47 billion before increasing again in 1984.[31]

Another new product authorized was the Super NOW account, which allowed an unlimited number of checks to be written against it. Thrift institutions were also allowed to make commercial loans and grant overdraft facilities—two more incursions into commercial banking functions. Perhaps most importantly, the legislation recognized the importunate need for financial deregulation and called for an accelerated timetable for the removal of interest rate ceilings. Rather than wait until 1986 for the total dismantling of ceilings, 1984 became the target date by which depository institutions would be free to offer deposit rates based on the market.

Mergers between banks within the same state or in different states was allowed under the legislation if one bank was closed or on the verge of closing. Different combinations were allowed; for example, a commercial bank could acquire a failing commercial bank or S & L, and vice versa, although the latter was extremely unlikely. The rationale behind this new principle was very practical: any bailout of an institution by another in the private sector was preferable to spending FDIC or FSLIC funds to accomplish the same end. At the same time, the new legislation gave the acquiring institution an opportunity to diversify its assets by acquiring institutions in a different geographical location.

On the surface, both parts of deregulation appeared to give thrift institutions extended powers at the expense of commercial banks. However, even in a period of relative financial stability the thrifts would need years to make serious inroads into expanded banking. By the end of the decade, the thrift industry would again face a crisis much more serious than that of the early 1980s. Neither were commercial banks yet out of the financial woods; in the same year (1982) they faced another crisis created by the aggressive lending policies to the Third World that they so actively pursued after the events of 1972.

No sooner had the deregulation been put in place than the banks again came under pressure. In October 1982, the government of Mexico announced that, without some assistance from its lenders, it would not be able to meet the interest payments on the sizable debt it had accumulated since 1972. Most of this external debt was in U.S. dollars and was owed to the banking community among whom it had been syndicated. The amount of the debt involved was estimated to be around $65 billion, most of which was granted originally on a floating basis. Mexico became the first notable international casualty of the worldwide recession. Gasoline prices had fallen more quickly than interest rates and the bank loan rates, based on short-term interest rates, remained high despite the drop in the price of gas.

The banks' overall exposure to Mexico was significant. The four largest lenders' loans outstanding amounted to approximately $9 billion, with Citicorp and the Bank of America accounting for slightly less than $6 billion. In both cases, that amounted to over 50 percent of their capital in 1982.[32] In addition to the revenues lost by an outright Mexican default, any write-off of the principal amounts involved could have effectively wiped out most of the larger lenders' capital as well. As a result, Mexico and its largest lenders began a series of debt renegotiations that lasted to the end of the decade. Most members of the original syndicates agreed to lend fresh funds so that current interest and principal repayments could continue rather than be written off. The smaller regional banks that had also participated all had to agree to any restructuring because they were legally the equals of the larger banks in the syndicates. Without their agreement to new terms, a legal default would have occurred. However, within a year, a new market had been established on an over-the-counter basis in which banks could sell their outstanding loans to third parties if desired. (More will be said about that market in Chapter 7.)

In the years following the momentous events of 1982, interest rates began to subside and by early 1986 a positive yield curve had again reemerged. Inflation had subsided, mainly due to the Federal Reserve's continuing tight monetary policy, and the stock market was at an historic high. But the commodity price deflation that accompanied the fall in inflation and interest rates had left many other Third World countries in dire economic straits. Most prominent among these were Brazil, Argentina, the Philippines, and many other Latin American and Asian countries whose export earnings had dropped dramatically. Many of them also negotiated debt restructuring programs by extending repayment periods, intended to forestall default. But the debt crisis claimed one commercial banking casualty that became the largest bank failure in U.S. history to date.

In the summer of 1984, the Continental Illinois National Bank ran into financial difficulties because of its loan portfolio. At the time, it was the seventh largest U.S. bank, measured by deposits of about $40 billion. Many of its loans, while adequately diversified, were in troubled areas such as foreign loans, agricultural loans, and energy loans—the latter to many domestic energy suppliers such as oil and natural gas companies. Compounding the problem was a group of bad loans the bank had purchased from another failing institution, the Penn Square Bank. As word of its financial plight grew, Continental lost several billion dollars in deposits in one week as many CD investors refused to roll over their deposits, demanding cash instead. As a result, the bank faced an enormous funding crisis and the regulatory authorities had to step in to prevent a technical failure.

In order to prevent an outright failure, the Federal Reserve provided Continental with emergency discount window loans and the FDIC agreed to insure all of its deposits, regardless of size. A syndicate of other banks was also formed to provide about $4 billion in emergency funds so that depositors would be assured that the institution would not fail. All of these emergency measures ensured that Continental would survive and that its weakness would not have a domino effect on other U.S. banks. Nevertheless, the measures adopted were extraordinary in that all depositors were protected, not merely those with $100,000 or less. The precedent that was set was repeated in 1988 when the FDIC again agreed to protect all depositors of two Texas banks close to failure, the First City Bancorporation and the First Republic Bank Corporation, both of which had fallen prey to the fall in gasoline prices and poor housing markets in their home state.

In the case of many bank failures, especially those in Texas, the provisions of the deregulatory legislation allowed many out-of-state banks to acquire these failing institutions. Many money center banks and larger regional banks were thus able to expand, while avoiding the prohibitions of the McFadden Act. The first major test case of the new deregulatory climate came in 1983, when Citicorp acquired Fidelity Savings and Loan of California and renamed it Citicorp Savings. Bank of America acquired Seattle First, a Washington commercial bank that would have otherwise failed without an infusion of capital from a willing buyer.

One of the major problems that arose from poor and nonperforming loans made by the banks was the erosion of their capital bases. As mentioned above, total loans to Mexico alone represented more than 50 percent of some of the major banks' capital in 1982. When combined with problem loans to other entities, the percentages were much higher and threatened many institutions' viability. As the Third World debt crisis became more pronounced, the Federal Reserve acted to increase bank capital in order to shore up their balance sheets and assure the financial markets of the viability of the financial system.[33] This was done in two distinct steps.

The first step came in 1985 when the Federal Reserve announced that a capital total assets ratio of 6 percent would be required. While the actual number required was somewhat arbitrary, one fact was obvious: the ratio had been declining steadily since 1960, when it stood at 8 percent.[34] During the same period, the number of assets at federally insured commercial banks had grown exponentially; thus, while the dollar amounts were greater, by 1982 capital adequacy had nevertheless declined. The new standard forced many banks to the capital markets to raise funds. It also caused many larger banks to scrutinize assets or other receivables on their books in order to raise cash (see Chapter 7).

In 1987, the Fed again decided to raise capital adequacy requirements. In this instance, it participated in an international agreement reached at the Bank for International Settlements with 11 other industrialized countries to establish uniform requirements on all banks by the target date of 1992. These measures required banks to apply risk measurements to their assets and contingent liabilities, including letters of credit and interest rate swaps. This accord was an acknowledgement of the efficiency of the euromarket in international borrowing and lending and of the internationalization of the bank marketplace in general. It sought to place all banks participating in that market on a level playing field, at least in terms of capital adequacy.

Despite the problems faced by banks in the 1980s, they nevertheless continued to expand by offering new products and services. Lending to the Third World obviously decreased during the latter part of the decade, being replaced by other sources of revenue deemed to be less risky. The most notable addition to bank revenues was the development of the interest rate swap and currency swap markets. Expansion was also accomplished through subsidiary companies that offered brokerage and other securities-related businesses to customers. As the regulatory authorities tightened the screws, the banks retaliated by opening an attack on the securities-related constrictions of the Glass-Steagall Act.

The swap market for both interest rates and foreign currency transactions developed quickly, with the first transactions occurring in 1983. Two borrowers, usually corporations, would swap their fixed and floating rate debt at advantageous terms; the banks entered the transaction as third parties in order to guarantee the swap. In return for the guarantee, banks received a fee based on the total value of the deal. This sort of banking transaction was different from traditional lending in that fees would immediately be generated although the actual exposure of the swap did not appear on the balance sheet of the banks involved. Only if the transaction went awry because of a default by one of the parties would the bank have to honor its commitment. Swaps, whether interest rate- or currency-related, were thus booked by banks as contingent (off the balance sheet) liabilities rather than as assets.

Swap fees became a useful source of bank revenue as the Third World loan market dwindled in the years after 1982. Although it is difficult to estimate the size of the international swap market, because swaps are essentially private transactions, by the end of 1989 it stood at around $700 billion in total swaps outstanding. Between 1985 and 1988, it was generating about $50–70 billion per year in new business and had established itself as a new major financial market in its own right.[35]

During the 1980s, banks continued to grow in size although the increased capital requirements did require some to retrench in order to raise their net worth. Total loans and securities had grown by $1 trillion, from $1.32 trillion in 1981 to over $2.4 trillion by the beginning of 1989.[36] Securities represented about 20–25 percent of the total throughout the decade, a far cry from the 1930s and 1940s when the proportions were reversed. But the increased competition for funds in the deregulated environment, and the rise of Japanese banks in particular in the international league tables of total assets, increased pressure on U.S. banks to find other profitable lines of business. This led them to increase their lobbying of regulators to allow them to reenter the corporate securities business once again.

Banks had made some inroads in gaining a foothold in the business they had been forced to leave in 1933–34 by acquiring brokerage houses. This enabled them to offer brokerage (usually discount) services to their retail customers. Brokers were acquired by bank holding companies and operated as subsidiary companies. However, they had to be individually capitalized so that depositors' funds were not placed at risk. While this form of expansion moved banks closer to the old concept of the financial supermarket, the most lucrative part of the securities business—underwriting—still remained beyond their reach. The only type of underwriting they had been able to participate in over the years was eurobond underwriting, engaged in by their Edge Act subsidiaries located overseas. Domestically, some had entered the commercial paper market as distributors of short-term corporate notes, but usually they did so only on the secondary market side.

The new-issues market for corporate bonds and stock provided a lucrative source of revenue for investment banks; the banks viewed it as one in which they too could realize substantial gains. For instance, in 1987 over $392 billion was raised in the primary markets, with $326 billion represented by new bonds and $66 billion in new stock offerings.[37] Assuming that the average underwriting fee for the total was about 2.5 percent, the total underwriting revenues exceeded $9 billion.

One of the banks' major arguments was that if they were allowed to reenter the business they would be able to raise this new capital for smaller fees than the investment banks normally charged. If fees could be reduced by one-half, over $4.5 billion could be freed for capital investment rather than for investment banking fees. While the argument was persuasive, it nevertheless ignored one equally persuasive argument in favor of the investment banks that had been brought out 35 years earlier in the case of the *U.S. v. Henry S. Morgan*. Investment banks had established historic relationships over time with their clients that gave them an intimate knowledge of those clients' financing needs and how best to achieve them. Commercial banks, lacking that specific sort of knowledge, would not be able to compete successfully in the new-issues market by underwriting and placing new issues. They had no track record and certainly the investment banks did not want to see them develop one at their expense.

Nevertheless, in 1988 and again in 1989, the Federal Reserve did allow commercial banks to begin underwriting commercial paper and corporate bonds on a limited basis. Corporate stocks, however, were not included in the rulings. Banks quickly seized the opportunity and formed their own syndicates to underwrite bonds in particular, usually through their merchant or investment banking subsidiaries. After 55 years of exclusion from the underwriting business they had finally gained a toehold, if not a foothold, in investment banking again.

Commercial banking has witnessed a long and varied history since 1934. The banks have grown in size and diversity and have weathered many economic and financial crises as the economy changed from a postwar manufacturing base to one dominated by service industries competing in an increasingly international marketplace. In this latter respect, they have been in the forefront of change as they reacted to consumer and industrial developments that helped shape the American economic ideal. At the same time, many of their original ambitions, originally forged during the growth years of the 1920s, have resurfaced in the 1980s. The ideas of "financial department store" and "universal banking" are again beginning to take shape and in many cases, have already reappeared as many of the original banking constrictions crumble in the wake of technological change and consumer demand for innovative financial services.

NOTES

1. Federal Reserve *Bulletin*, May 1934 and December 1937.

2. Ibid., December 1933 and December 1937.

3. Quoted in Harold B. van Cleveland and Thomas Huertas, *Citibank: 1812–1970* (Cambridge, MA: Harvard University Press, 1985), p. 204.

4. Ibid., p. 205.

5. See John Donald Wilson, *The Chase: The Chase Manhattan Bank, N.A., 1945–1985* (Boston: Harvard Business School Press, 1986), p. 17.

6. Jones related that the RFC attempted to enlist the commercial banks in lending to small businesses after it had been given official sanction to loan to business and industry after 1934. The results were less than satisfying. As he recalled later: "I sent a letter to every one of the 14,000 banks in the United States asking their cooperation in making loans to business. Only 1 percent acknowledged receipt of our letter. That hardly seems credible, because more than half of the banks had been directly assisted by the RFC and all had been indirectly assisted." See Jesse Jones with Edward Angly, *Fifty Billion Dollars: My Thirteen Years with the RFC* (New York: Macmillan, 1951), p. 183.

7. Marquis James and Bessie Rowland James, *Biography of a Bank: The Story of the Bank of America* (New York: Harper & Bros., 1954), p. 416.

8. Ibid.

9. Federal Reserve *Bulletin*, December 1947.

10. Parker B. Willis, *The Federal Funds Market: Its Origin and Development*, 3rd edn (Boston: Federal Reserve Bank of Boston, 1968), p. 15. Also see Herman

Krooss, *Documentary History of Banking and Currency in the United States*, vol. 4 (New York: Chelsea House Publishers, 1969), p. 2991.

11. Krooss, *Documentary*, vol. 4, p. 2978.

12. The Stephens Act divided New York State into nine districts within which banks could legally branch. The only way a bank could open a branch in another district was through merger, and not by opening a branch *de novo*. Since one of these districts was New York City itself, New York City banks were confined to branching only within the city limits. Official merger with other state banks would be the only way the major money center banks could expand. See Paul V. Teplitz, *Trends Affecting the U.S. Banking System* (Cambridge, MA: Ballinger, 1976), p. 166.

13. Cleveland and Huertas, *Citibank*, p. 249.

14. E. Wayne Clendenning, *The Euro-Dollar Market* (Oxford: Clarendon Press, 1970), p. 23.

15. Cleveland and Huertas, *Citibank*, p. 255.

16. Bank for International Settlements, *Annual Report*, 1969; and Morgan Guaranty Trust, *World Financial Markets*, various issues.

17. Ordinarily, an investor purchasing money market instruments outright would have had to invest in round lots that may have been out of reach of the ordinary investor/saver. Treasury bills usually required an investment of $10,000, while commercial paper required $100,000, as did negotiable bank CDs and bankers' acceptances.

18. Federal Reserve *Bulletin*, January 1975.

19. Federal Reserve System, *Flow of Funds Accounts*.

20. Wilson, *The Chase*, p. 213.

21. Morgan Guaranty Trust, *World Financial Markets*, 1978–79.

22. Federal Reserve *Bulletin*, January 1980.

23. The new categories were M–1A, including currency and demand deposits at banks, M–1B, including M–1A and checking deposits at other institutions (NOW accounts, automatic transfers), and the three larger measures, M–2, M–3 and L, all of which included eurodollar deposits held in the Cayman Islands.

24. George S. Eccles, *The Politics of Banking* (Salt Lake City: University of Utah, 1982), p. 248.

25. Ibid., p. 249.

26. Although this process was highly visible during the period of rising interest rates in the 1970s, it had in fact been occurring since World War II. In 1945, there were over 6,800 federally chartered banks, as compared with only 5,600 in 1980. Even during periods of relative interest rate stability many institutions had withdrawn from the Fed for essentially the same reasons. These reasons became much more pronounced after the original OPEC price rise and the subsequent spiral in interest rates.

27. The members of this committee included the Secretary of the Treasury, chairman of the Federal Reserve System, chairman of the Federal Home Loan Bank Board, chairman of the FDIC, and the chairman of the National Credit Union Administration.

28. The elimination of state usury laws helped pave the way for many lending institutions to begin offering adjustable rate mortgages. It also helped prompt the various mortgage agencies to begin purchasing adjustables as well; see Chapter 2.

29. Other than commercial banks, depository institutions includes S & Ls, savings banks, and credit unions.

30. United States League of Savings Institutions, *Source Book*, 1985.

31. The amount of money market mutual funds fell from $185.2 billion to $138.2 billion. This does not include institutional funds; however, they also declined by a similar percentage. One cause of the decline may have been the fall in interest rates during the same time period. Ninety-day commercial paper fell by 300 basis points and similar Treasury bills by 200 basis points. See Federal Reserve *Bulletin*, October 1985. The amount of money market funds outstanding has always moved in line with the trend of short-term interest rates: when rates rise, the amount outstanding rises, and when rates fall, outstanding money market funds fall.

32. The other two banks included Manufacturers Hanover, with $1.7 billion outstanding, and Chase Manhattan, with $1.4 billion outstanding, representing 52 and 37 percent of their capital respectively. See John Pool and Steven Stamos, *The ABCs of International Finance* (Lexington, MA: Lexington Books, 1987), p. 112.

33. Capital in this case is divided into two components. Those funds represented on the balance sheet by retained earnings, funds derived from the sale of common or perpetual preferred stock, loan loss reserves, and convertible bonds are classified as primary capital. Secondary capital includes bond borrowings outstanding but not yet repaid, and certain other classes of preferred stock. The simplest measure of bank capital divides the amount of capital on the books by the amount of loans outstanding. This gives the amount of capital as a percentage of loans outstanding.

34. FDIC annual reports, 1960–74; and *Bank Operating Statistics*, 1975–88.

35. See Charles R. Geisst, *A Guide to the Financial Markets*, 2nd edn (New York: St. Martin's Press, 1989), Chapter 7.

36. Federal Reserve *Bulletin*, September 1983 and April 1989.

37. Ibid., January 1989.

4

Financing the Castle: The Mortgage Agencies

Quality, single-family housing has become the most tangible element of the American dream, symbolizing freedom and space to grow. Spurred by the crowded conditions of nineteenth-century Europe, new immigrants placed housing high on their list of priorities and considered it the epitomy of what their adopted country had to offer. Over the years, many individuals have continued to place the individual castle at the top of their list of material needs. Perhaps no other single material goal has come to symbolize the American dream so succinctly. As a result, housing has become one of the United States' most vital industries and statistics related to it are closely watched signs indicating the health of the economy.

The story of housing is more complicated than simply building upon a dream. The availability of credit, the term structure of interest rates, the ability of mortgage-granting institutions to cope with economic conditions, and the individual's ability to service his or her mortgage debt all must be factored into the general discussion so that the peculiarly American method of funding mortgages since the mid–1930s can be properly understood. Aside from these standard factors that affect mortgage markets anywhere, the mortgage industry in the United States is uniquely assisted by the federal government. This assistance is offered through the vehicle known as the "agency" function, whereby a government-created agency intervenes in the marketplace in order to provide liquidity to the lenders of mortgage money. While this function may appear simple, it is in fact a complicated process that has come to be repeated many times in twentieth-century U.S. financial history. The soundness of the concept also proved itself internationally, beginning in the 1950s, when it became the model for many international development agencies. The concept of agency financing is American for all intents and purposes although it was quickly recognized that the same function that provided liquidity for the mortgage market could also be redefined to help provide funds for Third and Fourth World development. More will be said about this variation of the theme at the end of this chapter.

The development of mortgage agencies originally occurred, and has remained, at the wholesale level of mortgage funding. The agencies that have been created since the mid–1930s have operated between mortgage grantor, or "originator" in financial parlance, and the capital markets. On the retail, or individual, level mortgage borrowing has remained a private transaction between the individual and the banking institution. How and why banking institutions involve the agencies in the mortgage process involves both the fulfillment of a commitment as well as a response to monetary conditions, which sometimes can prove pernicious to the market as a whole.

Despite the growing presence of agencies through the middle part of this century, housing finance has remained in the private sector. Individuals have sought mortgages from the traditional sources of funds: commercial banks and especially savings and loan associations or savings banks. Thrift institutions have been integrally involved in mortgage lending since the nineteenth century and have in recent years suffered most because of their limited nature as depository/lending institutions dedicated almost solely to redirecting savers' funds into the housing market. Their plight over the years helped prompt the banking legislation of the early 1980s designed to help them cope with the interest rate effects of restrictive monetary policies and the subsequent damage caused to the expansion of the housing market as a whole.

In the nineteenth century, depository institutions devoted solely to granting mortgage loans were called building associations. The first was established in Philadelphia in 1831 and was called the Oxford Provident Building Association. The nomenclature used was British by design. U.S. building associations were modeled after the English building societies developed about 50 years earlier. The English institutions and their U.S. counterparts were organized as mutual societies; that is, the institutions were owned by depositors. They were not capitalized by the sale of stock and thus there were no public shareholders as such. The current capital structure of U.S. savings and loan associations still reflects this original model. In the mid–1980s, about 80 percent of all S & Ls were still operating as mutual societies.

The ownership of thrifts is not as important as are the organizational problems they pose for the housing market as a whole. Being mutual means that thrifts were, and still for the most part are, local institutions whose influence does not extend beyond the geographical area in which they operate. On the negative side, this means that mortgage lending is primarily local in nature, subject to a lack of standardization in lending rates. On the positive side, it suggests that credit analysis of potential homebuyers should be left to indigenous institutions that know the local market best.

In the period leading to the stock market crash of 1929 and the depression that followed, thrift institutions and banks were the primary sources of mortgage money. Loans made were booked as assets by the lending institution and remained on the books until final payment was made. But out of the financial turmoil of the 1930s rose myriad new financial institutions designed to provide a safety net against future unforeseen events. Essentially, these new institutions would leave the traditional mechanism of mortgage granting in place while providing another layer of previously unexplored governmental assistance in an attempt to ensure an orderly, growing market.

THE 1930s EXPERIENCE

In the decades prior to the Depression, S & Ls underwent a period of rapid expansion. In 1925, over 12,000 were chartered, a twofold increase over the decade before.[1] But they were ill equipped to cope with the period of business and monetary contraction that was to follow. In October 1930, the first of the decade's banking crises occurred, with over 600 banks failing in October and November alone, representing some $550 million worth of deposits.[2] The year culminated in the failure of the private Bank of the United States, the largest commercial banking failure in U.S. history up to that time.

As all depository institutions came under pressure, an idea that had been floating around for over a decade began to take tangible form. In the summer of 1932, the Federal Home Loan Bank Act was signed into law and the future of mortgage-granting institutions changed with this one piece of legislation. This act created the Federal Home Loan Bank System, a structure that somewhat resembled the organization of the Federal Reserve System.

The system as such included the Federal Home Loan Bank Board, 12 Federal Home Loan Banks organized on a regional basis, and the members of the system, the S & Ls for whom it was primarily created. The 12 banks created recalled the origin of the Federal Reserve although the geographic districts were not quite the same. The purpose of the system was to provide liquidity to member institutions suffering cash-flow problems. In this respect, it could transfer funds from one district to another in order to provide temporary relief.

Individual Home Loan Banks obtained the cash they needed to operate by selling stock to the member savings institutions. This made the individual member shareholders the owners of the local district bank. Thus, shareholders both provided capital and obtained loans if necessary. This consolidated the mortgage industry to an extent because all of the previously fragmented savings institutions were at least united under one national umbrella organization. The overall purpose of this institution was to provide a prop under both the construction industry and financial institutions at the same time.

Although the Home Loan Bank System served as a means of bringing support to savings institutions, it did not provide the agency function described earlier. The original agency function would be found in other developments of the early 1930s closely related to the institution of the Home Loan Bank System but which brought support closer to the individual. The first agency, the Home Owner's Loan Corporation, was founded in 1933 by the Home Owner's Loan Act. The second was inaugurated a year later with the Federal Housing Administration. Of these two agencies, only the latter survives to this day; the former was officially liquidated in 1954.

Homeowners benefited directly from the activities of the Home Owner's Loan Corporation. It was instituted primarily to ensure that the benefits derived by S & Ls from the creation of the Home Loan Banks would be passed along to the homeowners themselves. The corporation added liquidity to the marketplace by exchanging its own bonds for delinquent mortgages held by the originating institutions and then favorably changing the terms on the mortgages to benefit the mortgage holder. Within three and one-half years of its inception, this corporation purchased and refinanced over 1.8 million delinquent mortgages, amounting to $6.2 billion.[3]

The Home Owner's Loan Corporation ceased this activity in 1936, having exceeded its congressional spending limitation. It subsequently sold off much of its portfolio and was eventually liquidated in 1954. However, the concept that it had begun successfully did not pass out of existence but was picked up by two other agencies created for the purpose. One of these was the Federal Housing Administration, better known as the FHA. This agency came into existence in 1934. Although it is usual to think of the FHA as a mortgage assistance agency, its original purposes were a bit broader than its activities today. When FHA was first created under Title I of the National Housing Act, it was the first venture by the federal government into the area of consumer financing. Along with the Electric Home and Farm Authority, the FHA was an attempt by the federal government to stimulate the flagging economy by assisting the consumer.

Originally, the FHA provided insurance to banks or other depository institutions for home modernization loans made to homeowners. By the term "home modernization" was meant loans made to install indoor plumbing or lavatories. The purpose of this program was as much geared to upgrading health as it was to improving housing standards and providing economic stimuli. If the borrower subsequently defaulted under this program, the agency would reimburse the lender for a certain percentage of the loan's value. Given the depository institutions' new emphasis on retail lending, mentioned in Chapter 3, this assistance slowly began to introduce banks to retail lending on an even greater scale, as would another small agency created by similar legislation.

The Electric Home and Farm Authority was created by executive order under provisions of the National Industrial Recovery Act in 1933. Its major purpose was to encourage consumers to purchase electric appliances and use electric power, thereby stimulating both sectors of the economy. The stimulus was found at the retail level. A consumer would buy an appliance from a retailer who would then sell the financing contract to the agency for cash. The consumer in turn paid monthly installments to the local utility that supplied the power.

Both agency ventures were new endeavors for the federal government insofar as aiding the consumer was concerned. Although the FHA especially would become better known for providing mortgage insurance, the early agency functions nevertheless proved to be harbingers of financial practices yet to come. In 1936, the chief executive officer of the FHA remarked that the principal achievement of the agency seemed to be "the big thing," that is, familiarizing commercial bankers with small consumer loans amortized on a monthly basis.[4] Until the Depression era, consumer loans were provided mainly by private finance companies, and not commercial banks per se. Now with government assistance they had gotten a taste of small retail business and as Administrator George McDonald of the FHA put it, "I think the local banks which went into this business will never get out of it . . . and they will be enough to furnish competition to the finance companies."[5]

In the midst of the Depression a model was created that would lead to a broader form of consumer financing several decades later. The basic concept employed would be taken up by large finance companies specifically created by manufacturers to finance consumer purchases of their goods, such as electrical appliances and automobiles. By the early 1980s, these finance companies would prove successful enough to compete with the commercial banks in other traditional banking areas, such as commercial and industrial lending.

The next development in the early history of the housing agencies came in 1934, when Congress passed the National Housing Act specifically to provide federally guaranteed mortgage insurance. Administration of the provisions of the legislation was placed in the hands of the FHA. Rather than create a new administrative body, the FHA was designated because the legislation was actually opposed by the thrift industry. The building associations opposed it because they felt that the insurance provided would also apply to mortgages originated by commercial banks and insurance companies, allowing them to further encroach on traditional thrift industry profits.[6]

However, the act included provisions that the thrifts did support and this helped secure the passage of the legislation. The Federal Savings and Loan Insurance Corporation (FSLIC) was created to provide insurance for savers' deposits at S & Ls for $5,000 per account. The FSLIC set a premium to be paid by the participating institutions. By becoming members of the insurance corporation, thrifts were able to extend their credibility to the public and profit in a marketing sense as well. This was especially important to the industry as a whole because the Banking Act of 1933 had made deposit insurance available to commercial banking customers as of July 1, 1934.

From its inception in 1934 to year end 1944, the FHA made insured or direct mortgage loans of slightly over $7 billion.[7] In 1944, and again in 1948, new developments were occurring in the mortgage market that further shaped the market and brought it closer to its present form. While the 1930s certainly witnessed the origin of federal assistance in the mortgage market in the form of providing guarantees to mortgage originators, it was the 1940s that ushered in the idea of making a market in federally underwritten mortgages.

Prior to the 1940s, the newly developed agencies had made considerable headway in providing assistance to the housing market. In addition to the mortgages insured or guaranteed, their influence was also felt in the interest rates for new mortgages granted by lending institutions. Prior to the establishment of agencies, the rates attached to new mortgages depended on the lending institution. As a result, different rates were being charged in different parts of the country. For instance, the average contract rate charged on a first mortgage for an owner-occupied residential property granted by an S & L in Worcester, Massachusetts, in January 1934 was 5.65 percent. In Austin, Texas, the rate was 7.45 percent, while in San Diego, it was 7.19 percent. The same sort of differentials could be found in mortgages granted by commercial banks and savings banks as well. However, the rate was the same (5 percent) for all geographical areas on mortgages granted by the Home Owners Loan Corporation.[8] This led one commentator to remark in 1937 that "a leveling tendency among interest rates charged in different parts of the country appears to be in prospect, partly as a result of the extension of the activities of Federal agencies which have uniform rates for all their loans."[9]

As a result of the founding of the Home Loan Bank Board and the specific agencies themselves, the process of interest rate standardization of home mortgages became embedded in the U.S. housing market. This was true, however, only of those lending institutions that availed themselves of agency support. But in commercial terms many lending institutions would have to follow suit in order to maintain their lending policies in face of this competition.[10] Ten years earlier, the Farm Credit System had undergone a similar rationalization of interest rates. Agency intermediation had begun to have an effect in both the consumer and housing loan markets.

VETERANS' ASSISTANCE AND FANNIE MAE

The government's only attempt to provide mortgage assistance to a special group within society occurred with the establishment of the Servicemen's Readjustment Act of 1944. This legislation originally allowed veterans to purchase homes at prewar prices upon their return but was soon afterward expanded so that servicemen could obtain mortgages at lower interest rates than nonveterans. The agency entrusted with this function was the Veterans Administration (VA) established in 1930, which combined all federal agencies that up until that time provided services for former servicemen.

In contemporary terms, neither the VA nor any of the other agencies developed in the 1930s actually functioned in the manner that self-financing government-sponsored agencies do in the present market. The funds the agencies used for their support or insurance programs normally came from government sources, but not the public bond market. The funds spent by them came from insurance premiums levied, the sale of assets acquired in default proceedings, or appropriated funds. And until 1944, no secondary market capabilities were built into any of the institutions' charters.

The original market-related capacity was found in the charter of the Federal National Mortgage Association, or Fannie Mae as it is more popularly known, founded by Congress in 1938. Originally, the objectives of the organization were similar to those of the other established agencies—to increase the volume of new housing built nationwide, thereby aiding the construction industry and the economy. Also included in its objectives was the desire to provide a broad secondary market for FHA-insured mortgages. It was this latter objective that distinguished Fannie Mae from its predecessors.

The term "secondary market" can be somewhat misleading here. Since a large proportion of the funds raised by the various agencies today comes from the bond market, it is sometimes erroneously inferred that this is what is meant by secondary market function. What the term actually meant was the ability of an agency to purchase or sell mortgages from its own portfolio, with the mortgage originators being the counterparties. Simply put, the originators could either divest or acquire mortgages after they had been written by dealing directly with Fannie Mae. The secondary market prices of the mortgages traded were dictated by prevailing interest rates in the market as well as the terms and conditions of the obligations themselves.

Although Fannie Mae was founded in 1938, it was not until 1948 that it began to emerge from relative obscurity to assume a major role in mortgage financing. During its first ten years it purchased several hundred million dollars worth of FHA-insured mortgages, but that number was less than 5 percent of the mortgages the FHA had insured during the same period. During the war years, the agency was relatively silent and only resurfaced in 1948 after Congress authorized it to purchase VA-guaranteed home mortgages as well. In the period immediately following, the agency made its presence felt in the market. Between February 1949 and July 1950, FNMA acquired almost one-third of all VA loans closed and almost half of VA loans given for new construction.[11]

The Housing Act of 1949 changed the course and tone of U.S. housing policy for decades to come. The act stated that the national goal of housing policy would be to provide a decent home and suitable living environment for every American family. While never actually defining the term "suitable" specifically, it was assumed that this meant upgrading dilapidated housing by improving plumbing facilities and reducing overcrowding; the latter was measured by the number of persons per room.[12] This legislation, passed during the Truman administration, dominated U.S. housing policy until 1968, when new legislation further refined the aims of home building on a massive scale.

Almost immediately, Fannie Mae became the agency most easily identified with the American dream in two respects. First, it emerged as the premier federal agency concerned with housing; second, it was the only housing agency with a presence in the credit markets as a public-sector borrower. But its evolution into a unique U.S. federal agency took over a decade to accomplish. Fannie Mae continued to purchase FHA and VA mortgages until 1954, when its activities again came under the scrutiny of Congress. The agency was reorganized in that year under the Housing Act, which redefined its secondary market function and also envisaged its eventual sale to the public, or privatization. This latter goal would be achieved 13 years later.

To support its secondary market objectives, Fannie Mae was able to draw on three sources of funds. The first was the proceeds of a preferred stock sale made to the U.S. Treasury. As with all directly owned government agencies, the Treasury was the holder of the capital stock either in common or preferred form. The second source was its ability to borrow on the credit markets; it was authorized to borrow up to ten times its net worth. In 1954, this amounted to about $1 billion. Third, the agency could realize monies from net government investment and the sale of mortgages off its books. Until 1954, this third source was Fannie Mae's major source of funds, but it was replaced by bond market borrowings after the 1954 reorganization.

Despite the social advantages of Fannie Mae's operations, it was not universally popular in the mortgage industry itself. Between 1949 and 1959, the largest percentage of sellers of mortgages to the agency—also accounting for the largest percentage of volume of business done—were mortgage companies rather than banks or thrifts.[13] The depository institutions felt the pressure brought to bear by the leveling of interest rates and also objected to secondary market operations after 1954 that encouraged competition from nondepository mortgage originators. As a result they avoided Fannie Mae, especially when credit market conditions were conducive.

Fannie Mae also came under criticism at various times during its first ten years of secondary market operations. The major criticism was that it bought more mortgages than it sold, thereby providing more of a support function than a secondary market function. By being a net buyer of mortgages it actually competed with originators, evoking complaints of unfair government competition and meddling in the marketplace. Rather than making a market in mortgages, the agency became a market in and of itself.

Another vague area surrounding its operations was the role the agency was to play *vis-à-vis* monetary and fiscal policy. In periods of tight conditions in the credit markets, its role of providing liquidity could run counter to Federal Reserve policy or to government spending constraints. While this potential clash with policy may not have been foreseen when the agency was first founded, it became a major and persistent area of concern that led to the eventual sale of stock to the general investing public in 1968.

As the agencies became more entrenched in the housing market, the original objectives for which they were founded began to change. These objectives, of providing stimuli to both the construction industry and lending institutions, were slowly replaced with more socially oriented objectives. The notion that decent housing meant a lowering of the crime rate, a healthier population, and fewer transfer payments or other social costs became the major policy objective of housing policy. In theory, the upgrading of dilapidated housing would have beneficial social effects in the long run. To this end, Fannie Mae, as well as the other agencies, also provided special support programs for low-income housing so that homebuyers from many socioeconomic groups would benefit from its operations.

THE DEVELOPMENT OF MORTGAGE-BACKED SECURITIES

The pressure that developed over the years to spin Fannie Mae off to the private sector culminated in 1968 with the founding of the Government National Mortgage Association, better known as Ginnie Mae. The purpose of this agency was to assume the special assistance and liquidation functions that, up until that date, had been carried out by Fannie Mae. In addition, Ginnie Mae also guaranteed mortgages originally insured or guaranteed by the government through other agencies.

With the advent of Ginnie Mae, Fannie Mae was privatized through the sale of common stock to the investing public. Its shares are now held by investors and listed on the New York Stock Exchange. As of September 1, 1968, Fannie Mae was officially a private corporation operating under government auspices. Through privatization, the agency was freed of government budget constraints and able to expand its portfolio substantially.

The reorganization of Fannie Mae and the creation of Ginnie Mae were both precipitated by the Housing and Urban Development Act of 1968. The functions of the latter agency were overseen by the Secretary of Housing and Urban Development, a cabinet-level position that had been created three years earlier. While this piece of legislation is best known for the creation of the new agency that subsequently changed the face of housing finance, it also had an important social goal that has not substantially changed since the original agencies became operative 30 years before. The Housing Act of 1968, unlike its legislative predecessors, had a quantitative objective; it called for the construction or rehabilitation of 26 million new housing units within a ten-year period. The "decent home" goal of 1949 had been given specific form. As Lyndon Johnson was to note later in his memoirs, "We had high hopes for the new law but the experts had warned us . . . without the proper mixture [of responsible fiscal and monetary policies] the realization of a goal of 26 million housing units was doubtful."[14]

Under the legislation Fannie Mae now concentrated its efforts on its secondary market functions while Ginnie Mae continued to purchase mortgages backed by FHA or the VA. Additionally, Ginnie Mae was able to give assistance to low- and middle-income housing by acting in tandem with Fannie Mae. While the procedure used in this respect was somewhat complex it nevertheless illustrated the federal government's commitment to provide housing to potential homebuyers at all income levels.

The tandem program provided direct government assistance in the purchase of mortgages to provide housing for lower-income families. Ginnie Mae would issue a commitment to purchase the mortgages at par, or face value. Fannie Mae would then make the actual purchase at the market rate for the mortgages. These rates usually were below par, given that the interest rates attached to them were lower than those attached to traditional commercial mortgages. When the time arrived for the actual financing to be carried out, Fannie Mae would retain the mortgages if their market prices had risen to par. If they had not, Ginnie Mae would purchase them at par from Fannie Mae, thereby providing assistance using government money. The cost to the federal government would be the difference between the two prices.

Since Fannie Mae was no longer operating within governmental budget restraints, it now had freer rein to expand its activities in the market. Within two years of operating under this new system it had expanded its mortgage portfolio twofold, from about $6.5 billion in 1968 to slightly over $14 billion in 1970. But for the most part, the assistance provided was confined to FHA and VA mortgages. The specially assisted mortgages continued to form the bulk of its asset portfolio. Despite the fact that Fannie Mae had been privatized, it still had to keep its activities within the confines of its original legislative objectives.

Ginnie Mae also acquired an important market function that would be expanded several years later. The Housing Act authorized it to guarantee interest and principal repayments as securities issued by private mortgage institutions that were backed by pools of FHA or VA mortgages. This was the origin of what became known as the mortgage-backed security. A large market developed around these securities within the decade as the demand grew for fixed-income securities in general, especially for those with specific asset backing.

An additional fillip was provided to the mortgage market in 1970 with the passing of the Emergency Home Finance Act. Primarily designed to subsidize advances made by the Home Loan Bank System, this act broadened Fannie Mae's activities and created a new player in the mortgage market, the Federal Home Loan Mortgage Corporation, known in industry parlance as Freddie Mac.

As mentioned, Fannie Mae's activities in the market had been confined to the purchase of FHA and VA mortgages. The 1970 legislation enabled it to perform secondary market operations in conventional mortgages, that is, the traditional fixed-rate, 30-year mortgage not insured or guaranteed by a government agency. Freddie Mac was empowered to conduct secondary market operations in the same two categories, raising the funds necessary by issuing debt securities in its own name. The original function of providing assistance to guaranteed mortgages had thus been expanded into the general housing market.

Freddie Mac is a subsidiary of the Federal Home Loan Bank System and as such provides assistance to depository institutions and mortgage bankers approved by the Home Loan Bank Board. For the most part, it deals with thrift institutions, the constituent members of the Home Loan Banks. Apart from sharing similar functions with other agencies, Freddie Mac also issues similar sorts of securities in its own name. The nature of one of these particular securities effectively ushered in the contemporary era of mortgage financing.

Both Fannie Mae and Freddie Mac issue traditional debt securities in their own names, as does Ginnie Mae and occasionally the Home Loan Bank System. Traditionally, these are straight debt securities with semiannual coupons attached, issued for medium- and long-term periods. In credit market terms, they are backed by either the full faith and credit of the agency involved or by pools of mortgages purchased in the marketplace. Neither is directly backed by the U.S. Treasury as a direct government obligation. Ginnie Mae is the obvious exception, being the only mortgage assistance agency directly owned by the Treasury.

Since Fannie Mae has relied on bond borrowings as a source of funds since the mid- to late 1950s, and the new agencies with different mandates also required additional capital inflows, marketing of their names and debt securities in the marketplace was vital if they were to supply the secondary market for mortgages with a constant flow of funds. In order to do so, new types of bond products were developed to entice investors so that lenders could be assisted in the traditional manner. The new mortgage-backed security proved especially important in agency financing. Traditional borrowings by an agency were limited to a specific multiple of its capital on the balance sheet. In the case of Fannie Mae, it was set at twenty times capital in 1968. However, mortgage-backed securities did not fall under these guidelines since they were backed by pools of real property assets: mortgages and the property securing them. These new securities proved vital in continuing to finance the market, especially in times of tight credit, when investors might look askance at an individual agency's ability to service high coupon debt.

The Housing Act of 1968 gave the agencies the ability to issue mortgage-backed debt for the first time. In most cases, this meant that if Fannie Mae issued such securities they were in fact backed by a guarantee of Ginnie Mae. Soon thereafter Freddie Mac also began issuing similar obligations with the more specialized name of "participation certificates," or PCs. Originally issued in 1971, PCs are bonds backed by a large, diversified pool of quality mortgages designed to appeal to certain institutional investors. These obligations were designed specifically for depository institutions such as thrift institutions, offering them a diverse asset mix. They could be traded by investors in the secondary market and could also serve as collateral if presented to the Home Loan Bank Board.

Of the various types of mortgage-backed or related securities designed during this period, the pass-through certificate was to become perhaps the most popular of all, designed to appeal to a broad spectrum of investors. The pass-through was a somewhat revolutionary concept in bond financing in that it provided several new wrinkles for investors that had not been seen before in the marketplace. However, after the idea became accepted, issuing activity in them increased at a brisk pace well into the 1970s and 1980s.

A pass-through certificate is a bond that pays its interest monthly rather than semiannually. It originates in a manner similar to other mortgage-backed securities. Lending institutions pool together eligible mortgages and sell them to a mortgage agency. The agency in this instance pays for the pool with funds raised from the bond markets at a fixed rate of interest, normally extending from 15 to 30 years to maturity. Investors purchasing the bonds thus receive their interest payments from the mortgage borrowers, who are required by the lending institution to pay their interest once a month. In effect, interest is passed through from homeowner to bondholder.

Technically, the mortgage payer does not know that an agency is involved in this process at all since his or her counterparty was, and remains, the institution that loaned the money in the first place. The bank or S & L remains the collection agent because the agencies cannot deal directly with individual members of the public. Investors, however, have accepted new pass-through issues because they are the only standard U.S. bonds that pay interest on a monthly basis.

One of the more confusing aspects of these securities is the early repayment of principal, which normally occurs with no advance notice. Since individual mortgage borrowers may retire their mortgages at any time without prepayment penalty, the bondholder may in fact receive partial repayments of principal prior to maturity. As prepayments occur, the size of the original issue will begin to diminish and interest payments to all bondholders will decline as well. Thus, there is a disadvantage to pass-throughs in that they do not provide protection to the investor by necessarily guaranteeing fixed-interest payments over the life of the issue.

The natural tendency of mortgage borrowers to prepay their obligations can thus prove to be a disincentive to investors preferring the reliability of a traditional bond. When interest rates decline, homeowners are likely to refinance mortgages or sell their homes to realize a profit, creating chaos among the holders of pass-throughs, who begin to experience repayments from the agency. These holders of pass-throughs are thus susceptible to all of the usual forces that affect the bond markets in general plus the added uncertainty of having to base their cash flows on the behavior of individual members of the homeowning public.

Over the years the bond market has not treated pass-throughs as well as long-term direct obligations of the U.S. Treasury. Traditionally, pass-throughs trade at a yield premium to a comparable government issue because of this uncertainty factor. However, they have remained extremely popular because of the monthly interest factor and their well-diversified underlying support. Ginnie Mae has been the predominant issuer of pass-through securities. The other indirect federal agencies, Fannie Mae and Freddie Mac, normally issue mortgage-backed bonds or participation certificates ranging from about 15 to 30 years to final maturity. All mortgage agency bonds, dating from the earliest borrowings to the 1980s, were traditional fixed-rate financings. However, the complexion of mortgage borrowing began to change with the advent of adjustable rate mortgages (ARMs) and agency financing began to employ adjustable financings as well after 1982.

DEVELOPMENTS IN THE 1980s

The origin of adjustable, or floating, rate securities is discussed in Chapters 3 and 7. While the actual securities were imports from the euromarket, the concept of adjustable rates had been actively discussed domestically for at least 20 years prior to the introduction of the first adjustable-rate bond. Variable rates became a subject of discussion in relation to the effect of Regulation Q of the Federal Reserve on depository institutions. Although Regulation Q was effectively abolished with the passage of the Depository Institutions Deregulation and Monetary Control Act of 1980, it often prompted heated debate in the 1960s and 1970s concerning its effect on the ability of depository institutions to react to changes in interest rates. One major obstacle to the introduction of adjustables was the presence of state usury laws that, in some cases, placed a maximum rate on mortgages. It was not until DIDMCA became operational and the Garn-St. Germain Depository Institutions Act was passed that state usury laws were abolished and the mortgage agencies agreed to fund adjustable-rate mortgages with their own adjustable-rate borrowings in the capital markets.

Regulation Q enabled the Federal Reserve to determine the maximum rates that banks could pay on deposits. This power had been vested in the Fed since 1933 by the Glass-Steagall Act. Prior to the volatile markets of the 1970s, this effectively meant that the Fed could use Regulation Q as a technique of monetary policy. If the central bank decided to tighten credit and discourage banks from lending, it would simply leave current deposit levels in place as other money market rates moved higher. This would encourage savers to take their funds elsewhere to find a higher rate of return. Concomitantly, banks would have fewer funds available for lending. The net effect of this process was to discriminate against the small saver who had neither the expertise nor the ability to seek higher returns.

From the institutional side, arguments in favor of Regulation Q held that by keeping the depository institutions noncompetitive, the Fed was in effect assuring their liquidity. The savers' inability to react to rate changes worked in favor of the banks and thrifts. And since the savers did not react, or were presumed not to until that point in time, the housing construction industry would benefit from a constant flow of funds.[15] Given the behavior of interest rates since World War II, these assumptions proved correct. But the interest rate spiral that occurred after the OPEC price shocks of the 1970s helped destroy many time-proven notions about savers' behavior and the consequent supply of funds to the housing market.

Whether savers are able to respond to higher returns in the marketplace depends on whether they have the knowledge of precisely how to do so and whether there are instruments available for them to purchase in small denominations. Normally, money market instruments such as Treasury bills, commercial paper, or negotiable certificates of deposit came in denominations designed for institutional buyers rather than small savers. In a sense, it was not proven that small investors would not react to rate changes because the alternative—higher-yielding instruments—was beyond their reach in terms of the dollars needed for investment. But as already seen in Chapter 3, small investors did put intense pressure on depository institutions in the late 1970s and early 1980s by investing in money market mutual funds.

The institutional problem with Regulation Q ceilings was that they underscored the natural mismatching that thrifts (especially) suffered on their books as they funded long-term mortgages with short-term time deposits. The return on assets would be constant over the life of the mortgage loan while the rate paid on liabilities (deposits) would be current and subject to change. The only way that this mismatch could benefit the depository institutions was if the yield curve remained positive, that is, if short-term interest rates remained lower than long-term rates, on which mortgages were based. If this relationship was upset, so too would be the cash flows of mortgage-granting institutions.

As interest rates rose steadily throughout the 1970s and became negatively sloped toward the latter part of the decade, residential home purchases became increasingly popular, putting pressure on the thrift institutions to provide mortgage money. The boom in consumer spending that occurred especially after 1975 was accompanied by an increase in home purchases as many individuals hedged against inflation by using real property investments rather than securities. Between 1970 and 1984, the rate of return on a single-family home far exceeded that on a Treasury bond or an equity investment.[16] In order to meet this demand, many mortgage originators relied on the mortgage agencies by selling the newly created mortgages, leading to an increase in agency obligations outstanding.

As a result of this shift in investor preferences, many depository institutions became disintermediated; that is, funds that were once in their vaults or otherwise destined to be deposited were directed toward alternative investments. This disintermediation was most deleterious to thrifts because of their mismatch problems. Low-returning mortgages booked in the past were now out of line with new, higher, money market rates.

After 1982, adjustable-rate mortgages were introduced by thrift institutions to shore up their balance sheets. The new type of mortgage normally changed its interest rate once per year in line with a base reference rate, normally the Treasury bill rate or short-term Freddie Mac posted rate. The money market rates approximated the rates that were paid on deposits, while the mortgages yielded higher rates. The mortgage-fixing rate was usually several percentage points higher than the reference rate, thereby assuring the mortgage-granting institution a guaranteed fixed percentage profit regardless of the ultimate direction of the base rate. This ability to tailor the revenue on assets to the cash outflows on deposits gave the thrifts greater balance sheet flexibility. However, it did not prove a panacea to the thrift industry across the board since many were failing at the time and many more have failed since adjustables were introduced.

Adjustable-rate financing became so popular that these new types of mortgages often exceeded 50 percent of all new residential mortgages granted, especially in times of high interest rates. The agencies also helped in this respect by offering adjustable-rate bonds or notes of their own. Both Ginnie Mae and Freddie Mac developed adjustable-rate borrowings to be sold to the bond investor seeking to hedge against higher interest rates in the future. In 1986, Freddie Mac offered mortgage-backed securities to the market backed by mortgages tied to a one-year Treasury bill. These securities had the same features as the mortgages they represented, including a 2 percent annual rate cap. This meant that mortgage holders could not have their mortgage rate increased or decreased by more than 2 percent in any given year.

While adjustables helped the thrift industry recover from the crisis of the late 1970s and early 1980s, the industry as a whole suffered another crisis again in 1988 which had a profound impact on the entire financial structure. The housing boom of the 1980s had made many thrifts, as well as commercial banks, aggressive lenders in both the residential and commercial mortgage markets. As a result of the boom, many imprudent loans were made, based on inflated property values. A similar situation was also seen in the agricultural lending market several years before. The strains in the system began to appear as prices began to level off and even drop in some instances, leaving the lending institutions with sizable losses on nonperforming loans.

As many thrifts began to fail, increased pressure was put on the FSLIC, which found itself financially incapable of insuring the deposits of failing institutions. Finally, in early 1989 Congress passed the Financial Institutions Reform, Recovery and Enforcement Act, or FIRREA. This legislation signaled the most revolutionary changes in the thrift industry since the FHLBB was established in 1932. The FIRREA was nothing short of a revamping of the original system plus the establishment of a new agency to help fund the bailout of the industry.

Deregulation had proved of dubious value to the thrift industry in general. The expansion of thrift assets, mandated by the Garn-St. Germain Act, enabled the thrifts to broaden their assets by expanding their holdings of commercial real estate and corporate bonds. Many of the commercial holdings did not prove economically viable when the real estate market in general began to soften. And many thrifts invested heavily in junk bonds, a product that did not exist when the Garn Act was passed. As a result, the expansion into new types of assets proved more risky than the deregulation had envisaged. When coupled with extensive frauds perpetrated by many thrift officers nationwide, the industry was again shaken and on the verge of collapse for the second time in a decade.

The FIRREA was intended to restructure the regulatory framework of the industry. In place of the Federal Home Loan Bank Board, it created the new Office of Thrift Supervision (OTS). The FDIC took over the insurance of both state- and federally-chartered institutions, with the OTS taking on the role of primary regulator. This new regulator was expressly established as an office of the U.S. Treasury. This effectively made the FDIC the liquidator of thrifts that failed or were on the verge of failing. The act also allowed thrift institutions to convert to a bank charter and allowed bank holding companies to acquire savings institutions in order to take pressure off the FDIC.

On the liability and asset side, thrifts were required to meet the capital requirements of commercial banks and to maintain a core capital of at least 3 percent. They were also required to divest themselves of any equity investment or junk bond investment by 1992. This provision helped to create selling pressure in the secondary junk bond market that put a temporary halt to many new financings in 1989. In both cases, the intent was to reduce the portfolio risk that many thrifts had assumed since 1982 and return them to a more solid, and solvent, footing. Any thrift that could not maintain the new standards risked being closed by the FDIC and sold to another institution or a third-party investor.

The major problem faced by the new OTS and the FDIC was one of funding. The bailout of the industry would prove expensive, with estimates ranging from $50 billion to $300 billion. The wide range of estimates only underlined the complexity of the problem the industry had become. The bailout also was structured during the first year of the Bush administration. The President proclaimed that he would not raise taxes in order to support the industry, meaning that private sources would have to be employed in order for the reorganization to be successful. Given that the mortgage market was at stake, both the needs and restrictions pointed in the same direction: a new agency would be required to provide the necessary funding. .

For the second time within the decade, a new agency was created to cope with an agency-funding problem. The disposal of thrift assets was placed under the aegis of the Resolution Trust Corporation, a mixed-ownership government corporation designed to dispose of thrifts put under the receivership of the FDIC. Actual funding was to be provided by the Resolution Funding Corporation (REFCORP). This agency was originally authorized to borrow up to $50 billion to be used for liquidations. As Farmer Mac two years before (see Chapter 5), this agency was to be guaranteed by the Treasury but in a slightly different manner. REFCORP was authorized to purchase zero coupon bonds issued by the Treasury, using retained earnings of the Federal Home Loan Banks in order to defease the principal of its own borrowings. Through this technique, itself a product of the financial innovation of the 1980s, its own borrowings would be collateralized by Treasury bonds, meaning that the principal and interest would be guaranteed by the Treasury.

Although this new agency was created as an off-balance-sheet enterprise of the Treasury, it did not have the same stature as the existing mortgage assistance agencies that continued to function as they had in the past. REFCORP did not provide secondary market mortgage assistance or purchase mortgages from lenders. The Resolution Trust Corporation itself was intended to be an emergency financial enterprise that would cease operations at the end of 1996. In this respect, it was more akin to the emergency farm credit assistance provided by the Agricultural Credit Act of 1987 than it was to its mortgage agency cousins.

Since the expansion of Fannie Mae's activities in the late 1950s and early 1960s, agency bonds have become popular investment vehicles. They rank second only to direct Treasury obligations in terms of creditworthiness, trading at the smallest risk premia over comparable Treasury bonds. While investment distinctions are made between the agencies themselves as well as the types of obligations they offer, mortgage agency bonds find a broad spectrum of investors.

Part of their popularity has to do with the amount of outstanding issues in the marketplace. Because of the large number of them issued over the years, the secondary market for them is both broad and usually highly liquid. These characteristics appeal to institutional investors, who are the largest investors in agency issues. As the housing market has grown stronger and mortgage debt increases, so too does the amount of mortgage agency bonds outstanding. For instance, at year end 1988, there was an estimated $3.2 trillion worth of outstanding mortgage debt in the United States. Of that amount, approximately $2.1 trillion represented mortgages on one- to four-family residential dwellings—the type predominantly financed with agency assistance. The holders, or originators, of these residential mortgages were thrift institutions (holding $645 billion), commercial banks ($654 billion), and life insurance companies and finance companies ($49 billion). The balance was held by the agencies themselves. Ginnie Mae held the largest outstanding amount, accounting for approximately $325 billion on a pass-through basis and another $43 billion in traditional holdings; Fannie Mae accounted for a total of approximately $162 billion. Freddie Mac was the other substantial holder, accounting for $214 billion. The other agencies held a far less significant amount, totalling about $25 billion.[17]

In mortgage market terms, the agencies held about 40 percent of one- to four-family residential mortgages outstanding. As financial intermediaries, their support of the market has been significant in providing liquidity and helping to establish uniform long-term mortgage rates. The long-term rates, as those on their shorter bonds, help establish a national mortgage rate that no longer varies with geographical area or the peculiarities of the local banking system.

In bond market terms, the mortgage agencies had a combined float of some $700 billion worth of debt securities in the market at year end 1988. This amount makes the mortgage agency market the third largest bond market sector in the country (behind the Treasury market and corporate bond market) in terms of similar creditworthiness of securities traded. The bonds themselves are considered investment grade for most fiduciary investors and depository institutions nationwide. Pass-throughs especially have been popular with the general investing public because of their monthly interest feature. Many bond funds have been created to take advantage of this feature and advertise the monthly payment as one of the major advantages over their competition in the traditional semiannual product.

The first 50 years of mortgage agency history saw the institutions grow from small specialized bureaus designed to stimulate the Depression and post-Depression economy to become dominant factors in the mortgage industry. Along the way, their mandates changed and their focus of attention sometimes shifted to social goals more specific than simply boosting the construction industry and providing more units of housing on a nationwide basis. They now provide perhaps the best example of the way in which the private investment markets help indirectly fund the housing sector with government assistance. Other U.S. agencies have also been developed, using the same general concept to aid different sectors of the economy. The general model has also been used by international development agencies created after the Bretton Woods Conference, designed to provide funds for Third World development.

Institutions such as the International Bank for Reconstruction and Development (World Bank), the Inter-American Development Bank, the Asian Development Bank, African Development Bank, and the European Investment Bank all employ an agency function in their basic borrowing and lending activities. The World Bank was the first of these to be founded, tracing its lineage back to the Bretton Woods conference of 1944. The European version, originally the European Coal and Steel Community, was instituted by international treaty in 1951, to be followed by the establishment of the European Community and the European Investment Bank at Rome in 1957.

All of the development banks or agencies employ the same basic model in their operations. The institutions themselves are owned by sovereign states but operate independently. Their major purpose is to make infrastructure loans to developing areas in need. In order to do so, they borrow funds on the international bond markets and lend the money to the borrower at essentially the same cost. Because of their sovereign ownership, their credit ratings are all of the highest order. This enables them to borrow term funds at the lowest rates. When they lend money to a poor or developing country they are performing an alchemy of sorts, lending AAA money to those with poorer credit ratings. This is the essence of the international agency function.[18]

When individual governments enter into agreement to form these international development agencies, they perform much the same function, obviously on a different level, that the United States government did domestically in the mortgage market. Assistance is provided by making relatively inexpensive funds available to those in need with the goal of stimulating the international economy. The private markets are tapped, using the sovereign guarantee to alleviate fears concerning the default of principal and interest. Through this device, poor countries without any legitimate credit standing can obtain funds at the same rate as their lenders.

The agency function, as originally developed by the U.S. mortgage agencies, has had a long and varied history, both in terms of stimulating the housing market as well as providing a model for other U.S. agencies and international institutions. It has proved to be one of the most successful financial concepts developed in the twentieth century. But because of its institutional nature, it has remained almost invisible to the general public eye. However, without its presence since the post-Depression period one can safely assume that the face of American housing, and indeed the American dream, might indeed be radically different.

NOTES

1. United States League of Savings Institutions, *Fact Book*, 1973.

2. Milton Friedman and Anna Schwartz, *A Monetary History of the United States, 1867–1960* (Princeton: Princeton University Press, 1963), p. 308.

3. Walter J. Woerheide, *The Savings and Loan Industry* (Westport: Quorum Books, 1984), p. 4. Also see Thomas Marvell, *The Federal Home Loan Bank Board* (New York: Praeger, 1969), especially Chapter 2.

4. Quoted in Joseph D. Coppock, *Government Agencies of Consumer Installment Credit* (New York: National Bureau of Economic Research, 1940), p. 5.

5. Ibid.

6. Woerheide, *Savings and Loan Industry*, p. 5.

7. George F. Break, "Federal Loan Insurance for Housing," in G. F. Break et al., *Federal Credit Agencies* (Englewood Cliffs: Prentice Hall, 1963), p. 6.

8. David L. Wickens, "Developments in Home Financing," *The Annals of the American Academy of Political and Social Science* (March 1937): 79.

9. Ibid., p. 78.

10. On the topic of interest rate standardization see also Charles R. Geisst, *A Guide to Financial Institutions* (New York: St. Martin's Press, 1988), p. 105, for a general discussion. Also see P. H. Hendershott and K. Villani, *Regulation and Reform of the Housing Finance System* (Washington, DC: American Enterprise Institute, 1977), p. 44.

11. Jack Guttentag, "The Federal National Mortgage Association," in Break et al., *Federal Credit*, p. 69.

12. For a more detailed discussion of the problem of dilapidation and improvement see, for instance, John C. Weicher, *Housing: Federal Policies and Programs* (Washington, DC: American Enterprise Institute, 1980), especially Chapter 2.

13. Guttentag, "The Federal National Mortgage Association," p. 84.

14. Lyndon Baines Johnson, *The Vantage Point: Perspectives of the Presidency, 1963–1969* (New York: Holt, Rinehart & Winston, 1971), p. 331.

15. For a defense of Regulation Q in this respect see Allan Meltzer, "Regulation Q: The Money Markets and Housing," *Housing and Monetary Policy* (Federal Reserve Bank of Boston, 1970), p. 44 ff.

16. For an example, see Geisst, *Guide*, p. 77.

17. Federal Reserve Bank, *Bulletin*, January 1989.

18. The original international agency function was first performed by the European Coal & Steel Community, the European Railway Consortium EUROFIMA, and the International Bank for Reconstruction and Development (World Bank). By borrowing on the capital markets and then passing along the proceeds to entities in need of development funds, they were able to perform the same sort of function that Fannie Mae had originally performed in the U.S. housing markets. While the nature of the guarantees of the agencies differed, all international agencies developed subsequently were able to adhere to the original, basic formula and supply funds to needy, less than creditworthy entities using their own intermediary status to satisfy investors concerning the integrity and creditworthiness of the organizations.

5

Financing the Breadbasket: The Farm Credit System

The broad range of mortgage market assistance described in the previous chapter is the type that most investors are most familiar with—agency securities backed in some manner, mean, or form by real property assets. Normally these types of securities represent mortgages of single-family dwellings. However, they are not the only type of mortgage loans supported by federal agencies. During the Depression era, another agency was created to deal with the special financing needs of U.S. farmers. While the residential housing market benefited from agency support, the support was not intended to help homeowners at their place of business or employment. However, when the support system was developed originally for farmers it was broader in scope than the ensuing residential mortgage agency function in that it provided farmers with financing for both home and work at the same time since the two were inextricably interwoven.

The term "support," in reference to farm credit mortgage assistance, needs to be qualified here so as not to imply price supports or subsidies provided to farmers by the federal government over the years. Agriculture has been the beneficiary of two-sided support since the 1930s. On the one hand, it refers to the assistance provided to farmers to enable them to purchase land and equipment in order to engage in agricultural production. On the other hand, it means financial assistance by government to ensure prices for farm products or, in other cases, subsidies for *not* producing in order to keep agricultural prices stable. The present study is interested only in the former activity, being related to the financial markets rather than the market for agricultural products as a whole.

In organizational terms, the Farm Credit System, as it is known today, is the oldest of the U.S. federal credit agencies. Having undergone many metamorphoses since its inception in 1917, its impact on U.S. agricultural financing has been significant over the years. In many ways, it has remained somewhat anonymous in the world of financial markets while its mortgage counterparts have become much better known. This backstage treatment is even more unusual given the fact that agricultural financing has been, on average, much more volatile than residential mortgage lending over the years.

The plight of the Farm Credit System in the 1980s will remove some of the obscurity and push the agency into the forefront. When the Federal Land Bank of Jackson, Mississippi, requested assistance from the Farm Credit System in December 1987, it became the first fatality of a component of the system since its founding 70 years before. Six months later, several more Land Banks also requested assistance. How these failures occurred, how Congress responded, and how the financial markets were involved in funding system debt obligations over the years will determine the success of government-sponsored agricultural financing in the last decade of the twentieth century.

The Farm Credit System was not alone in requesting federal government assistance in 1987. The Export-Import Bank of the United States, better known as the Eximbank, also served notice to Congress that its lines of credit at the U.S. Treasury would have to be increased by 1988 if it were to remain solvent. How these disparate sorts of agencies came to grief at about the same time is more than simple coincidence. What is not sometimes clear is why these problems surfaced when interest rates were lower than they had been for a decade. When interest rates spiralled between 1979 and 1985 the repercussions for financial institutions were clear, agencies included. But it was only several years after rates had fallen that the resulting balance sheet problems began to surface. In the cases of the Farm Credit System and Eximbank, the loan portfolios were vastly different and the purposes of the agencies themselves were equally diverse. The one trait they shared in common was a time lag as the consequences of high interest rates began to catch up with them and affect their balance sheets several years after many loans had been made.

The juggling act that many lenders face when interest rates rise and then plummet was certainly not a new experience for the Farm Credit System, which had suffered similar problems before. But the failure of one of its component banks only underscored the fraility of the system after almost five years of a negatively sloped yield curve. And the impact was not limited to the Farm Credit System alone. Commercial bank lending to LDCs, natural oil and gas drilling companies, and students in institutions of higher learning also suffered the same "lagged" effect for many of the same basic reasons. The reason that the agricultural sector is often singled out as the prime example of this phenomenon is that borrowing and lending have occurred for the same reasons many times over the last 60 years, usually with the same catch-up effect.

THE EARLY YEARS: 1917–33

As many of the agencies created by the federal government during the Depression years, the Farm Credit System was not created by one bold stroke of the pen but took several decades to evolve into the agency that is in existence today. Being the first of the federal credit agencies, it also relied on non-American concepts, a process that curiously would be reversed 30 years later when many of the international and regional credit agencies looked toward the U.S. mortgage agencies as a model for promoting international economic development. In the planning stages during World War I, its architects actively studied European methods of providing credit and support to the agricultural sector.

President William Howard Taft began the process in 1912 by requesting the U.S. ambassadors to various European countries to report on the means by which those nations provided agricultural credit to their farmers. Those reports plus the findings of two commissions, one congressionally sanctioned and one private, paved the way for the Federal Farm Loan Act of 1916, passed during the administration of Woodrow Wilson. The one European model most closely followed during the drafting period was the *Landschaft* of Germany, the government-sponsored rural cooperative credit system.

At the signing of the legislation in 1916, Wilson noted, "The farmers . . . have occupied hitherto a singular position of disadvantage. They have not had the same freedom to get credit on their real estate that others have had who were in manufacturing and commercial enterprises."[1]

This phrase alludes to the two problems faced by farmers in the nineteenth- and early twentieth-century United States. The first was the availability of credit; lenders were diverse and the interest rates they charged varied widely as well. Prior to the passing of the legislation, farm mortgage credit in particular ranged from 7 to 12 percent per annum, depending on geographical location and the nature of the lender. The second problem was the actual term of the credit. Mortgages did not exceed five years in most cases, meaning that the farmer was susceptible to changing interest rates and roll-over financing for the outstanding principal amount at the end of the loan.

One of the major institutional forces behind the passage of the Farm Loan Act was the organization of the Federal Reserve System in 1913. By dividing the country into 12 reserve districts, the Federal Reserve Act brought all national banks under the aegis of the newly reconstituted central bank. The Farm Act was similar to the purposes for which the Fed was created in one respect: by using federal legislation to create a "system" as such it sought to do away with local geographical discrepancies and provide more uniform interest rates across the country.

The Farm Act provided for the creation of 12 Federal Land Banks under the supervision of the Federal Farm Loan Board, consisting of five members to be drawn from both major political parties. The banks themselves were capitalized at $750,000 each, represented by shares denominated at $5 each. Most of the original shares were bought by the U.S. Treasury. The Farm Loan Act was very specific, however, in stating that the ownership of the Land Banks was not to be in government hands longer than necessary. With this intent in mind, the banks were required to retire the government's holding in their institutions with subsequent sales of stock as quickly as possible after the initial phases of organization had been completed. But it was not until 1947 that all government involvement in the Land Banks came to an end and the system truly could be said to be in the hands of the public—that is, the farmers themselves.

The Land Bank system grew rapidly after the geographical lines for the districts had been drawn. The number of banks applying for charters to operate within the districts (called Federal Land Bank Associations, or FLBAs) proliferated to 2,100 by the end of 1917 and by the end of 1918 the number stood at over 3,300. The amount of loans made exceeded $147 million.[2] In the early years, the Federal Land Banks raised capital by issuing bonds, but early attempts at raising external funds were blunted by World War I. Federal government war bonds provided the most popular magnet for many investors' funds and as a result the newly organized Land Banks had a difficult time in the marketplace, having been crowded out by the government's borrowing needs and the lure of risk-free securities that had no default risk attached to them. As a result, the Treasury itself, by necessity, became the largest initial investor in Federal Land Bank bonds, a situation that persisted until about 1921.

In order to entice investors thereafter, Land Bank bonds were given an exemption from federal income tax so that interest payments and any capital gains on principal repayments were free from tax. Essentially, this meant that the early agency bonds were treated as municipal issues are today. The exemption was lifted in 1941 and securities issued after that time were subject to federal taxation on both counts.

By the beginning of the second decade of the century, the effects of the newly created Land Banks and the FLBAs began to be seen in the composition of farm mortgage debt and its major sources. In 1915, about $4.5 billion of outstanding farm mortgages was held by three lending groups almost exclusively. Some $3.75 billion was held by "individuals and others," a financial term used to designate a noninstitutional lender, whether a private loan made by a family member or by another private individual granting loans on commercial terms. Another $500 million was held by commercial banks, and the balance was held by life insurance companies.[3] Ten years later, farm mortgage debt had grown to an outstanding $10 billion. Of that amount, about half was held by individuals, and another $3 billion by commercial banks and life insurance companies. But the balance of $2 billion was held by Land Banks, which had begun to compete with individuals successfully and impose more standard rates on the industry than had been seen in previous years.[4]

In 1923, new legislation expanded the Land Bank system. The Agricultural Credit Act of 1923 gave the Farm Loan Board the ability to create 12 intermediate credit banks that would be supervised by the Federal Land Banks themselves. The purpose of these institutions was to discount short-term and medium-term agricultural paper and notes for institutions making agricultural loans, and to make loans to farmers' cooperatives. In order to raise funds, these intermediate credit institutions were authorized to issue their own short-term debt obligations.

The 1923 act also made structural changes in the nascent system that helped expand its power and organization. For instance, it increased the number of members of the Loan Board to seven from five, raised the amount of money that could be lent to an individual farmer, and reorganized the cost accounting of the Loan Board and the individual Land Banks. Early in its development, it could be seen that the agricultural credit agency was going to progress much as agencies that would be devised in the 1930s— that is, by a patchwork of legislation over the years that would continually add to its power as its functions expanded in an ad hoc fashion.

The Land Banks faced a difficult task almost from the outset on more than one score. In the first several years of operation, an agricultural crisis occurred that severely affected agricultural prices. Beginning in 1920, prices collapsed by over 50 percent. In May 1920, prices stood at 237 on an index based on 100 as of a four-year period ending in 1914. By mid-June 1921, prices had fallen to 111.[5] Prices began to recover several years later but the drop in farm income caused many foreclosures and the number of distressed farm mortgages increased sharply, in some cases by four times over the course of the decade.

This early crisis, the first of many faced by farmers since the end of World War I, also made Land Bank bond obligations somewhat difficult to sell in the early years. This caused special problems for new financings in particular. Since many of the debt financing techniques used in the bond markets today were not practiced prior to the stock market crash of 1929, borrowers had to be particularly careful when deciding when to come to market for fresh funds, especially if a decline in interest rates was anticipated. If a Land Bank anticipated a decline in interest rates it might decide to wait until rates fell before assuming any new fixed coupon debt. These sporadic delays in financings plus early investor resistance began to disappear as the system became better known and developed a track record for success. Although not the sole measure of success, the traditional agency spread between the cost of funds and revenues received (that is, the interest paid on borrowed money as opposed to the revenue received from loans made) was quite healthy in the first decade of operation. For instance, in 1928 and 1929 the Federal Land Banks paid an average of 4.43 percent on bonds issued while booking loans at an average rate of approximately 6 percent.[6]

The second major crisis for the Land Banks was the Depression and the havoc it wreaked on farm valuations and agricultural prices. The collapse in prices brought many farmers to financial ruin and forced foreclosures on their properties. Between the years 1929 and 1932, farm prices fell below prewar prices of 1910–14.[7] This meant that the banks granting the mortgages lost a revenue-producing asset and had to accept the farm as collateral in a period of depressed land values. Besides creating an unprecedented number of bank failures in the agricultural sections of the country, the growing number of foreclosures were socially unacceptable, creating yet more unemployment and impoverishment. As a result, Congress acted in 1932 to shore up the Land Banks to avoid further catastrophe.

The first attempt to offset the rise in mortgage foreclosures came in 1932 when Congress made funds available to grant extensions to farmers so that they could service their mortgage debt and pay taxes that were in arrears. But the relief was only temporary and was supplanted in 1933 by a presidential order creating what is known today as the Farm Credit Administration. As with many of the agencies functioning today, this new body was born out of necessity during the Depression. In later years it proved to be a viable tool by attempting to protect farmers against the vicissitudes of economic cycles and all of the pitfalls that accompany them.

THE MODERN SYSTEM EMERGES

The executive order creating the structure of the modern system was in reality a reorganization of the Land Banks and the local cooperative banks. The 12 Land Banks became responsible to this new, enlarged agency that now was headed by a single chief executive officer, Henry Morgenthau, Jr. The purpose of the centralization was to bring all of the activities of the banks under the aegis of this new body, which was responsible for seeing that the credit needs of farmers were better coordinated than they had been in the previous 16 years. The achievements of the early years had not been insubstantial. Credit was now available that was more properly suited to the needs of agricultural producers, whether it be mortgage money or shorter-term funds needed for working capital. But the Depression helped underscore the fact that the system as it originally stood was too disparate and required a central authority.

In mid–1933, Congress passed the Emergency Farm Mortgage Act, which specifically sought to slow the rate of foreclosures. Funds were made available to help tide farmers over the collapse in prices by granting extensions to their credit. If the Land Banks suffered losses as a result of these actions they were to be reimbursed by government appropriation. In addition, the rate charged on loans by the FLBAs was lowered from 5 or 6 percent to 4.5 percent per annum. The same subsidy principle was used here: if the banks suffered losses as a result of the new rates they would be reimbursed by the government.

Technically, this was not the typical agency function as it would subsequently be practiced. The positive spread between the cost of funds and the revenues produced by loans became negligible and the difference was made up by appropriation. But without some form of government intervention, the farm sector would have been headed for total collapse. As mentioned above, prices by 1932 had fallen below their prewar levels. Farm mortgage debt, however, had risen dramatically over the same 20-year period. In 1910, mortgage debt stood at about $3.32 billion. By 1930, the number had almost tripled to $9.24 billion.[8] Equally important was the amount of equity, on average, that farmers maintained in their properties. During the early years, the Land Banks could only lend 50 percent of the appraised value of the property offered as collateral. With the passage of the Emergency Farm Mortgage Act this percentage was increased to 75. At the same time, the amount of equity in those properties held by owners began to decline. Equity declined between 1910 and 1930 from 90 percent of value to only 80 percent of value.[9] While those absolute numbers may seem quite conservative by standards of the latter part of this century, they were based on escalating land values. The aggregate amount of farm property taxes received nationwide between 1920 and 1930 illustrates the problem. Taxes received between these two dates increased from $452 million to $629 million, a rise of 39 percent.[10] Assuming for a moment that land values rose by a similar amount, equity could decline nationwide as a percentage of appraised value. A farm worth $10,000 in 1920 could have been purchased with a Land Bank loan of $5,000, the equity being 50 percent. If the value of the property rose to around $14,000 in 1930 (its appraised value), the farmer now had equity of about 36 percent of value, assuming no debt amortization in the ten years. While only a crude illustration, the simple example shows that rising prices increase these debt/equity ratios, enticing farmers to borrow based on the run-up in appraised values. When the fall eventually came, the debt remained in place while the income required to service it declined dramatically.

While values rose, income derived from the selling of farm products was much more unstable over the same general period. In 1919, the annual gross income from farm production was at an historic high of $17 billion. Two years later, it had dropped to $9 billion. It rose again to $12 billion in 1929, and then dropped drastically to about $5 billion in 1932.[11] The large amount of debt accumulated by farmers in good times only proved a millstone around their collective necks when the Depression arrived.

This ten-year swing in farm prices and income did not occur only during the Depression but had already taken its toll beginning in the early 1920s. Between the beginning of 1921 and the end of 1933, over 14,000 banks failed in the United States, many from rural areas. For example, in the northwest-central states of Minnesota, Iowa, Missouri, North Dakota, South Dakota, Nebraska, and Kansas, 47.5 percent of the banks active in the area had failed by 1933. That percentage was matched by a similar figure in the south Atlantic states (Delaware to Florida), while the mountain states were not far behind at 45 percent. At the same time, only six percent of New England banks failed as did only 13 percent of those in the middle Atlantic area, sectors involved more in manufacturing than agriculture.[12]

The private marketplace was enlisted to help shore up the Land Banks in 1934 through the passing of the Federal Farm Mortgage Act. This legislation created the Federal Farm Mortgage Corporation, empowered to issue bonds bearing the guarantee of the U.S. Treasury. These new securities were to be used in different ways to benefit the Land Banks. Primarily, this body was able to borrow money through bonds with a government guarantee and lend to the Land Banks if market conditions proved prohibitive for the banks themselves. But the history of the corporation was fairly short-lived; it was abolished by Congress in 1961.

The early years of the Farm Credit System witnessed several layers of federal control being added to the basic structure of Land Banks and intermediate credit banks. The Farm Credit Act of 1933 established the Production Credit Associations (PCAs), which were able to discount farmers' loans with the Federal Intermediate Credit Banks. Over the years, the PCAs have come to provide short-term credit to the same group for which the Land Banks provided mortgage credit. While most of the funds extended were for working capital purposes (one year or less), the PCAs provided intermediate credit for terms of up to ten years.

The 1933 legislation also provided the groundwork for the establishment of 13 banks for cooperatives that would be able to provide financing for agricultural cooperatives. Loans made to cooperatives could be for marketing support, supplies, and other services. Importantly, they also helped to finance the export business of their borrowers. The Central Bank for Cooperatives, located in Denver, Colorado, worked in conjunction with the district banks to provide loans that may have exceeded the individual bank's ability to lend. In this respect, the Central Bank behaved in much the same fashion as the Federal Home Loan Bank or the Federal Land Bank. According to Farm Credit System estimates, the Bank for Cooperatives still provided about 65 percent of all credit used by U.S. cooperatives as of 1987.

REORGANIZATION AND CRISIS—AGAIN

Prior to the outbreak of World War II, President Franklin Roosevelt intervened in the organization of the Farm Credit System (FCS) by issuing an executive order in 1939 that effectively ended its agency status. Jurisdiction over the agency was passed to the Department of Agriculture and it remained under cabinet jurisdiction until passage of the Farm Credit Act of 1953. While politics of the period inspired the change in status, it was not long before the FCS found itself with a new agricultural cycle on its hands: the rise of farm prices due to the war and the subsequent flow of funds back to the Land Banks as a result of rising farm incomes.

Fortunes began to change for farmers and farm production in the 1940s as prices and incomes again began to rise dramatically. Prices rose faster than costs and farmers were able to pay off their debts, in some cases far ahead of debt schedules. Between 1940 and 1946, prices received by farmers rose 146 percent, while production rose 24 percent, and net incomes rose an average of 230 percent. The numbers continued to increase after the war as well. By 1952, prices were up by 188 percent over 1940, production by 32 percent and incomes by 233 percent.[13]

The major cause of this round of price rises and increase in incomes was the demand for farm products caused by the war itself. But increases in agricultural technology and farming methods also played a major role in increasing production. Developments such as improved mechanization, greater use of lime and fertilizers, conservation practices, better feeding of livestock, and improved control of insects and disease had all gathered momentum in the years preceding the war. Their original impact had been obscured by the drought and Depression of the 1930s but by the outbreak of war they all converged to create an unprecedented increase in output.[14] This period became known as the second American agricultural revolution, the first occurring at the end of the Civil War almost a century earlier.

The higher prices received by farmers and the increased production caused by the war had a profound impact on the balance sheet of U.S. agriculture as a whole. Between 1940 and 1946 assets rose from $53.7 to $107.2 billion while the real estate component rose from $33.6 to $61.8 billion. At the same time, liabilities in the form of real estate debt actually declined from $6.6 to $4.8 billion.[15] In addition, the percentage of total farm mortgage debt held by the Land Banks and the Federal Farm Mortgage Corporation dropped from 48 to 16 percent.[16] As a result of the increased cash flows, the Land Banks made a concentrated effort, beginning in 1944, to pay off what remained of the government capital on their books. By 1947, they were all successful and were all farmer-owned.

In the wake of the Land Bank success, both the Intermediate Credit Banks and the Production Credit Associations also made progress in reducing the amount of government ownership, although a substantial reduction would not be seen until the 1950s. However, despite the inroads made in reducing debt overall, by 1953, the year that the Farm Credit System passed out of Department of Agriculture hands, debt again began to mount. However, it presented less of a structural problem for farmers' balance sheets than it had during the prewar years.

Between 1946 and 1953, the debt burden of farmers again rose by almost 100 percent although the amount of that debt was less than 10 percent of the estimated value of total assets.[17] The debt burden was increasing but it appeared not to have an effect on farmers' leverage, still being a small proportion of assets. But the overall balance sheet of U.S. agriculture in general does not shed light on the plight of the smaller farmer, whose amount of outstanding debt had roughly doubled. By 1952, farm prices and incomes had again begun a decline.

The Farm Credit Act of 1953 returned the system to agency status and removed it from the auspices of the Department of Agriculture. The express purpose of this act, and the Farm Credit Board it established, was to ensure that the system was wholly farmer-owned as soon as possible. This legislation included not only the Land Banks but the Intermediate Credit Banks and the Production Associations as well. This goal did not become a reality until 1968, when the last PCAs paid off their remaining government capital. During that fifteen-year period, the Land Banks, PCAs, and Banks for Cooperatives expanded their activities at a steady rate. In each case, the average rate of growth in loans granted rose by about 24–29 percent per annum.[18]

After the system was in the hands of farmers rather than the U.S. Treasury it could no longer be said that system borrowings were in any way guaranteed by the government. In fact, as the system moved toward private ownership over the years, bonds and notes issued were perceived as "quasi-" U.S. government obligations, or to use the more popular phrase, "indirect" obligations rather than bearing direct guarantees. Thus, more risk was associated with its borrowings than those of, for instance, Fannie Mae. But as the federal government passed more and more legislation to expand the system, the borrowings of the Farm Credit System were looked upon in the same light as those of Fannie Mae or (later) of Freddie Mac.

After five decades of somewhat ad hoc growth, the system underwent a revision in 1974. Congress passed the Farm Credit Act of 1971, designed to eliminate outdated parts of the system and eliminate bureaucratic overlaps. Many of the former responsibilities of Congress were now passed directly to the Federal Farm Credit Board and the district boards in turn. The passing of the executive mantle meant that the boards would be able to respond to system needs faster than Congress had been able to do in the past. The new legislation also broadened the powers of the system.

Most noteworthy in this latter respect was an expansion of services offered by the system. The Land Banks and PCAs were now able to offer credit to nonfarm agricultural homeowners and commercial fishermen. The Banks for Cooperatives were also allowed to lend additional funds to cooperatives. These additional powers enabled the system to achieve a greater share of financing within the agricultural sector than ever before. By 1975, the number of new loans was double that of 1971; the total amount borrowed from the Land Banks in 1975 was 353 percent more than in 1971, increasing from $1.3 billion to $4.6 billion.[19]

The growth and eventual privatization of the Farm Credit System was aided in no small part by its ability to borrow funds on the bond markets. But as an agency dedicated to providing mortgage and credit to farmers it began to face many of the problems encountered by other mortgage lenders in the late 1970s and 1980s. The problems faced by the savings and loan industry, and the FHLB and FSLIC in the residential housing sector were also experienced by the farm credit banks, Land Banks, and the Farm Credit System as a whole. The negatively sloping yield curve and the high value of the dollar on foreign exchange markets began to take their tolls on all institutions involved in lending to farmers, as well as on the farms themselves. These problems caused an investor reaction regarding the creditworthiness of Farm Credit System bonds as a whole.

What had become almost a cyclical problem for farmers in the twentieth century reappeared in the 1980s as the negative yield curve affected farm cash flows. Once again, balance sheet erosion took place and the industry began to suffer. At year end 1982, farm real estate and holdings were valued at approximately $749 billion; in the following five years they began to decline steadily, reaching a five-year low of $510 billion at year end 1986, a decline of 31 percent.[20] During the same period, total farm debt also declined from $190 billion in 1982 to $155 billion in 1986, a decline of 18.4 percent. But the equity component of farm real estate also decreased, as would be expected, from $771 billion in 1982 to $537 billion in 1986, a decline of some 30 percent.[21]

On the income side, the picture for the same period was somewhat brighter but not bright enough to offset the balance sheet declines. Between 1983 and 1986, net farm income increased from $12.7 to $37.5 billion. But this income figure is composed of actual cash receipts as well as noncash items such as inventory changes, nonmoney income, a decline in farm expenses, and direct government payments. If the actual cash item is isolated, the picture changes. Farm cash receipts declined marginally during the same period from $141.1 to $140.2 billion. Measured more realistically, net cash flows also declined marginally over the same period, decreasing by $200 million.[22]

The high value of the dollar on the foreign exchange markets also contributed to a confused trade picture for farmers. Between 1981 and 1987, world grain output increased by 180 million metric tons and foreign grain production increased by 194 million tons. But U.S. output actually declined by 14 million tons, illustrating the damper put on exports by the dollar's value. The U.S. agricultural trade balance as a whole declined from $26.6 billion in 1981 to $5.4 billion in 1986.[23] If adjusted for inflation, the decline became even more pronounced in real terms.

The balance sheet erosion and the declining competitiveness of U.S. agriculture on the international markets created the debt crisis of the Farm Credit System in the mid–1980s. By 1987, direct government payments in cash and commodity certificates represented almost 40 percent of net farm income. As income declined in real terms and equity was devalued, many farmers exercised their rights under their borrowing agreements with their FCS lenders to restructure loans. Many were not able to remain solvent at all. By 1986, the system had recorded a loss of $1.9 billion after several previous years of stress. In 1987, the losses swelled to $2.7 billion, accounting for a total running loss of $4.6 billion by year end 1987. As a result, provisions for loan losses were increased and actual net interest income declined from $1.3 billion in 1985 to $509 million in 1987.[24]

The farmers' dilemma and the strains it caused on the lending institutions were taken up by Congress when it approved the Agricultural Credit Act of 1987. In very general terms, this act was the agricultural equivalent of the legislative aid provided to S & Ls by the Depository Institutions Act of 1982, or the Emergency Home Finance Act of 1970, which created the Federal Home Loan Mortgage Corporation. Its passage was certainly propitious in that it preceded the requests for assistance made by several Land Banks later in 1987.

The Agricultural Credit Act of 1987 was signed into law on January 6, 1988, to provide sweeping structural and functional changes to the way in which U.S. agriculture was to be financed in the future. Assistance was provided on several levels: assistance to the Farm Credit System itself and to system borrowers. In addition, it provided for an eventual restructuring of the system and the development of a secondary mortgage market for farm mortgages.

The Farm Credit System was aided by the establishment of the Farm Credit Assistance Board, which provided aid to system institutions when their stock falls below par. If the stock of a system bank fell by no more than 25 percent below par, the institution could apply for the ability to issue preferred stock and receive further assistance so that it would not be financially impaired. If the stock fell below 75 percent of par value, it would be forced to apply for assistance on a nonvoluntary basis.

The second aspect of assistance, that to system borrowers (banks or other institutions holding stock in the district Land Bank), protected their holdings by requiring the Land Banks to retire their stock at par after any outstanding loans made to those institutions were paid back in full. It is useful to remember here that loans made by Land Banks are made to constituent members that are also stockholders. In either case, the assistance package was expensive and the U.S. Treasury was enlisted to provide help in making funds available.

Funds for the guarantee of borrower stock as well as other assistance monies were to be obtained by the sale of fifteen-year uncollateralized bonds whose interest and principal was guaranteed by the Treasury. A total of $4 billion of bonds was authorized, originally sold to the public beginning in the summer of 1988. The agent for the borrowing was the Farm Credit System Assistance Corporation, established by the act to provide the capital for institutions whose functions had become impaired.

Restructuring the Farm Credit System was another provision of the act which changed the traditional structure of the 70-year-old institution. The act required the Federal Land Bank and the FICB in each of the districts to merge by the summer of 1988. By the same deadline, the PCAs and Federal Land Bank Associations in each district were also required to submit merger proposals. Similarly, the Banks for Cooperatives were required to develop proposals to merge into a National Bank for Cooperatives.

Perhaps the most drastic part of the restructuring changed the traditional complexion of the system itself. By the summer of 1989, the 12 federal farm credit districts were required to reorganize themselves into six districts. When enacted, the Farm Credit System was no longer the agricultural equivalent, in terms of numbers, of the Federal Reserve or the original Home Loan Bank Board.

The last part of the act of immediate interest here was the establishment of a secondary market for agricultural mortgages. The Federal Agricultural Mortgage Corporation (FAMC) was created within the Farm Credit System to develop a secondary market for agricultural mortgage loans. Its sobriquet quickly became "Farmer Mac." This body was empowered to sell off mortgage loans to loan "poolers," who in turn would package the eligible loans to serve as backing, or collateral, for securities offered to the investing public. Previously, the Farm Credit System had provided mortgage loans to farmers but had never developed a secondary market for them. Thus, its previous bond borrowings had not resembled the more popular Ginnie Mae, Fannie Mae, or Freddie Mac bond obligations. But in keeping with the now popular agency function, the bond obligations were guaranteed by the FAMC. With the development of this institution, the U.S. mortgage agency sector had come full circle to include almost all types of residential mortgages.

Of all the U.S. agencies, either direct or indirect, the Farm Credit System was the slowest to develop the secondary market activities normally associated with the traditional residential mortgage agencies. As a result, it only recently began to offer mortgage-backed securities in its own right. Regardless of the reasons for this twenty-odd-year delay, the farm crisis of the 1980s was met with a traditional legislative response and apparatus that had been used successfully many times before. As of this writing, it is too Early to determine whether the Agricultural Credit Act will prove successful, but if past history is any indication it should help the farm system weather its most recent storm. The success of the financing package will ultimately depend on investors' perception of farm mortgage risk.

THE ROLE OF COMMODITY FUTURES MARKETS

The bond markets are not the only source of assistance for farmers provided by the financial community. The traditional commodity futures markets also play a crucial role in financing agriculture, although on a different level. The futures markets aid the agricultural industry by providing markets where commodities may be traded (bought or sold) for delivery at a future date, in contrast to the cash or physicals market, at which products are sold for immediate delivery. But in contrast to the traditional securities markets, the futures markets do not trade actual securities representing capital market instruments but rather trade futures contracts that are "derivatives" of the actual commodities they represent.

Commodity futures markets originated in the United States in the nineteenth century when farmers began to sell their crops on a "to-arrive" basis; that is, the buyer of a farm product was actually buying a crop that was not ready for immediate delivery. This method of trading was initiated so that the producer of the commodity could sell in advance of harvest to protect against a potential price decline of the crop itself should market conditions change in the interim. The buyer was guaranteed the price regardless of market conditions. However, both parties still faced risks in the process. Since these markets are organized as hedging markets, the economic function they perform is basically different from investment in the stock or bond markets. For example, if the physical price should rise, the producer loses any additional profit he might have made by waiting until the commodity was ready for delivery. If the price falls, the buyer loses because he could now buy the product in the cash market at a cheaper price than he paid on the "to-arrive" basis. In either case, both buyer and seller are committed to the price at which the deal was originally struck.

Given the inflexibility of this arrangement, futures markets developed that gave either party the opportunity to close out their position in a secondary market designed to trade the contract. The original seller could buy back his contract at the current price (not necessarily the original contract price) or the buyer could sell his contract on the same basis. Either party could incur a gain or loss in the process but the new market allowed either one to change his mind and take a gain or loss prior to the delivery date. This made the original contract trading less rigid and also presented opportunities for nonfarmers or nontraditional users of commodities to speculate on agricultural price movements.

Futures trading has developed over the years to the extent that contracts are traded on most staple agricultural products and their derivatives. Most trading is conducted at one of the exchanges in Chicago and, to a lesser extent, New York. Contracts exist, *inter alia*, on cereals, fibers, livestock, beans, juices and a bevy of derivative products such as soybean oil and rapeseed oil. While the products differ, the mechanics of their trading has been standardized regardless of the commodity itself or the exchange at which it is traded.

In its simplest sense, commodity futures trading benefits the producers of agricultural commodities and those needing to refine them into consumer products, such as food processors or wholesalers. At this level, the markets aid farmers by providing downstream demand for their products. However, the markets have aided in another, somewhat broader sense. In addition to the natural sellers and buyers, the markets also appeal to speculators who add liquidity to the trading floors of the exchanges. Without speculators, the markets would still resemble the earlier form of "to-arrive" trading originally developed in the nineteenth century.

Speculators are attracted to futures trading because of low margin requirements, which offer the potential for highly leveraged profits. For example, a trader who wants to trade in corn futures contracts is required to put down only a small fraction of the contracts' current market value, perhaps as little as 3 to 5 percent, in order to open a position. If the contract should appreciate in price he is able to take advantage of the entire gain by selling the position, using only a small amount of money as trading "equity." In such a manner, he is able to buy and/or sell contracts prior to their maturity simply looking for price movements, rather than having to take or make delivery as a farmer or processor would be expected to do.

In the classic economic sense, speculators add liquidity to the market floor of a futures exchange while the natural users of contracts utilize the markets for hedging purposes. This is another example of the way in which the markets bring external forces to bear to aid in support of agricultural prices. But this sort of "support" is not on the same level as that provided by the Farm Credit Administration. And it should not be assumed that the futures markets aid in *price* supports for farmers. The best assistance they render is to provide the facilities and the liquidity for farmers to hedge the one variable that has caused severe strains on both their own personal balance sheets and the Land Banks in general—the uncertainty surrounding the price of agricultural products, which itself has a direct impact on farm incomes and the ability to service agricultural debt.

Because of their unique nature as derivative markets, the commodity futures exchanges have their own regulatory body distinct from the Securities and Exchange Commission discussed in Chapter 1. The original Banking Act of 1933 and the Securities Exchange Act of 1934 did not include futures trading because it does not fall within the ambit of either banking or eligible securities dealing. Instead, the futures exchanges are regulated by the Commodity Futures Trading Commission (CFTC), created in 1974 by the Commodities Futures Trading Commission Act. This body is composed of five full-time commissioners appointed by the President and has jurisdiction over all futures exchanges in the country.

This commodity version of the SEC developed somewhat late but the futures markets were nevertheless regulated earlier in the century. The farm crisis of 1920–21 and the intense speculation in grain futures that it created prompted Congress to pass the Futures Trading Act in an attempt to reduce wide price movements and excessive speculation in grain futures. However, the Supreme Court ruled that the act was unconstitutional and Congress responded by passing the Grain Futures Act of 1922. That piece of legislation enabled the U.S. Department of Agriculture to enforce rules of procedure on the exchanges themselves.

This original set of regulations applied to grain futures only, leaving a wide variety on nonagricultural and metallic commodity futures still unregulated. Finally, in 1936 Congress passed the Commodity Exchange Act, designed to extend regulation to all the exchanges, not just those for grains. Most of the legislation was geared to protect against manipulative practices by traders, to prevent excessive positioning, or speculation, and to provide criminal liabilities to miscreants. The Commodity Exchange Act would reamin the sole piece of legislation until Congress broadened it in 1968 and passed the Commodity Futures Trading Commission Act of 1974.

As their counterparts in the mortgage market, the farm agencies have had a long and varied history. The structure of the institutions has changed many times over the last 70 years as crisis and competition have dictated financing needs unforeseen in the earlier part of the century. The widespread problem that farm lenders faced is no different from that faced by thrift institutions over time. Despite the fact that the local indigenous banks were united under a system, they remained at heart local lenders, subject to the vicissitudes of their local economies. While commercial banks were able to break out of that cycle of locality, farm banks have been unable to do so. As a result, the need for an effective system of control has become all the more apparent if the Farm Credit System is to survive and provide the assistance that farmers require in the future.

NOTES

1. Quoted in *The Federal Land Bank System, 1917–1967* (Washington, DC: Farm Credit System, 1967), p. 5.

2. Ibid., p. 10.

3. Lawrence Jones and David Durand, *Mortgage Lending Experience in Agriculture* (Princeton: Princeton University Press, 1954), p. 8.

4. Ibid.

5. Ibid., p. 9.

6. Federal Farm Loan Board, *Annual Report*, December 1929.

7. Jones and Durand, *Mortgage Lending*, p. 10.

8. U.S. Secretary of Agriculture, *The Farm Debt Problem* (Washington, DC: U.S. Government Printing Office, 1933), p. 5.

9. Ibid., p. 14.

10. Ibid., p. 20.

11. Ibid., p. 23.

12. Ibid., pp. 29–30.

13. Jones and Durand, *Mortgage Lending*, p. 13.

14. Wayne D. Rasmussen, ed., *Readings in the History of American Agriculture* (Urbana: University of Illinois Press, 1960), p. 277.

15. Ibid., p. 14.

16. W. G. Hoag, *The Farm Credit System* (Danville, IL: Interstate Publishers, 1976), p. 254.

17. Jones and Durand, *Mortgage Lending*, pp. 17–20.

18. Hoag, *Farm Credit*, p. 260.

19. Ibid., p. 269.

20. Farm Credit Administration, *Economic Perspectives* 1988, p. 9.

21. Ibid.

22. Ibid., p. 8.

23. Ibid., pp. 6–7.

24. Ibid., p. 16.

6

Financing the Mortarboard: Higher Education

If residential housing is the real property element of the American dream, education is its most important intangible element. During the twentieth century, it has become the major means of social mobility for a growing population that has witnessed the structural and social changes brought about by the demise of the industrial revolution and the rise of the technological revolution. It is also the one area that almost all politicians, regardless of party affiliation, recognize as being of fundamental importance to both the well-being of the nation as well as to their own political fortunes. In his memoirs, Lyndon Johnson was proud to claim that because of his programs, a million and a half young people were able to attend college who otherwise would probably not have been able to afford it because of family circumstance.[1] George Bush also recognized its importance and proclaimed that he wanted to be remembered as the "education president" almost immediately after entering office in 1989.

Education in the United States has a long and varied history, with the government beginning to play a general role at all levels in the nineteenth century. Prior to 1957, government financial aid to education was geared primarily at assisting the states in vocational education and "Americanizing" the student, at whatever level. Given the vast number of immigrants entering the country and the shortage of skilled labor in certain sectors of the economy, this influence, achieved mainly through government assistance programs, was certainly logical enough. However, one distinguishable fact characterized education prior to 1957: assistance to students in paying their education costs was indirect. A teachers' college or agricultural college that succeeded in providing training for a large number of potential teachers or farmers usually did so because the institution was accessible in terms of cost. This meant that both the states and the federal government funded those institutions so that the tuition cost remained fairly low for the student, below what a private institution would charge for a similar education. The myriad indirect subsidies that were developed often created tension since many Americans were educated at sectarian institutions; detractors claimed that aiding students at those institutions or the institutions themselves violated the hallowed separation of church and state.

While education is part and parcel of the American dream at all levels, higher or tertiary education will be the focus here because undergraduate and postgraduate training have been the beneficiaries of financial market intervention in much the same way that housing has benefited from agency intermediation. However, assistance to this sector of the economy developed rather late in comparison with the Farm Credit Administration or the mortgage agencies. The reason for this late development is twofold. First, as with agriculture and housing, a crisis was needed in order to prompt government action that would lead to a market for student loans at the university and postsecondary vocational level. Second, this new form of intermediation as first devised was fundamentally different from the agricultural and mortgage markets in that it was not based on real property assistance but an intangible. However vital that intangible was to the national interest, it would take time to develop it in a similar framework so that the markets would lend their full support.

The Farm Credit System as such owed its original development to World War I and the agricultural crises of the 1920s and early 1930s. The mortgage agencies owed their development to the Depression and social legislation spanning the period 1938 through 1968. Education, however, owed its post–1950 development to an external event that shook the American dream as much as any economic or military occurrence. Despite two world wars and the Korean military crisis, perhaps no single historic occasion troubled American perceptions of progress and international relations as much as the "Sputnik crisis" of 1957. The United States had been beaten in space exploration. The repercussions would be felt at all levels of society but perhaps nowhere greater than at the level of education.

The role of the financial markets in the funding of education is only a small part of the overall history of the subject itself but nevertheless marks a turning point in the accessibility of higher education for the general population. As far as the markets are concerned, only higher or tertiary education has been eligible for the type of intermediation seen in previous chapters on housing and farming. To date, this has meant that the markets have been able to purchase student loans from lenders through a government-sponsored intermediary. This process involves the originator of a loan being able to sell the obligation to an agency that borrows in the marketplace in order to make the purchase. In short, student loans for college, graduate, or certain types of postsecondary professional training can be used as collateral-based borrowing in the markets in much the same way as home or farm mortgages. The agencies obviously differ but the principle nevertheless remains the same.

Unlike farm or home mortgages, however, student loans have always been considered more risky than real property-backed loans because they rely solely on the borrower to pay them back in point in time and are not collateralized. On the face of it, this would appear to make them too risky to be used by an agency as backing for its own debt obligations. This problem was recognized quite early and special guarantees by the federal government had to be put in place in order for the eventual intermediation to be successful. While the process appears to be quite similar to the securitization provided by the mortgage agencies, it nevertheless has its own peculiar form of intermediation, making it more akin to the original Fannie Mae or Veterans' Administration rather than to Ginnie Mae, Freddie Mac, or the Farm Credit System.

In the wake of the first Soviet Sputnik launched into space in 1957, U.S. education underwent an agonizing process of reappraisal at the governmental level. The question most often asked was how such a powerful industrial democracy, which prided itself on its ingenuity and productive capacity, could have been beaten in scientific exploration. The immediate policy response was to create a program to help finance higher education, especially in mathematics and the sciences, so that the national pride would not be embarrassed again by having to concede first place in such scientific enterprises.

THE ORIGINAL STUDENT LOAN LEGISLATION

The response to Sputnik came in 1958 with the passage of the National Defense Education Act (NDEA). On the tertiary education side, this act provided about $1 billion of services to college students to be disbursed over four years through Title 11 of the act. The purpose of the funds was to provide loans for undergraduate and graduate students intending to become college teachers. The intent of the legislation was clear: the country was perceived to be lagging in science, mathematics, and language training. This new loan package, submitted under a piece of defense legislation, was intended to close the gap. In its response, Congress had in effect declared war on its second-best status in science. This structural response would be echoed in the Eisenhower, Johnson, and Carter administrations in later years.

The actual distribution of the funds, as loans, was not a simple matter. It employed the matching principle whereby each state in which a borrowing student resided was to match from its own resources the federal amount provided. However, the borrowers themselves applied to their educational institution in the first instance and were assessed on the basis of educational costs and family means. Early in the program, need became the major criterion for a loan. If granted, the institution through which the individual applied provided 10 percent of the amount, with the federal government providing the balance. If the student decided to take up teaching in the public school system upon finishing his studies, all or part of the outstanding amounts could be cancelled. This latter provision, along with low rates of interest and fairly long pay-back periods, provided a great incentive for potential teachers who otherwise might have sought more lucrative professions.

The nascent student loan program was enhanced in 1965 by the Higher Education Act, which expanded opportunities for borrowing. Under Title IV of this legislation, the government entered what has become known as the direct student loan program. Rather than employ the educational institution that the student was attending as an intermediary, the government adopted the more proven method of using commercial banks as intermediaries for the loans. Students in need would apply to banks for the loans under federal criteria and, if approved, the government would then guarantee the loan to the lender. In such a manner, student loans fell under the same general framework as loans made to veterans under the original VA and FHA guidelines established several decades before.

Complicating matters in this process was the role of the states in guaranteeing lending. If the individual state in which the student resided had a student loan agency of its own, the guarantee was originally made by the state agency, with the federal government standing behind 80 percent of the amount guaranteed if the borrower defaulted. If the state did not have such apparatus in place, the government would guarantee all of the principal amount plus interest to banks originating the loans. Thus, the student loan program had two distinct elements: the general level of guarantees through the states was known as the Guaranteed Student Loan Program, while the direct level of guarantees to banks became known as the Federally Insured Student Loan Program.

Despite the new ground broken by these two pieces of legislation, the problem of students repaying these loans was always of primary importance to legislators. Naturally, this topic would become more hotly debated as the programs themselves became larger in the 1970s and the 1980s, but it was already evident early in the history of guaranteed lending. In the senatorial hearings preceding the passage of the Higher Education Act in 1965, an examination was made of the six years of lending to students under the original NDEA to determine whether the program was being abused or providing benefits as originally envisaged.

From its inception in 1958 until mid–1964, the NDEA had made $443 million in loans to some 640,000 borrowers. Of that amount, 10 percent was granted by the educational institutions involved, with the balance provided by the program. In 1964, $243 million was outstanding to students still in various stages of education, $191 million was due to be collected, and $9 million was cancelled because students fulfilled their obligation to teach in the public schools. Some $3 million was considered to be in default. While the latter number may seem rather small in relation to the total amount granted over the period, it represented almost 15 percent of the amount of cash actually being collected at the time that the Education Subcommittee of the Senate Committee on Labor and Public Welfare held its hearings. Even though the report of the hearings avoided comparing this delinquency rate to that of commercial banks collecting consumer loans, the problem was nevertheless obvious. Too many students were deemed to be avoiding repayment of their loans, for whatever reason.[2]

The delinquency problem was exacerbated by the terms and conditions of the loans themselves, which were designed with a heavy federal subsidy. For instance, under NDEA students could borrow up to $5,000 for their undergraduate years and up to $10,000 for graduate or professional training. Normally, repayment was to begin nine months after studies ceased and could be extended to a maximum of ten years. Interest was paid at a rate of 3 percent only after graduation; the interest was paid at 0 percent while the student was still enrolled in the program itself. Thus, the rate of interest and the repayment terms were more generous than any sort of consumer loan extended by commercial lending institutions at the time.

Although the Higher Education Act added a new dimension to the granting and the guaranteeing of student loans, the two programs in tandem provided the nucleus for lending. The terms and conditions of direct student loans were not materially different from those of the National Defense Student Loan (NDSL) program and both continued to consider the need of the student in determining the amount of aid, if any, to be provided. Both programs proved to be immensely popular in the late 1960s as the postwar baby boom generation became of college age and the pressure on higher education increased. But one problem persisted as new methods were devised to provide for the increasing demand for funds: student loans, vital for the intellectual life of this particular generation, were still considered to be among the most risky for lenders to originate due to the collection problems they presented. Although guaranteed to a large extent by federal government programs, continued demand for them would only exacerbate the situation. As a result, the intangible part of the American ideal presented a collection problem that, if left unsolved, could eventually vitiate the original intent of the 1958 and 1965 Higher Education Acts.

THE POSTWAR BABY BOOM

The demand for higher education created by the generation born after World War II was the most intense witnessed by U.S. educators since the

1920s, when the demand for college education and number of degrees granted grew exponentially. In 1919–20, the population stood at 104 million, slightly over 500,000 of whom were enrolled as full-time students in higher education institutions. Demographically, that represented only 7.88 percent of the population in the age group 18–21. Ten years later, the number of students had jumped to 1.1 million, representing 11.89 percent of that age group. The growth continued until the outbreak of World War II, when it tapered off before beginning its upward trend shortly thereafter. By 1963, almost 34 percent of students aged 18–21 were enrolled in higher education of some sort.[3] While the NDEA program aided over 600,000 students between 1958 and 1965, it alone did not add greatly to the numbers of students attending college.

The same is true of the growth figures after the direct loan program began in 1965. While the numbers increased each year, the actual percentage rates of growth were about the same. Therefore, the growth in student numbers cannot be solely attributed to the loan programs but reflect a general trend in population. But costs were another matter. Between 1973 and 1981 the total number of students in the country increased from 9.6 million to 12.3 million, an increase of 25 percent. During the same period, federal government costs for maintaining the two programs increased over eight times, from $306 million to $2.5 billion. The enormous growth in subsidized costs was accounted for by rising institutional costs. Put another way, the loan programs accounted for only a small fraction of total college revenues nationwide. If the students the programs actually assisted were removed from college entirely, college revenues would not have been seriously affected. However, the programs did enable many students to attend who might otherwise not have been able to do so because of a lack of funds.

The problem with student loans lies in their dual nature as socioeconomic stimulants on the one hand and as consumer loans (assets) for lending institutions on the other. Although the default risk is guaranteed by the federal government, lenders do not necessarily view them as the most desirable of assets because once the student himself is responsible for the repayment of interest and principal, the probability of default immediately rises. The time period within which a loan may be finally classified as in default is considerably longer than a normal, nonguaranteed consumer loan. Thus, even if the bank is eventually able to get its money back by invoking the guarantee, opportunity losses will arise nevertheless. The intermediary lender could also suffer unrealized losses by a default even if it is eventually compensated by the federal government.

Given the clash between the desirability of continuing the loan programs on the one hand and the repayment problems on the other, it became obvious that the programs required the assistance of an intermediaries' intermediary if they were to continue to provide long-term social and economic benefits. Fortunately, many programs were already in place that could be used as models to provide liquidity to the institutions originating student loans in the first place. Out of this need, the student loan version of Fannie Mae was born, employing private financial market investment with federal guarantees.

THE DEVELOPMENT OF SALLIE MAE

Of all the federally related agencies providing market support services, the Student Loan Marketing Association, better known as Sallie Mae, is the only one that does not deal with mortgages and consequently does not use real property as collateral for its borrowing operations. Instead, it uses government guarantees as collateral and raises money through the capital markets to fund its operations. Historically, Sallie Mae came into existence in much the same way as its mortgage predecessors—that is, through legislation. The association was created by the Education Amendments of 1972 and its original capital stock was held by the Treasury. In keeping with previous models, it was quickly privatized in 1982 after being enlarged during the intervening ten-year period.

The actual mechanics of Sallie's operations are a bit more complicated than they appear on the surface. While providing a secondary market for guaranteed student loans, it does so on the state level, not directly at the federal level. Although the system involves the ultimate guaranty of the federal government, the first layer is found at the state agency level, presuming that the state in which the student borrower lives in fact possesses such an agency. Thus, in the first instance, guaranteed student loans are secured by a state agency to the actual lender of the funds. The state agency, or in some cases another nonprofit guarantor agency, then "reinsures" the loan with Sallie Mae to protect the lender against default. While this reinsurance program is similar to that provided under the FHA or VA programs using Fannie Mae, the term "reinsurance" becomes significant when discussing student loans because of the lack of collateral associated with this particular type of lending.

Because of the state agency level of intermediation, another level of financing appears in addition to that employed by Sallie Mae in the capital markets. What appears to be a fairly straightforward matter of financing in fact has a totally separate level of intermediate financing between the Sallie Mae guaranty and the lender's willingness to create such loans in the first place. As with all U.S. agency financing, this intermediation illustrates the complexity of agency operations in the marketplace. As with the original mortgage agencies, a pyramid is created that consists of the loans themselves at the bottom and the ultimate guarantor at the top.

The state intermediaries' activities in the loan market increased dramatically from 1970 to the mid–1980s. Prior to that time, the programs proceeded in much the same general way as described here: lenders made loans and the federal government guaranteed them, providing a subsidy to those students still attending college. Beginning in 1969, interest rates began to rise and the Congress passed the Emergency Student Loan Act. This piece of legislation provided what is known as the Special Allowance Payment (SAP). These payments were made directly from the government to the lenders to help offset the increased cost of funds as interest rates began to rise. Ordinarily, these SAPs had a limit of 3 percent.

Shortly thereafter, many states, through their state student loan agencies, began to borrow on the municipal bond market. The coupon rates of interest were low since the bond interest was exempt from federal taxation. The states were able to raise cheap funds solely to purchase loans from the originators. Inadvertently, the SAPs allowed the states to make money on the purchase operation by having their revenues exceed their costs on the operation. As soon as the various state authorities realized the potential for profit, the number of state student loan bonds began to proliferate.

The states were further aided by federal legislation as well. The Tax Reform Act of 1976 officially allowed state agencies to issue tax-exempt bonds for the express purpose of purchasing guaranteed loans. But more importantly, the legislation exempted the SAP from the tax codes, effectively allowing the states to make a profit on the transaction. The only proviso was that any profit realized was to be used to purchase additional student loans or to be turned over to the states themselves.[4]

Continued congressional dedication to the student loan program thus proved to be a windfall to the states, which were reaping unrealized profits by combining the tax-exempt financings with the SAPs. Only with the passing of several tax changes, including the Tax Reform Act of 1986, were these loopholes closed and the windfall profitability erased. The technical term for such operations is arbitrage—in this case, interest rate arbitrage. By allowing the states to arbitrage the difference in the rates, the tax code was effectively using taxpayers' money to subsidize education, resulting in a state profit. When the arbitrage level was narrowed through the 1986 tax reform, states were still allowed to make marginal profits but not as large as those made previously.

Despite the intermediation provided by the states or other nonprofit agencies organized expressly for the purpose, Sallie Mae is the only agency organized at the federal level to deal with the purchase or "warehousing" of student loans. It can purchase the guaranteed student loans outright or make advances against them to the lending institution, known popularly but somewhat cumbersomely as "warehousing advances." As a government-organized and government-related agency, it uses its own good name in the market to borrow funds in order to perform its intermediary functions. On the surface, Sallie Mae would appear to be one of the riskier agencies, due to its purchasing of nonsecured student loans. On the contrary, however, its standing in the bond markets is considered to be of the highest order because the loans in its own portfolio are in fact government guaranteed. Thus, its risk of doing business are operational rather than loan-oriented.

Despite the fact that Sallie Mae's operations appear to be more of a reinsurance function than those of other mortgage or agricultural agencies, the liquidity function it provides is an important element in stimulating local lenders to continue to make student loans. During its short operational history, it has grown substantially in size so that by the mid–1980s, it was estimated to have purchased slightly less than 20 percent of all guaranteed loans, the balance being retained by various state entities. The important periods of Sallie's growth are the ones just preceding and then following its full privatization in 1982. From 1980 to the end of 1987, assets, including student loans and warehousing advances, grew from $2.1 billion to over $22.8 billion. Shareholders' equity rose from $46.7 million in 1980 to over $684 million in 1987. Net income rose from slightly over $16 million to $181 million during the same period. Obviously, debt also rose as these operations were funded in the money and bond markets. Total debt rose from about $2 billion in 1980 to slightly over $22 billion in 1987.[5]

Growth in the balance sheet and revenue statements obviously gives an indication of Sallie Mae's growth in relation to the market but it is the comparison with other sorts of commercial banking institutions that gives a true indication of its ability to intermediate and of the financial markets' acceptance of its role. Measured in comparative terms, Sallie Mae fared quite well after privatization and produced financial ratios that were the envy of many commercial banking institutions, especially in a period characterized by the developing bank crisis of the early and mid–1980s.

For example, in the 1980s Sallie Mae constantly produced a return on equity (book value of equity) of over 30 percent on average. That return far outstripped those of most banks with at least $5 billion in assets, including the money center banks.[6] However, these sorts of returns were accomplished with relatively low equity-to-asset ratios, when compared with those of commercial banks. During the period 1979–83, Sallie Mae's equity-to-assets ratio (excluding preferred stock) ranked below those of commercial banks with balance sheets of $5 billion or more. Beginning in 1984, the ratio did begin to rise to a comparable level.[7] It rose as the Federal Reserve was putting pressure on the banks to increase their ratios to even higher levels to cushion against the potential threat of nonperforming loans to Third World countries. As with many agencies, Sallie Mae was able to operate on a basis that would not have been acceptable if it had been a commercial banking institution.

The return on equity figures are indicative of two distinct yet different trends that can be found in all federal agencies. In the first case, one of the basic principles of finance can be seen in its pure form. As the amount of leverage in an organization increases (the use of bonds or preferred stock financing), the return on shareholders' equity naturally increases. From 1979 to 1987, Sallie Mae's long-term bond indebtedness jumped from $8.8 million to over $14 billion. During the same period, its shareholder's equity rose from $40 million to over $684 million. Obviously, the percentage changes in the two increases are not at all comparable. But the borrowing nevertheless helped enhance the agency's profitability. In 1981, Sallie reported earnings per share of 52 cents; in 1987 it reported $4.14 per share.

In the second instance, Sallie Mae has become perhaps the best-known example of an agency that is the closest to being risk-free of any of the government related agencies. It is the "off-balance-sheet" nature of the organization that helps in this particular case. Trading in the marketplace with an implicit federal government guarantee, Sallie Mae has accomplished two ends: it has been able to provide liquidity for student loan lenders while at the same time using its market stature to provide a subsidy for those loans to the student borrowers. This type of liquidity/subsidy function is due to the fact that the bond market has high regard for the agency, viewing it as a borrower with little chance of outright default risk.

SALLIE MAE IN THE BOND MARKET

Regardless of the intricate nature of any agency, the funds it employs in its liquidity operations come from the bond markets. How the markets view the particular agency spells the ultimate success or failure of its operations. In Sallie Mae's case, it is viewed as a prime credit for investors and often has traded with the smallest spread on its borrowings over U.S. Treasury securities of any of the other agencies, Ginnie Mae included. As a result, it has had access to a low cost of funds although the loans it supports often have the highest default rates of any market sector supported directly or indirectly by the federal government.

As obligations of a federal-related agency (although it is indirectly related), Sallie Mae's bonds are exempt from the registration requirements of the Securities Acts of 1933 and 1934. They are also eligible to be used in open market operations of the Federal Reserve if it chooses to use them. They are also eligible for purchase by fiduciary institutions, which must hold the predominant part of their portfolios in (mostly) risk-free or investment grade securities. But unlike obligations of the mortgage agencies or the Farm Credit System, Sallie's bonds are shorter in maturity because the types of loans it funds are shorter. For the most part, its outstanding bond borrowings are more intermediate in nature than those of the other agencies.

For instance, at year end 1987, the longest interest-bearing bond the agency had outstanding was due in 1998. The longest of all its bond obligations was a zero coupon bond due in 2022 but that represented a small portion of its total long-term indebtedness. Of the total amount of long-term indebtedness, about 60 percent was in the form of floating rate, or adjustable, notes which periodically readjust their interest above a comparable Treasury bill. The heavy reliance on floating, or adjustable, instruments, points out the one risk that Sallie faces in its day-to-day operations, that of interest rate risk in the form of mismatching on its books.

Because of the absence of perceived default risk, the spread that Sallie Mae pays over Treasury bills is one of the smallest in the bond markets generally. The interest rate risk in terms of a mismatch is therefore of little concern to investors unless it persists over a long period of time. By receiving a small spread, perhaps no more than 0.35–0.50 percent over a Treasury bill, Sallie is able to make a profit on the loans it purchases or warehouses as long as the student loan rate in general remains at a spread of 2–3 percent over bills. Thus, the agency is able to parlay its high credit standing into the ability to make money as well as assist the market. That small spread translates into increased earnings per share, which investors view favorably.

This low spread raises the question of the nature of the subsidy provided by Sallie Mae. Without the layer of government-guaranteed student loans that it purchases, the cost of funds would be higher and the earnings per share would be lower. By allowing the agency to borrow with the implicit guarantee, a subsidy is provided by the government both at the agency level as well as at the student borrower level. In market terms, this means that the investors in Sallie Mae obligations are receiving less of a return than a similar mortgage agency or Farm Credit bond may yield, but they are also assuming less ostensible time risk. One source has estimated the subsidy to Sallie to have cost the government, and consequently the taxpayer, an average of approximately $40 million per year between 1982 and 1985.[8] This figure is obtained simply by comparing Sallie's cost of borrowing with that of an equivalent private borrower and multiplying that savings spread by the amount of debt outstanding. Calculated on that basis, the implied subsidy rose to almost $250 million in 1987.[9]

In addition to student borrowers, the beneficiaries of the subsidy are the shareholders. They are broken down into three classifications—holders of voting common stock, nonvoting common stock, and adjustable rate preferred stock. Holdings of voting common are confined to educational institutions and financial institutions that participate in student lending programs. Nonvoting common stock has been sold to members of the general public and trades on the New York Stock Exchange, as does the common stock of Fannie Mae. In total balance sheet terms, the amount of paid-in equity capital remains somewhat small; the majority of Sallie Mae's funding is accomplished through the bond and note markets.

By the mid- to late 1980s, the success of the student loan program was evident. In the academic year 1986–87, over 23 percent of all U.S. undergraduates received some sort of federal loan, almost evenly split between men and women. The average loan was approximately $2,125.[10] But after almost 30 years of assistance, loan collections still presented a problem. In 1985, the United States Department of Education released a study showing the amount of student loans in default by institution on a state-by-state basis.

While the default rate varied greatly from institution to institution, many trade schools, especially cosmetic or beauty schools and secretarial schools had high numbers of their graduates in default when compared with the state or national average for all institutions. The default rate can be viewed as an indirect measure of success in determining whether a postsecondary institution is adequately preparing its graduates for the labor market after completion of studies.

Because of the increasing default rate, the Secretary of Education made certain amendments to the Guaranteed Student Loan Program through the authority of the Higher Education Amendments passed in 1986. These rule changes effectively changed the name of the program to the Stafford Loan Program. Under the new rules, the Department of Education tightened up the reporting surrounding student loans made by originators with an eye to ensuring more timely collections in the future.[11] As a result, the Department began to publish on an annual basis the default rates at each institution of higher learning in the country at which students qualified for loan assistance. This became necessary because the default rates at certain institutions had risen to as high as 40 percent of all students with loans outstanding.

The demand for student loans has risen as the costs of postsecondary education have risen. By the mid–1980s, over 50 percent of all U.S. high school graduates were enrolled in some sort of collegiate or other postsecondary educational programs. That figure can be compared with the 1920s' estimate of less than 10 percent. The costs at private institutions rose dramatically, beginning in the late 1960s, to reach almost $20,000 per year at the more expensive or elite universities in 1989. This fee could be twice the amount charged by a state-supported institution. Because of these increases, and the relatively small amounts that could be borrowed on a total basis, many institutions also offered students various financial packages to help finance their educations in addition to the basic student loan programs. In some cases, the fear of escalating costs also prompted some colleges to adopt financial packages that owed much of their design to products and practices developed in the financial markets since 1980.

One of these methods was derived directly from the present value concept that had originally proved so popular in personal pension schemes created by the Employees Retirement Security Act of 1974 (ERISA). Using a declared present value to ensure a future value, some colleges offered parents of students packages that would ensure a fixed tuition rate when the child was ready to enter college on a full-time basis. For a lump sum payment paid when the child was still in elementary school, the college would guarantee that that amount would cover the student's tuition bill when he reached college age. This method of payment was devised both to help parents finance future education costs and to aid in college planning in a time of estimated declining enrollments.

The principle employed was that used in the zero coupon bond. By purchasing an instrument at a distinct present value, the investor would receive a definite future value. The trade-off in this case was interest; zero coupon bonds pay no interest but do mature at face value at a definite future date. Since the parent's money could be collected when the child was still young, the college could in turn invest the funds. Once the parent had paid out this amount, the child's enrollment could be planned in advance by the college or university.

Although not universally popular, this sort of advanced payment program showed the gradual reliance of educational planning on what had become standard practices in the pension and insurance industries. Other innovations included the opening of "education banks," which were dedicated solely to providing the same sort of future value service without requiring the parents to commit themselves to a specific educational institution. In many cases, these special sort of depository institutions created forms of tax-deferred deposits that paid out lump sum benefits to students when they became of college age.

The success of Sallie Mae in aiding students as an accepted borrower in the bond markets illustrates the investors' tacit acceptance of off-balance-sheet financing by the federal government. Perhaps its greatest success in its relatively short life is in its reinsurance function, which enables lenders to sell off loans that have a spotty history of repayment. However, while the agency itself may well continue to prosper, the federal government is still saddled with any loans that are in arrears or have defaulted. In this respect, a cost that in many cases is indeterminate is added to the outright level of subsidies at both the student borrower and agency level.

The problem facing originators of student loans under the guaranteed programs has had many parallels in other federally-guaranteed programs, notably the farm assistance programs and the mortgage lending programs. As the demand for higher education has grown, especially since World War II, the demand for assistance has also grown, putting strains on lenders who may be reluctant to grant funds in times of inflation or financial uncertainty. The time lag between the graduation of a student and the time that he begins to repay can be highly uncertain because it is contingent on the job market for new graduates, as well as on the individual's willingness to repay the debt. Although these cash-flow uncertainties are peculiar to the student loan market, they nevertheless have parallels in other agencies' financings.

Future default rates can be expected to be high in a period beset with inflation or economic uncertainty, translating into a poor job market. The value of intermediary agencies such as Sallie Mae is that they are able to smooth this transition period by ensuring that funds continue to flow into the student loan market in order to guarantee lenders against default while at the same time providing a national resource of sometimes uncertain, but nevertheless necessary, value.

Sallie Mae's value in assisting higher education is considerable because education loans are, for the most part, still predominantly made by commercial lenders. When market conditions become poor, or other forms of lending become more desirable, those lenders would naturally be expected to curtail student loans in favor of other opportunities. But by providing liquidity for those institutions, the agency is able to ensure an orderly flow of funds into education, regardless of credit conditions. And while guaranteed student loans do not pay the total educational bill for students, it is safe to assume that without them the American dream of higher education would have been less accessible than it has been since 1958.

NOTES

1. Lyndon Baines Johnson, *The Vantage Point: Perspectives on the Presidency 1963–1968* (New York: Holt, Rinehart & Winston, 1971), Chapter 9.

2. U.S. Office of Education, *Report on Collection of National Defense Student Loans* (Washington, DC: U.S. Government Printing Office, 1965), especially pp. 2–9.

3. National Center for Education Statistics, *Digest of Educational Statistics* (Washington, DC: U.S. Department of Health, Education, and Welfare, 1972), p. 75.

4. Pearl Richardson, *The Tax-Exempt Financing of Student Loans* (Washington, DC: Congressional Budget Office, 1986), p. 7.

5. Student Loan Marketing Association, various annual reports.

6. Marvin Phaup, *Government Sponsored Enterprises and Their Implicit Federal Subsidy: The Case of Sallie Mae* (Washington, DC: Congressional Budget Office, 1985), p. 24.

7. Ibid., p. 25.

8. Ibid., p. 34.

9. Assuming a spread of about 35 basis points as compared with an implied spread of about 135 basis points for a comparable corporate or agency obligation times a total debt of $22 billion.

10. National Center for Education Statistics, *Digest of Education Statistics* (Washington, DC: U.S. Department of Education, 1988), pp. 254–55.

11. See specifically the Federal Register, November 10, 1866, and June 5, 1989.

7

Two Decades of Financial Innovation

The financial services revolution of the early 1980s, beginning in the United States and quickly spreading to Europe and Japan, had its direct origin in the deregulatory legislation passed by Congress in 1980 and again in 1982. In this case, it was a true revolution in the postwar American sense in that it attempted to redress a problem (a balkanized, constrained banking system) by legislating to enable commercial banks and thrifts to cope with a new market environment and increased international pressures. But the true economic and financial origins of this revolution lie in two international developments dating back almost ten years earlier.

As the old adage has it, "necessity is the mother of invention," but Shakespeare probably put it better by stating that "necessity must obey nature." The OPEC oil price rises of 1974 and 1979–80 provided the catalysts for much of the financial innovation and deregulatory legislation that occurred in the next decade. They also provided an impetus for financial developments taking place in Chicago that until that time were considered somewhat tangential to the real world of financial markets. But the effects of the price rises were cost-push inflation and the eventual spiral in interest rates that accompanied them. This uncertainty provided the unmistakable *sine qua non* for all subsequent financial developments—investor uncertainty. On the back of that uncertainty came many new methods and financial techniques designed to cope with it.

The first OPEC price increase in 1973 raised the price of oil from $3.65 to $11.65 per barrel. At the time, OPEC accounted for 57 percent of the world's production. Global demand for oil was high and viable substitutes were not yet available so the rise immediately catapulted the previously relatively obscure coterie of oil producers into the public eye. The worldwide recession of 1974–75 and the spurt in consumer prices experienced in all of the OECD countries quickly assured the OPEC nations a central place in all future economic and financial developments.

The second round of oil price rises came in 1979–1980 when oil reached its postwar peak of about $35 per barrel. During the intervening years, OPEC production actually fell from about 57 percent of world production in 1973 to about 48 percent in 1979. During the same period, U.S. domestic oil production also slipped slightly, from about 16 percent to 13 percent. The shortfall was made up by exports from the Soviet bloc, Britain, and other Third World producers. A great deal of the OPEC dollar surplus was invested outside the producing countries. OPEC money found its way into most financial and real property investments in the United States and Western Europe. But perhaps the greatest single recipient of these surpluses was the eurobanking system, located mainly in London and the other major European money centers. By offering rates of interest on deposits that were marginally higher than U.S. rates and by withholding no tax at source on the interest paid, the banks were able to attract a large portion of the liquid OPEC surplus. For instance, the total size of the eurodollar deposit market in 1970 was $110 billion; by 1978 it had increased to over $835 billion.[1]

Aside from the domestic price inflation caused by the tenfold rise in oil prices, a large pool of funds was accumulated offshore that had a significant effect on foreign exchange values by the early 1980s. The sudden movement of these funds from one capital center to another, chasing a high rate of return wherever it was to be found, had a profound impact on financial markets and the monetary policies of all the major industrial countries. On a smaller but equally significant scale, it would also have a pronounced effect on the balance sheets of many U.S. and foreign multinational companies.

While the rise of the oil price cannot be minimized, it followed hard on the heels of the international monetary crises of the early 1970s. These crises combined with the oil push inflation to add an increased volatility to the value of the U.S. dollar on the foreign exchange markets. After the breakdown of the Bretton Woods system of pegged exchange rates in the summer of 1971 and the eventual demise of its successor, the Smithsonian Agreement of 1972, the price of gold began to rise and many foreign holders of U.S. dollars began to divest in favor of other hard currencies and gold as well as art objects and other real property assets.

The breakdown of the fixed exchange rate system and the advent of floating exchange rates, when coupled with new levels of intenational liquidity, heightened the volatility of the financial markets. By 1974, the brief U.S. experiment with ad hoc capital controls in the form of the Interest Equalization Tax (1963–74) and controls over direct foreign investment (1965) in the form of "voluntary restraints" was finished and capital flowed freely in and out of the country, unfettered by government control.

Superficially, the absence of capital controls and the relatively easy access for the foreign investor to U.S. financial markets should have benefited the domestic economy by ensuring a constant flow of foreign investment funds. But the situation was complicated by the U.S. withholding tax leveled against interest and dividends paid to foreign holders of domestic securities. Although the 30 percent tax leveled at interest and dividends paid to foreigners was retrievable if the investor's country had a double tax agreement with the United States, opportunity losses could still lower the rate of return until tax returns were actually filed. In addition, the Interest Equalization Tax, leveled against Americans who held non-American securities issued in the domestic market, proved that the United States was still somewhat parochial in its attitudes toward things foreign in the financial markets. As Robert Solomon noted, the Interest Equalization Tax (IET) had a striking impact by discouraging domestic investors from buying foreign securities.[2]

While the avowed purpose of the IET and the voluntary controls on foreign investment was to stem the flow of dollars out of the United States, this aim was thwarted by the effect in the markets of the new exchange rate environment. Due to newly discovered swings in currencies' values, investors were now apt to switch funds and currencies from one capital center to another on short notice, creating what has become known as "hot money," that is, funds placed in short-term portfolio (securities) investments only. Being highly liquid, these funds could be moved to alternative investments on short notice.

Despite the roots of market volatility, the major focal point became movements in U.S. interest rates that gradually rose throughout the 1970s. By 1981, both long-term and short-term interest rates had reached postwar peaks. Even more pronounced than the actual level of rates was the fact that the yield curve became negative in slope; in this condition, short-term rates actually exceed yields on longer-dated bonds. The negative curve was the phenomenon that produced a drastic shift in U.S. balance sheet values and investor attitudes.

The irony in these developments was that high real U.S. interest rates helped engender even higher volatility in the foreign exchange markets. Real rates of interest in the United States were higher than in any of its industrialized hard currency counterparts. As a result, foreign investors flocked to U.S. investments, particularly Treasury bills and bonds in the first instance, despite the presence of the withholding tax.

The financial innovation that began in the early 1970s and continued well into the next decade took many forms and variations. In the earlier stages, innovation centered around institutional developments, although later it was concentrated on developing new techniques and products intended to respond to continuing problems within financial institutions. In the early stages, the products and techniques were not actually new; however, the new investment environment was, and it was the structuring of new exchanges especially that drew the most skepticism from within and without the investment community.

NEW EXCHANGES AND PRODUCTS

In 1971, President Richard Nixon suspended the convertibility of the U.S. dollar into gold, ending the Bretton Woods agreement that had been in force in the foreign exchange markets since 1947. The successor agreement, the Smithsonian Accord, had a short life and collapsed in 1972, giving way to the floating exchange market that now prevails for hard currencies and some of the major soft currencies as well. In the new market environment, currencies "float" against each other; the market determines rates on a supply and demand basis rather than adhering to the International Monetary Fund's standard use of fixed parities against the dollar. This new environment had the potential for extreme volatility from the outset.

The first innovation following the breakdown of Bretton Woods was a financial future that appeared in 1971 on the International Monetary Market (IMM). This particular exchange dedicated itself solely to the development and trading of myriad financial futures over the next 15 years, but the original instrument that it traded was a foreign exchange future. Both the exchange and the contract were new although the concept employed was traditional. Foreign exchange futures applied the fundamentals of traditional foreign exchange forward trading to time-proven methods normally employed to trade agricultural and metallic commodities. The interbank foreign exchange market determined the spot price for one currency against another and the futures markets then used that price as the major determinant for extrapolating a price for delivery in several months' time. The new market for foreign exchange was not intended to replace the interbank forward market; neither could it have replaced it. What it sought to accomplish was to expand the idea of trading beyond the traditional participants in that market, namely, multinational corporations and the banks themselves.

Currency volatility and the deleterious effect it could have on corporate balance sheets was certainly not confined to the largest of international traders. Many small and medium-sized businesses also had extensive aggregate foreign exchange needs that could not be adequately served by the traditional forward market, in which the average transaction may well have been beyond the reach of their working capital capacities or needs. The new futures market allowed investors to trade smaller lots of currency on a contract basis that might only amount to a small percentage of the average interbank forward trade. In addition to contributing to innovation in general, the new foreign exchange future also brought a new dimension to what had traditionally been a purely institutional market. It introduced the smaller trader or company and attempted to cater to these somewhat different needs by using a combination of traditional forwards and traditional futures.

The introduction of this new market was indeed well-timed. In the four years following 1973, the dollar declined on a trade-weighted basis by about 9.3 percent while the Japanese yen rose some 32 percent and the Swiss franc rose about 22 percent.[3] In addition, individual currency volatility increased and the newly emerging alignments in the marketplace quickly affected trade balances and economic geography as a whole. The new futures market also provided investors with a crucial aspect of trading that the traditional market lacked—secondary market liquidity. In the forward market, contracts had to be delivered as specified; that is, if a company bought sterling forward as a hedge, it had to take delivery. It was not able to lay off the contract to a third party if the original need for it changed over time. The futures market was able to develop secondary trading and use it as one of its strong selling points, especially for the smaller trader.

The value of the IMM increased for the smaller company or trader after the introduction in 1975 of new accounting rules designed to deal with foreign exchange gains and losses. Financial Accounting Standard 8 (FAS 8) was officially introduced after the breakdown of the Smithsonian agreement to deal with the balance sheet and revenue statement effects of the new exchange rate regime. The standard introduced was subsequently replaced with a simpler method nine years later (FAS 52) but the behavior it generated among all sorts of foreign exchange market participants was ideally suited for the new contracts and helped ensure their success.

The major problem faced by businesses of all sizes was the effect that floating exchange rates would have on their dealings with foreigners in non-U.S. dollar currencies as well as the valuation of overseas assets and liabilities. FAS 8 attempted to come to grips with the problem by imposing what became known as the "temporal" method of accounting for gains and losses. It required all nonmonetary assets and liabilities (not current items on the balance sheet) to be valued at the historic exchange rates prevalent at the time of booking if those assets and liabilities were held outside the United States. All monetary items (current) were to be valued at the exchange rate prevalent at the time of valuation. In other words, two rates could be and were used in valuing overseas assets and liabilities. Since the gains or losses produced by the temporal method had to be realized on the income statement of the companies involved, this method permitted a great deal of foreign exchange hedging by companies with international dealings. Balance sheet hedging became fashionable as companies attempted to preserve the value of their overseas assets and liabilities by selling or buying currencies forward against their assets and liabilities on a quarterly basis. This increased posturing in some cases only added to the volatility of the market itself.

The futures market enabled smaller firms to indulge in the same sort of behavior on a smaller scale. While not a surrogate for the forward market, the foreign exchange futures market did carve out a niche in the financial markets nevertheless, and established a track record of limited success that would be expanded in other types of financial instruments.

The foreign exchange problem quickly spilled into the realm of fixed-income instruments such as bonds and money market obligations. The new exchange rate regime made it abundantly clear that interest rates would become as volatile as their foreign exchange counterparts and that the exchange rate mechanism could easily import inflation into the U.S. domestic economy. The bond and money markets themselves were ill equipped to deal with this problem since they had never had techniques or special instruments by which investors could hedge against falling prices. The traditional methods employed by professional traders were not adequate to cope with the new volatility rising in the markets since the fixed-income markets had been essentially stable for more than three decades.

Of all the interest rate instruments in the credit markets that could theoretically be hedged, the Ginnie Mae long-term bond was the first to have a future specifically designed for it. The GNMA futures contract was introduced in 1975 at the Chicago Board of Trade (CBOT) and has the distinction of being the first and oldest of interest rate futures. Of all long-term bonds issued in the United States, this was the most common variety of a single borrower other than the Treasury obligations of the U.S. government. Investors in them included many financial institutions, especially thrifts that bought them for investment purposes. The ability to hedge these bonds was therefore of vital importance to investors, who were in effect helping to provide liquidity to the mortgage market.

As with foreign currency futures, GNMA contracts were offered with three-month expiry intervals. This meant that an investor could use the market to buy or sell contracts expiring in the near future, depending on the length of time he needed to cover his interest rate exposure. The amount of time chosen by the investor depended on his expectations for interest rates over the near term and the anticipated price effect on his holdings.

Over the next ten years GNMA contracts proved to be less popular than other types of interest rate contracts that were issued subsequently. However, in the early stages of market development they were considered to be the most vital because they could help in providing liquidity to the housing market, which was vital to the continued health of the economy. If investors had a means by which they could hedge their holdings of Ginnie Mae securities they would continue to purchase mortgage obligations without fear of capital loss.

In the same year that the Chicago Board of Trade announced the mortgage contract, the IMM introduced the second of its innovative contracts, the future on 90-day U.S. Treasury bills. A similar contract was also introduced on the Chicago Mercantile Exchange. This contract became the most popular of all early financial futures contracts and remained so for the next ten years because its attraction was somewhat more broadly based than that of the others. The T-bill contract appealed to a wider spectrum of investors than the holders of bills alone; it was the only method by which all sorts of investors could cover their exposure to short-term interest rates in general by taking positions based on their expectations.

Holders of Treasury bills include almost all those in the financial markets who invest their working capital in short-term securities, whether in banks and other depository institutions, investment funds, or individuals. The 90-day Treasury bill is the most popular of all short-term Treasury issues. It is given its own statistical symbol in technical finance language—Rf—which signifies the risk-free rate against which all other short-term investments or interest rates are measured.[4]

Among financial institutions especially, the need to protect short-term assets against precipitous changes in interest rates was most pronounced. In 1975, an estimated $357–$360 billion of commercial banking assets were deemed susceptible to moves in short-term interest rates.[5] Under adverse conditions, a 1 percent rise in interest rates could reduce these assets by some $3 billion. Given that Treasury rates alone would rise by almost 9 percentage points over the next six years, the value of these figures became apparent as market conditions became volatile. Banks, corporations, and foreign central banks holding short-term U.S. assets would utilize the new futures markets to protect the integrity of their balance sheets. But one qualifying factor was apparent to all market participants early on in the development of the markets: the markets might not have the liquidity necessary to accommodate all of the financial institutions or other investors that might decide to adopt a similar hedging strategy at the same time.

Despite technical problems that provoked some skepticism about the markets' usefulness, innovation in the futures markets continued during the 1970s. In August 1977, the Chicago Board of Trade introduced what was to become the other most popular interest rate future, that on the long-term U.S. Treasury bond. The long bond, usually represented by the most current 30-year issue borrowed by the Treasury, represented the other volatile end of the yield curve. While short-term Treasury bills would immediately react to changing conditions in the credit markets, the longer-dated bonds would react more to secular changes in the interest rate structure. If they did, the resulting deterioration of investors' principal could take a substantial amount of time to recoup.

Bond futures, as bill futures, found a ready clientele in the professional trading community that made its living quoting secondary market prices in these obligations. Prior to the advent of the formal futures markets, investment banks and commercial banks that maintained markets in Treasury securities had practiced their own form of forward trading in various sorts of long- and short-term obligations but had never extended this trading to the general investing public. Although the new markets both remedied and formalized previous practice, futures instruments on both currencies and interest rate instruments were still quoted away from the home markets of their underlying instruments. It was a long way from the organized over-the-counter market for Treasury securities in New York to the pit environment for financial futures in Chicago.

The complexity of many of these new futures instruments proved a stumbling block to their early acceptance. Both bond and GNMA futures suffered from this product malaise until market conditions dictated that knowledge of their intricacies could actually help investors. Details such as deliverable grade, spot and nearby pricing, margin requirements, and delivery procedures were much more complicated than practices in the regular cash market for bonds, and if not understood correctly could present considerable risks themselves. In some cases, newly developed futures contracts failed to develop investor interest and never generated the liquidity necessary for a viable market.[6]

In the two years immediately following the introduction of the long bond contract, the market remained relatively quiet. But as the second phase of OPEC price rises forced up inflation and interest rates, the volatility of long-term bonds started to become painfully obvious to the investment community. When the bond contract was first introduced in the summer of 1977, the U.S. 30-year bond yield was about 8 percent. Four years later, it reached its postwar peak of slightly more than 14 percent. For a bond purchased as a new issue in 1977, that rise in interest rates created a capital loss of 44 percent.

Given the success of the previously mentioned futures, contracts on other instruments soon followed in their wake. Futures were also introduced on ten-year Treasury bonds, 90-day eurodollar deposits, commercial paper, and U.S. bank negotiable certificates of deposit. In all cases, the intent was to enable investors to hedge or speculate on interest rate risk. But the need to hedge equity investments also became crucial because the economic factors that affected foreign exchange values and interest rates also had a pronounced effect on individual equity values as well as on the overall stock market itself. During the same period, product development also focused on equity hedging instruments.

Derivative equity instruments underwent two distinct stages of development. The first stage occurred almost at the same time as the currency futures contracts were launched. In April 1973, the world's first options exchange was opened at the Chicago Board Options Exchange. Its purpose was to enable investors to buy and sell call and put options (options to buy or sell) in a central, organized exchange environment. Of the two types of options, calls were the first to be traded. These instruments allowed investors to trade stocks on a forward basis and were structured similarly to a futures contract. Contracts expired at three-month intervals in the future and had a contract (or striking) price as well as a market price. Investors had the ability to buy a stock for future delivery at a price established by the usual market supply and demand factors.

The establishment of this exchange was risky in two respects. First, options had been traded for years on an over-the-counter basis and this new market was encroaching on established financial territory. Investors would have to be enticed by the new exchange environment and its centralized potential for mitigating risk. Second, over the 18 months following the inauguration of the Chicago Board the stock market underwent one of its steepest declines in postwar history. The Dow Jones Industrial Index fell from 1051 in 1973 to 880 by the end of 1975. In the longer run, this sort of volatility would help underscore the usefulness of options in general, but in the shorter run it could have spelled financial ruin for the nascent organization.

The major attraction of options to an investor was that the amount of risk incurred was limited to what he had paid for the contract. This enabled a broad range of investors to play the stock market in miniature, that is, to speculate on a stock's rise or fall for a fraction of the equity's market price. This limited risk factor helped the market survive in its early days despite the overall direction of the stock market itself.

The early success of the Chicago Board prompted other U.S. exchanges to open trading. By 1974, Chicago was trading almost four million calls per day and the American Stock Exchange soon announced that it would open option trading facilities as well. Shortly thereafter the regional stock exchanges also opened trading facilities, sometimes offering their own listed options while in other cases duplicating contracts on the other two exchanges.

Options provided the investment community with two distinct benefits. The ability to trade a stock for potential future value for only a fraction of its current value was only one side of the coin, however. In a broader perspective, it also allowed portfolio managers to mitigate individual equity risk by using options in tandem with the actual stocks themselves to protect (at least partially) against unforeseen future losses. This gave money managers an additional tool in their quest for maximizing gain while avoiding undue risk.

Despite the growth and acceptance of traded options on individual stocks they did not protect investors against all of the risks intrinsic to equity investments. During the 1950s, the principles of modern portfolio theory were developed by Harry Markowitz. In a series of quantitative studies he showed that portfolios holding a number of different stocks were highly preferable to those that were exposed to only a small number. The basic assumption was that a broad range of holdings was less susceptible to the market forces than a narrow range; therefore, safety of investment could be found in diversity.

While options provided an additional tool for mitigating portfolio risk they were not able to help investors hedge against the second type of risk also intrinsic to equity investments—that of the market itself. The attempt to tackle that problem through more innovative product development was the second stage of derivative equity-linked instruments. In the spring of 1982, the Kansas City Board of Trade took the initiative and introduced a stock index futures contract. This innovative instrument was not based on a single underlying stock but on a market index. In the original case, the Kansas City contract used the Value Line Stock Index as its basis.

This new instrument developed initially as a futures instrument. It allowed investors to speculate on, or hedge against future market movements by selecting a future delivery date and either buying or selling the contract market price. In such a manner, market movements and the potential exposure they presented to investors could be hedged. In theory, investors could now hedge against a specific stock risk or that of the market as a whole.

Shortly after the Kansas City contract was launched other exchanges announced their own new contracts. The Chicago Mercantile Exchange offered a contract on the Standard & Poor's 500 Index while the New York Futures Exchange offered one on the New York Stock Exchange Composite Index. In almost all cases, the contracts were at least qualified successes. In the second six months of 1982, both Chicago and New York futures had traded over a million contracts; in Chicago's case the number approached almost two million.

Encouraged to build on the success of the first generation of options and futures on financial instruments, the markets entered a second phase in the early 1980s. Options were subsequently offered on Treasury bonds, foreign currencies, and stock market indices. The former two products met with a limited demand, while smaller investors flocked to the latter. The various exchanges quickly discovered that there was a limit to the amount of technical information and innovation that investors could assimilate concerning new products. Consequently, the second phase of development did not attract the investor interest that the original instruments engendered. This was especially true of the later instruments introduced, especially the options on futures of different types.

Financial innovation since the breakdown of the Bretton Woods system had another dimension that was not confined to the development of new products on domestic U.S. exchanges. This dimension was originally inspired by developments in the international capital markets and involved the grafting of foreign concepts onto U.S. financial instruments, a practice that would have been unthinkable a decade earlier. The focus of these innovations was not the general investing public in traditional securities but banks and other financial institutions serving in their traditional roles as intermediaries in the savings and investment process.

SECURITIZATION AND ASSET REALLOCATION

The rise in the price of oil during the 1970s also created a new class of debtor nations. When one speaks of the less developed countries (LDCs) and their appetite for funds that created the borrowing/lending explosion of that decade one is in fact speaking of roughly 100 nations in different stages of economic and social development. Their one common trait was the need to borrow in order to offset the balance-of-payments disequilibrium created by the oil price shocks.

The major suppliers of these funds were the international banks of various countries operating both from London, the heart of the euromarket, and from their domestic bases. In 1970, the non-OPEC LDCs had borrowed some $300 million from the banking system. By 1977, the figure had grown to an excess of $13 billion.[7] Individually, Argentina, Brazil, Mexico, Chile, the Philippines, and South Korea accounted for the largest amounts borrowed over the period. The geometric growth in the debt levels, which would increase from the period 1977–82 to even higher levels, led one commentator to conclude in 1977 that "the linkage of our banks with developing countries not only makes it difficult for them to walk away from us; it also makes it unlikely that we could walk away from them."[8]

Banks were willing to lend funds to the LDCs using one of several criteria. If the borrower was oil-based, its borrowing was assumed to be safe because the downstream price of oil would in fact cover payments of principal and interest. If the borrower was commodity-based, the same assumption was made. The genuinely poor, falling into neither category, were allocated funds on a crude portfolio basis; that is, if a particular bank's exposure to that country or geographical area was not particularly high, the added exposure was not considered too risky.

The funds available for this sort of lending came in large part from the OPEC countries, which deposited much of their newly found surpluses in the eurodollar deposit market. The banks, awash with funds, needed assets to balance these liabilities. Large-scale lending became prevalent, especially since these expatriate dollars were not subject to domestic U.S. reserve requirements, being held offshore. And in order to package these loans in large amounts, the loans were syndicated in much the same way as securities issues were traditionally packaged. The large amounts borrowed at any one time were arranged by one bank and sold off, or syndicated, in turn to other banks that bought a portion of the loan for their own books.

Another inducement for international lending was the obvious profit motive. In addition to being lucrative, international loans, and indeed the overall international operations of many U.S. banks, helped the parent holding companies remain profitable in the face of severe domestic banking pressures. The rise in the amount of deposits placed with the banks necessitated large loans to be booked as assets. The result was, in many cases, a borrowers' market.

It was not only LDC borrowing that increased during this period; the 1970s in general witnessed an unprecedented growth in borrowing by all sorts of organizations, commercial and not-for-profit. After 1977, the syndicated loan market for LDC loans continued at a brisk pace. As Mexico's ability to repay its $65 billion debt to the banking system became doubtful, lending to LDCs in general began to fall. By 1986, it had fallen to $15 billion, down from almost $25 billion in 1983.[9] But at the same time, lending to the OECD countries by international banks had increased, and borrowing on the international, or eurobond, capital markets had increased substantially from the decade prior.

Bond borrowing began its upward trend after 1972. The eurobond market, for example, was born in 1963 when $75 million equivalents were issued. By 1972, the outstanding figure had increased to $4.9 billion. In 1986, the number of new issues stood at the equivalent of $180 billion, not taking into account the amount already outstanding in the secondary market. Included in this were bonds of different varieties in addition to the traditional straight borrowing—variable coupon, or floating rate, notes, multicurrency bonds, zero coupon obligations, and an international resurrection of the old 1815 British war bond, the perpetual issue.

Almost all of the Third World debt incurred during this period was in the form of bank loans: bond borrowings were usually reserved for those entities from OECD countries. This debt distribution illustrates one of the ironies of financial markets during this period especially: borrowers of high credit standing could access the bond markets, while the less creditworthy relied instead on bank loans. This phenomenon became a problem when banks found themselves overextended to certain borrowers. Ultimately, the banks' shareholders had to bear the burden of nonperforming loans.

The debt explosion of the 1970s created two classes of financings. The first consisted of the multinational company, developed sovereign borrower, or international financing agency using the international and domestic bond markets to obtain the cheapest possible cost of long-term debt financing. On the other side of the coin were the less privileged, borrowing in antic- ipation of higher inflated earnings from their oil or commodity exports, or simply attempting to balance their payments. The structural differences in the way they borrowed would eventually become the basis for innovation in itself.

Financial innovations also developed in the international arena for the same reasons they had developed domestically. But since the international capital market was still in its early, formative years the developments con- centrated around new products developed by banks for banks, rather than techniques of hedging or mitigating risk for the general investing public. The basis for almost all of this syndicated bank lending originating in the euromarket was the variable rate, or floating rate, loan.

This type of bond was long-term in nature and paid its interest on a variable basis over a predetermined "reference rate." This base rate was usually the offered rate on three- or six-month eurodollar deposits. Through this method, the investor purchasing it was always guaranteed a current coupon at a slight margin over the prevailing money market rates.

In such a manner, banks could tailor a bond borrowing to the loan they anticipated making. For example, a seven-year loan at a specific spread over six-month dollars could be funded for the entire term by paying marginally less over the same rate to the bondholders. But most importantly, this sort of bond was considered a note. It usually ranked equally with deposits in the event that the bank was liquidated. Unlike most long-term bank bond obligations, it was not subordinated; it represented senior debt of the borrowing institution and would be treated as a long-term deposit of sorts. By issuing this type of security, banks had securitized bank funds over a medium or long term in much the same way that negotiable CDs had traditionally securitized shorter-term deposits in the money market. In the case of CDs, banks had added an element of marketability to short-term deposits. A floating rate bond or note was a longer-term version of the same concept.

During the early 1970s, floating rate notes were issued predominantly by banks, although some other types of borrowers also issued them on a trial basis. Their features illustrated that they were an ideal way of funding long-term assets with short-term interest rate-sensitive instruments while still being able to weather severe shifts in the interest rate structure. It was this feature that made them ideal for export to the United States to be applied to a financial services sector especially beleaguered by term/rate mismatching.

Ironically, the same funding principle that fueled lending on a syndicated basis helped prop up a part of the U.S. financial industry that had been damaged severely by the rise in interest rates and the consequent disintermediation that occurred among many financial institutions in the latter part of the 1970s.[10] American thrift institutions underwent a dramatic consolidation beginning in 1975. Their numbers dwindled from 4,900 institutions active in that year to only 3,400 by 1984. The rise in interest rates and their subsequent shift into a negative yield curve caused the profit margins of FSLIC-insured savings institutions to fall from an average 6 percent in 1975 to a −7 percent in 1981 and a −5.6 percent in 1982 before returning to an average profit in 1983.[11] The drop in average profitability forced many of the smaller, marginally capitalized thrifts to merge with the larger in order to survive. Failing that, some ceased operations entirely.

The major factor plaguing thrifts was the natural mismatching that occurred on their books as they directed short-term deposits into the long-term mortgage market. As long as short-term rates remained below the long term, mortgage assets provided a higher revenue than the rate paid to depositors. But when interest rates began to rise, profit margins began to fall, severely affecting thrifts' ratios. The major culprit in this process was the long-term fixed, or conventional, mortgage.

Mortgages traditionally account for 70–80 percent of a savings and loan association's assets. As has been discussed, the originating institution could retain the mortgage or sell it to one of the mortgage agencies. The original form of securitization provided by the mortgage agency, as it used those mortgages to back its own bond market borrowings, protected the market by providing liquidity. But it could not help the lending institution regain profitability. All that the lender could accomplish was to sell off the mortgage, shifting the interest rate risk to the agency and the investors who bought its bonds. Thus, the assistance that the mortgage agencies provided could not improve or maintain profitability; only liquidity was provided. Since the U.S. experience with rates was based on a positive yield curve, the negatively sloped structure required a different sort of response if the tradition of quality housing was to survive the challenges posed by the new environment.

The housing industry's answer to the challenge came in the form of the adjustable rate mortgage, first introduced on a large scale in 1983. Adjustables grafted the concept of a floating rate borrowings onto a traditional asset/liability mix. The new mortgages charged interest at a specific spread over a base rate and were changed periodically to reflect movements in money market conditions. This enabled lending institutions to avoid the mismatching that usually occurred by being exposed to different parts of the yield curve.

The popularity of adjustables among borrows proved their worth to the mortgage lenders. By 1985, approximately 70–75 percent of all new mortgages were granted on an adjustable basis. That proportion declined in 1986 and 1987 as interest rates declined and long-term fixed mortgage rates fell into single digits for the first time in a decade. But as with all market-related phenomena, the actual effects would prove themselves only with the passing of time.

The direct applicability of a floating rate note came on the funding side of these new mortgages. Apart from being able to adjust mortgage interest due as interest rate conditions changed, many mortgage institutions began to issue long-term debt on a floating rate basis using either the domestic capital market or the euromarket, depending on which offered the cheapest cost of funds. When they first appeared in the early 1980s, American floating rate bonds marked a milestone in the history of U.S. capital markets for two reasons. First, they were the first debt instruments issued domestically on an adjustable basis. Second, they represented only the second form of securitization in the country since the appearance of the original housing agency issues.

Under the terms and conditions of adjustable mortgages, lending institutions had been protected to some extent against future rate rises. But at the same time, the interest rate exposure risk had been shifted to the mortgage payer. The ability of the homeowner to absorb future increases in his interest would obviously depend on his future cash flows. Ironically, adjustable rate home mortgages put the homeowner in much the same position as Mexico and other developing countries had been in a decade earlier.

Securitization is a technique that has been best employed during times of financial crisis. When carefully applied, it has helped traditional asset holders mitigate risk by providing a new secondary market for assets that were previously illiquid. At the same time that adjustable bonds appeared in the markets, other new instruments were also introduced, all having the same purpose: to help banks raise liquidity at relatively low rates in order to bolster their capital bases at the behest of regulatory authorities.

Although a bank "crisis" as such was anticipated for several years prior to 1982, it was the Mexican debt crisis in October of that year that ushered in the most serious round of the bad loan problems that banks would suffer. But Mexico was certainly not the first brush with default by a sovereign borrower that the banks had experienced. The 1975 default by Zaire and the 1980 rescheduling of Poland's outstanding bank loans had served as a harbinger of events to come. But Poland's $35 billion of outstanding loans was minuscule in comparison with Mexico's $65 billion outstanding. The potential Mexican default, averted by rescheduling its debt into more favorable (longer repayment) terms, did point out, however, that U.S. banks were undercapitalized if large loan losses were incurred in the future.

As depository institutions in general came under pressure in both the stock market and the credit markets, their ability to raise new capital was seriously undermined. New issues of common stock were treated warily by investors. Since the latter 1970s, the stock market priced the earnings of large bank holding companies below those of corporate earnings in general.[12] Consequently, debt capital became more expensive for banks and the borrowing countries that had come to rely on them for funds. As portions of LDC debt became nonperforming, reserves had to be created against loss. These reserves were created out of net income and had a deleterious impact on retained earnings. In short, the banks were in need of capital and had few traditional avenues open to them because of increased investor resistance.

This situation was compounded by the fact that any capital raised would be required for the long term. If a U.S. bank issued a long-term bond, it would be a subordinated issue by definition. This would escalate its cost of funds regardless of the credit rating of the bank at the time. Few investors would be enticed by the prospect of a long-term obligation of an institution with loan portfolio problems. Even fewer would be enticed by the prospect of a new equity issue that would see increasingly fewer retained earnings in the foreseeable future.

With this problem looming on the horizon, as the traditional methods became too expensive, banks turned to securitization as a means of raising funds. With the assistance of investment bankers, they used those assets on their books that were performing as backing for debt issues. They were thus able to raise funds by creating an asset-backed security. The concept was not new; it was simply a rebirth of the agency pass-through concept using assets other than home mortgages.

Many depository institutions employed the idea in a variety of novel ways. Savings and loan associations issued bonds guaranteed by the principal and interest payments of government or agency securities in their investment portfolios. Commercial banks did the same, pledging payments (receivables) on such assets as automobile loans outstanding or credit card receivables. Investors were guaranteed payment by passing through borrowers' payments to them. But the major problem with this type of asset-backed loan was that they most often represented the best of a bank's assets—the type that would not ordinarily be sold under better conditions. When these assets became securitized, the bank lost them as performing assets and the profitability that accompanied them.

This sort of financing began in 1983–84 in the wake of the Mexican debt crisis. Although novel, the techniques used were not unfamiliar in corporate finance. The packaging of automobile loans is a case in point. This is a form of long-term factoring in which a holder of receivables sells them to a third party in order to raise cash. However, traditional factoring does not involve the issuance of a security. But this procedure does illustrate how securitization employs the marketplace to provide liquidity for assets traditionally considered illiquid by their very nature.

Despite the novelty of such financing techniques, they could not in themselves provide banks with all the funds required in the face of increasing demands by regulatory authorities for capital. By 1985, the Federal Reserve determined that banks should hold, on average, about 6 percent capital as a proportion of total assets, as seen in Chapter 3. At the time, some U.S. money center banks had capital ratios only of about 4.5 percent to 5 percent. Given that the 12 largest banks had assets of around $650–$700 billion at the time, even a 1 percent increase would require them to raise an additional $6.5–7 billion in the marketplace. And this amount is a crude estimate, depending on the exact nature of the capital-to-asset ratio employed.

Adding a greater element of uncertainty to the matter was the fact that the new levels of capital would also be affected by international factors. In the winter of 1986, the Federal Reserve and the Bank of England agreed that ratios should be similar for institutions on both sides of the Atlantic.[13] This was a recognition of the internationalization of the marketplace that had occurred since the deregulatory legislation of 1980 and 1982 in the United States and in 1986 in the United Kingdom.

In 1983, a market began to develop for loans that banks no longer wished to keep in their portfolios. Technically, this was called the secondary loan market, but it could also have been called another form of securitization.[14] It provided the means whereby a bank could offer its loans in a newly created secondary market, usually at a discount from face value. Purchasers could then bid for the loan at a yield commensurate with the potential default risk of the borrower, normally a developing country. This method allowed banks to divest themselves of some exposure to possible defaults; it held out the greatest potential for banks to realign their portfolios. However, if assets were disposed of in this way, a loss would still be incurred because the amount of discount at which the loan was sold would have to be written off against net income. This put banks in the ticklish position of having to decide whether to keep the loan on the books at face value, hoping for a positive outcome from the borrowers' downstream earnings, or to sell the loan and realize the loss in the current quarter.

Selling loans was only one side of the coin in this process. There still remained the matter of finding potential bidders for dubious loans. If the process was to be of serious economic value, it would have to be beneficial to the LDC borrower and/or the purchaser in point of time. Some debtor countries already had mechanisms in place that dovetailed with this emerging trend. The most fully developed plan was that of Chile. Since 1977, it had allowed external creditors to capitalize debt claims on Chilean entities by converting them into equity.[15] This was known as the debt/equity swap, enabling the holder of debt to convert it to equity in a developing country. The new equity investment would be denominated in the local currency rather than in dollars.

Other LDCs quickly seized this opportunity. By allowing multinational companies that had bought discount loans from the commercial banks to convert them into local equity investments, they were able to achieve two ends. First, the conversion spurred direct foreign investment in their countries. Second, the conversion itself allowed them to retire that portion of their external debt at less than face value, thereby reducing the total amount of debt outstanding. In this case, they were able to achieve those ends without recourse to another hard currency. The swaps were between dollars and the local currency only—almost invariably the latter was not easily convertible on the foreign exchange market.

The concept of securitization became more and more popular as the debt crisis became more pronounced. After Citicorp announced that it would begin writing off a portion of its outstanding Brazilian debt in the summer of 1987 by attempting to sell those loans in the secondary market, Brazil itself announced that it would be willing to offer its creditor banks long-term bonds to replace their outstanding term loans. The intent was to convert the floating-rate loan debt to fixed-rate securities that would not be subject to interest rate changes in the future.

Not all of the innovation in the post-Bretton Woods era involved securitization or the development of derivative products. Two of the most notable products developed were the interest rate swap and the currency swap, both involving securities. These two techniques were discussed in Chapter 3. They both gained popularity quickly in the financial markets, particularly the euromarket, because they afforded borrowers a viable means of reducing their cost of funds while at the same time providing banks with much-needed revenue in the wake of the Mexican debt crisis of 1982.

Of the two, the interest rate swap was the more frequently used. Two borrowers, one with fixed-rate debt and the other with floating debt, arranged to swap their respective interest payments. The fixed-rate borrower took on the floating payments and vice versa. If the terms were arranged favorably, both parties were able to reduce their original cost of funds below what their credit ratings might otherwise suggest.[16] The same was true of a currency swap. A U.S. borrower might issue bonds in Japanese yen at favorable rates and then swap the funds with a Japanese company holding dollars. A successful swap would see both parties lower their cost of funds below what the market would otherwise have suggested.

Swaps benefited both parties but created a potential risk for the commercial banks. Each swap needed a guarantee so that the new arrangement would be acceptable to all parties involved. Commercial banks provided these guarantees for a fee, usually ranging from about 0.25 of 1 percent to 0.75 of 1 percent of the total transaction size. These fees became a useful source of revenues for the banks after 1982 as lending to the Third World in general began to diminish.

The problems that arose because of these guarantees surfaced about the same time that the Federal Reserve began to insist on higher capital-to-asset ratios for the banks in general. These swap guarantees were booked by banks as contingent liabilities, that is, off their balance sheets. When included with other contingent liabilities such as letters of credit, it was possible that these items could exceed the capital of a bank by a ratio of 20 or 30 to 1. The controversy that began in 1982 as banks began guaranteeing swaps therefore had strong economic arguments on both sides. Detractors claimed that these contingent liabilities were nothing more than a loaded gun pointed at the corporate heads of the banks and could lead to another debt crisis in the years ahead. Those who viewed them as a godsend to revenues in the midst of the Third World debt crisis had only to point to the money earned for nothing more than a contingent liability.

JUNK BONDS

Many of the developments in the period of deregulation involved products that for the most part were invisible to the public eye. Swaps were but one example. However, one innovation became part of the jargon of the decade and was most prominent during the wave of mergers and acquisitions that preceded and followed the market break of October 1987. This was the development of "junk bonds" and the large primary and secondary markets that developed around them. As with many financial products, the concept was not new but the applications became far-reaching and created a unique market.

Junk originally was a designation given to secondary market bonds that had fallen from their original issuing quality and consequently sold at a discount in the secondary market, reflecting a new price/yield level. These instruments were no longer considered to be of investment grade; their falling credit ratings made them speculative by nature. But despite this fall from grace, they were often favorite investment vehicles for speculators who would buy them at a discount, hoping for an eventual return to grace by the borrowing company that would raise their prices and lower their yields. While popular, they nevertheless formed a very small segment of the corporate bond market because their low ratings put them out of reach for most mainstream investors.

The innovative element entered when the concept of a junk bond was applied to a new issue. The corporate bond market was normally restricted, on the primary side, to issues of investment-grade companies. Thus, junk bonds, by definition, were those trading in the secondary market. Beginning in 1983, Drexel Burnham Lambert, a New York investment bank, began experimenting with bonds that would be issued at a discount, allowing companies of less then investment grade to borrow in the new-issues market. These new bonds were issued at less than face value, or par, bearing coupons in line with those of investment-grade firms. But when the buyer calculated the yield, the discount price gave him a greater return than those of more highly rated instruments. Originally, these new instruments were called "original issue discount bonds" (OIDs), a more positive name than junk.

Junk bonds quickly became popular with companies needing cash for expansion but not rated highly enough to gain entry into the traditional corporate bond market. Investors also found them attractive because of their relatively high yields. As a result, the new-issues market grew rapidly. By 1989, the total market was valued at around $300 billion. But despite their popularity, investors faced sizable risks when purchasing them because of their high potential for default. However, if the cash raised helped the borrower to higher credit rating in the future, sizable gains could also be expected as their prices would be expected to rise and yields expected to fall.

In addition to their speculative appeal, junk bonds also figured prominently in the wave of mergers and acquisitions that characterized the 1980s. They became the favorite financing vehicles for those who needed to raise large amounts of cash in order to finance an acquisition. By issuing OIDs at prevailing rates, those involved in an acquisition were able to raise funds that would otherwise not have been available except perhaps through bank lines of credit. After the acquisition was complete, the new owners of an acquired firm would be faced with debt service payments that could seriously impede their future cash flows. Normally, the newly acquired company would be sold off in part to rationalize its operations, using the proceeds to retire the high-yielding debt. While this process was carried out, junk bonds proved beneficial because their artificially low coupon payments saved the companies' cash flows until the newly acquired firm could be restructured. In investors' eyes, some of these types of junk bonds could be considered less risky than those of companies that had always been poorly rated since their prospects for the intermediate term were probably better after the acquisition.

Both corporate demand for funds and investor demand for high-yielding instruments made the junk bond market the most popular innovation of the 1980s—at least with the general investing public. A fairly active secondary market for them developed and many junk bond funds (or unit trusts) were developed around them. The Garn-St. Germain Act of 1982 inadvertently proved of help since it allowed some depository institutions to purchase corporate bonds for the first time since pre-Glass-Steagall days. Thus, many savings and loan associations began to acquire OIDs for their own portfolios. After the Resolution Trust Corporation was established in 1989, thrifts were forced to divest themselves of junk bond holdings by 1992.

Developments in the financial markets in the post 1972–73 era attempted to come to grips with the uncertainty and inflation created by floating exchange rates and the rise in the price of oil. While not being able to eliminate the growing risk in investment and capital formation, they did nevertheless provide a limited means for investors to protect against capital loss. But perhaps the single greatest benefit of all these innovations was to help depository institutions maintain their operations during difficult economic times. While savings and loans associations especially owe a great deal to floating interest rates on both the asset and liability side of their balance sheets, however, it cannot be said that adjustable financings saved them. Many institutions did not survive the economic environment of the later 1980s. Yet floating rate instruments, as well as asset sales, helped many traditional U.S. institutions remain afloat and continue to provide their basic range of services to the public. The traditional theme of the financial markets had again been found in an environment more uncertain than many preceding it. Innovation helped both institutions and individuals to offset risk in a financial climate that had become increasingly volatile and, at times, inhospitable. The deregulatory climate helped foster the innovation in almost all cases, whether it was the official deregulation of 1980 and 1982 or the more de facto type such as the breakdown of the Bretton Woods system.

NOTES

1. Morgan Guaranty Trust, *World Financial Markets*, various issues; estimated gross size.

2. Robert Solomon, *The International Monetary System, 1945–1976* (New York: Harper & Row, 1977), p. 48.

3. See for instance Brendan Brown, *The Dollar-Mark Axis on Currency Power* (London: Macmillan, 1979), Chapter 1.

4. In this case, "risk free" means free of default risk rather than business risk.

5. Stanford Research Institute, *Preliminary Findings on Hedging Demand for Domestic Interest Rates and Foreign Currencies* (San Francisco: Stanford Research Institute, 1978).

6. For a discussion of the prerequisites for a successful trading market see, for instance, Brendan Brown and Charles Geisst, *Financial Futures Markets* (New York: St. Martin's Press, 1983), Chapter 5.

7. Morgan Guaranty Trust estimate; see *World Financial Markets*, 1978–79.

8. David O. Beim, "Rescuing the LDCs," *Foreign Affairs* (July 1977): 731.

9. OECD estimates; see *Financial Market Trends*, February 1987.

10. For an examination of the effect of the increased use of debt in the United States see John Ciccolo, "Changing Balance Sheet Relationships in the US Manufacturing Sector, 1926–77," in Benjamin Friedman, ed., *The Changing Roles of Debt and Equity in Financing US Capital Formation* (Chicago: University of Chicago Press, 1982).

11. United States League of Savings Associations, *Source Book*, 1985, p. 52.

12. Richard Davis, "The Recent Performance of the Commercial Banking Industry," Federal Reserve Bank of New York, *Quarterly Review* (Summer 1986): 5.

13. See Gary Haberman, "Capital Requirements of Commercial and Investment Banks: Contrasts in Regulation," Federal Reserve Bank of New York, *Quarterly Review*, (Autumn 1987): 1–10.

14. For a discussion see Christine Cumming, "The Economics of Securitization," Federal Reserve Bank of New York, *Quarterly Review* (Autumn 1987): 11–23.

15. Maxwell Anderson, Russell Kincaid, Caroline Atkinson, Eliot Kalter, and David Folkerts-Landau, *International Capital Markets: Developments and Prospects* (Washington, DC: International Monetary Fund, 1986), p. 62.

16. For a more technical description see John F. Marshall and Kenneth Kapner, *Understanding Swap Finance* (Cincinnati: South-Western Publishing Co., 1990).

8

Republicans, Democrats, and the Markets

Popular financial folklore holds that Republican and Democratic administrations have different effects on the financial markets. Stock and bond prices react differently to different administrations, usually characterizing Democrats as meddlers and spenders, and Republicans as cost-cutters willing to let the markets find their own direction. Stock and bond prices tend to rise when Republicans govern and fall when Democrats assume power. While the generalization overlooks many factors, a quick glance at the 70-year period of financial history covered here tends to support it to an extent. The bull market of the 1920s coincided with the Republican administrations of Warren Harding, Calvin Coolidge, and Herbert Hoover. The bull market of the 1950s and the 1980s occurred during the administrations of Dwight Eisenhower and Ronald Reagan. However, the bear markets of the 1970s occurred during both the Nixon and Carter administrations. The 30-year period between these major market changes remains somewhat inconclusive on this level.

A simple chronological argument obviously overlooks the fact that the original stock market crash and the Depression occurred during the later years of the Hoover presidency. The market break of 1987 also occurred during a Republican reign, as did the depressed markets of the early 1970s. The erratic bull market of the 1960s coincided with the Democratic administration of Lyndon Johnson that was committed to increased spending through the "Great Society" programs. While history may be slightly on the side of Republicans over the last 70 years, the folklore actually has two distinct historical periods. The first covers the period up to the crash of

1929, while the second dates from World War II. Ironically, the effects remain the same but the parties change hats. Prior to the crash, Republicans were indeed good for the markets. Since World War II, Democrats at first appear to have had the upper hand during the Roosevelt years prior to Eisenhower. Put another way, the American dream appears not to bear a distinct party label.

Simple generalizations naturally invite a host of criticisms and examination of more plausible factors. Rather than attribute growth and well-being to political parties, should the policies of the Federal Reserve be included as the real driving force behind the financial markets? Monetary policy and its effect on interest rates has always been the single most important influence on securities prices and capital formation. Yet the members of the Fed themselves are political appointees. Do the members of the Federal Reserve board of governors reflect the political leanings of those who appoint them? Perhaps they do initially, but it becomes apparent that the composition of the Fed's governing body is closely akin to the political composition of the Supreme Court. Although political appointees, Supreme Court Justices have not always toed the ideological line of the President who appointed them. However, it would be incorrect to assume that ideology does not play a central role in determining the way in which the Fed reacts to a government's fiscal policies.

In this chapter, the role of ideology will be examined to determine what sorts of policies the financial markets have reacted to most favorably. But this is not necessarily the sort of ideology that bears a particular party stripe. U.S. political history in the twentieth century has proven highly partisan in some respects and remarkably homogeneous in others. Underlying the political arguments of both parties has been the consistently stable vision of the American dream—economic well-being and access to social and economic betterment and mobility. Achieving this dream could only have been accomplished through a strong sense of pragmatic politics and economic ideology. Faced with the economic consequences of a disastrous stock market crash and massive bank failures, it was a Republican, Herbert Hoover— otherwise the epitome of a consensus-oriented, administrative president— who presided over the birth of the Reconstruction Finance Corporation, later to become a mainstay of the Democratic New Deal. Faced with massive farm failures and the unravelling of the thrift industry, it was Ronald Reagan and George Bush who presided over the creation of new federally supported agencies designed to provide assistance on traditional, time-proven New Deal lines. Put in simple institutional terms, ideologies certainly have consequences. A society's ideologies shape its social and political institutions.[1] But in the U.S. experience, no one particular party ideology helped shape the structure of the government-sponsored agencies that have intermediated in the markets and played such an important part in promulgating the American dream. Neither has any particular ideology imprinted itself on the financial markets as a whole. These institutions, especially the agencies, have survived both time and many political attempts to change their basic organizational structures. Yet pragmatism survived and Republicans and Democrats came to embrace the agency and market function as part and parcel of the American dream.

Despite all of the pitfalls surrounding sweeping generalizations, the markets' overall performance has rarely been plotted against various administrations over time in order to gauge the reaction of investors. Obviously, one administration inherits the legacy of those immediately preceding it and passes the mantle to its successor, giving rise to the age-old political dispute of who bequeathed what to whom. But singling out investor reaction to politics is convenient. On one hand, it provides a simple framework to determine why investors reacted—whether they reacted to economic and social policy, monetary policy, extraordinary measures such as credit restraints, or (obviously) a combination of all. On the other hand, it helps to point out the extremely pragmatic nature of U.S. economic ideology, whether it is at the policy level or at the market level. If one accepts the notion of the American dream, it becomes apparent that that vision is somewhat transcendental in nature. Party politics become secondary as politicians react in a surprisingly similar nature to financial crises and the potential diminution of wealth and savings.

POLITICS AND SECURITIES PRICES

The influence that investors have always had is rarely discussed in political terms. Most often, their impact is confined to economic and financial discussion. Nevertheless, investors are able to cast votes on a daily basis. If they are disillusioned with government measures concerning taxation, fiscal policy, or foreign affairs, they create price volatility in the financial markets—a force that governments must acknowledge. Unlike normal vote casting, they register their views on a continuing basis rather than wait for an election. While it may be argued that this sort of voting is short-sighted, ignoring true cause and effect, the cumulative effects of the markets on the political fortunes of those in power cannot be underestimated. This type of reaction gives rise to the folklore concerning Republicans, Democrats, and the markets.

This sort of "voting" can be seen in money market and bond market prices. If the slope of yields between short-term interest rate and long-term rates is positive (short rates are lower than the long rates), the outlook for the future is optimistic. If, however, the slope is negative, then the outlook is clouded. Investors purchasing fixed-income instruments must constantly adjust their returns for inflation and constantly monitor political and economic events. Perhaps no other single indicator gives such a clear view of investor expectations concerning the future.[2]

Stock prices also follow suit. The movement of major stock market indices is the equity market equivalent of the yield curve in the bond and money markets. Movements in either direction give a clear signal of investor expectations. Although both the yield curve and the market indices are indicators of secondary market activity, the price levels established in either market also serve as surrogates for the new issues, or primary, markets where new capital is raised. If the stock market is weak, companies will not raise new equity capital because the prices they could potentially receive are too low. If bond prices are also low, indicating high yield levels, borrowing will cost more. If both conditions are present at the same time, capital expansion and investment by companies will decline until prices and/or yield levels recover.[3]

The first presidential election in the time period discussed here is a case in point. In the November election of 1920, Warren Harding soundly defeated Democrat James Cox for the presidency. Harding's victory came on the heels of the Senate's rejection of Woodrow Wilson's advocacy of U.S. entry into the League of Nations. The United States, having emerged from a late entry into World War I, was returning to a period of relative isolation. Harding would later say that the United States sought no part in directing the destinies of the world. In 1920, the last year of Wilson's administration, the Dow Jones Industrial Average, then composed of 20 stocks, stood at about 70.00.[4] It started to rebound in 1921 and climbed to a high of 81.50 before rising almost 20 percent more in 1922. Corporate bond prices also began to rise and yields fell. Between 1920 and 1922, yields on high quality bonds fell by 1 percent, from 6.59 to 5.59 percent.[5] The bull market of the postwar years had begun.

The Wilson years preceding this rise were not necessarily characterized by poor markets, however. Other than a difference in the range of highs and lows for the year, the Dow's range was much the same in 1922 as it had been in 1919. But the years following 1922 were unprecedented, as has been discussed in previous chapters. Merely to isolate Harding's first year or so against Wilson's last year would be misleading. Wilson had served two terms and had seen the country through the war successfully. Harding was chosen to run by Republican party bosses, not by the rank and file of his party. But once elected, his adherence to America first found solid support from the markets and would pave the way for further Republican successes.

During Harding's administration the Dow continued to climb; however, the rise was characterized by some volatility. In 1923, the high for the index was 105 while the low was 85, a swing of almost 20 percent between March and October. Much of the volatility can be attributed to scandal and corruption in the Harding administration, which is probably remembered more for the Teapot Dome scandal than for any of its policies. Harding died in August of that year after suffering from ptomaine poisoning and was succeeded by Calvin Coolidge. The markets took almost no notice of his demise, with the Dow declining only one point the day after his death. But by 1924, the bull market had begun in earnest and by year end the index stood at 120.5. Corporate bond yields also continued to fall to an average of 5.44 percent for the year.

Coolidge's presidency was marked by the largest stock market rise in U.S. history to date. The market rose steadily in 1925 and closed the year at 156. A year later it closed at 157, and by the end of 1927 it closed at 202. The speculative fever originally discussed in Chapter 1 intensified in 1928, when the market closed at 300. In the last five months of the year, the index never retreated, fuelled by excessive margin trading. Many in both government and business became increasingly wary of the speculation taking place, but to no avail. Coolidge's years were marked by strong support for business and the market. One of his last pronouncements before leaving office stated simply that he thought the market was still a good buy at current levels.

And so it was in the eyes of investors. Herbert Hoover succeeded Coolidge in 1929 and the market continued its phenomenal rise, touching a same-day high of 358 on October 11. Then the crash occurred. By the end of the month, the index had retreated to 273 for a three-week loss of almost 24 percent. Corporate bond yields continued to fall, touching a postwar low of 4.5 percent. While the stock market did rally temporarily several times in the following two years, it always did so on an otherwise downward trend. By July 1932, it had reached its post-crash low of 43.

Contrary to popular opinion, Hoover's reaction to the massive bank failures and bankruptcies caused by the crash was fairly swift, if not comprehensive. In 1931, he outlined an 18-point program designed to stabilize the economy. Among the proposals were increased funds for the Farm Intermediate Credit Banks, the establishment of the Reconstruction Finance Corporation, and the establishment of the Home Loan Banks. All three of the proposals eventually passed Congress, although not in the original form that Hoover had envisaged. The seventy-second Congress that convened in 1931 was Democratic-controlled, with Democrats holdings 220 seats to the Republicans' 214. This was a dramatic reversal of the previous Congress, in which Republicans had held a 100-seat advantage. The Senate was still nominally in Republican hands with a majority of one. In the previous session, Republicans had held a majority of seven. Republican popularity was waning, as were the markets.

Hoover's problems in passing the legislation were legendary. Although he tried to rally bipartisan support for the legislative package, Democrats and break-away Republicans insisted on deletions or insertions in the programs, which Hoover felt were inappropriate. One example concerning the RFC provides an example. The Democratic Speaker of the House, John N. Garner, insisted that a provision be inserted in the legislation requiring the RFC to list, on a monthly basis, the names of any institutions that borrowed money from it. "I objected," Hoover remarked later "that this would create fear that any institution borrowing was in difficulties and might cause a run upon any borrower bank or business."[6] Although it was finally agreed to keep that list secret, "Garner reversed this undertaking a few months later—and many runs on banks ensued."[7]

Hoover's defeat by Franklin Roosevelt in the election of 1932 by 472 electoral votes to 59 marked the end of Republican domination of the presidency and the equation of Republican principles with healthy markets. The returning Congress was also heavily Democratic, holding a 310 to 177 seat majority in the House and a 60 to 35 plurality in the Senate. But the stock market did not react immediately to Roosevelt's victory. It was not until April 1933 that the index began to rise, following the banking moratorium of March. In that month alone, the Dow rose from 55 to 77, a better than 40 percent gain. The rally continued slowly yet steadily until August 1937, when it hit its Depression peak of 190.

Adding to Republican woes during the last years of Hoover's administration and the early years of Roosevelt's were the Pecora hearings in Congress, examining the causes of the crash. Many of the bankers interviewed by the committee were Republicans and the proceedings were well covered by the press. Those who only several years before had claimed that financial panics were a thing of the past, because of the Federal Reserve Board's ability to constrain credit, were now in full public view attempting to explain what had gone wrong. Charles Mitchell, president of National City Bank of New York and a member of the Federal Reserve Bank of New York, came under special scrutiny for his activities during the 1920s. The focus of long-standing differences between the Federal Reserve Board and the New York Fed can be seen in Mitchell's actions prior to the crash in August 1929.

Following a decline in the Dow in March 1929, when the index fell from 325 to 293 over a two-week period, Mitchell announced that his bank was ready to lend $25 million to the call market "whatever might be the attitude of the Federal Reserve Board." The announcement was viewed at the time as open defiance of the Board.[8] The Board itself was in favor of raising interest rates to discourage further speculation. Mitchell's statement was viewed as a clear conflict of interest and his resignation as a director of the New York Federal Reserve Bank was called for by Senator Carter Glass, among others. In August 1929, the Board did raise the discount rate to 6 percent, but to no avail. As Herbert Hoover starkly noted, "the real trouble was that the bellboys, the waiters, and the host of unknowing people, as well as the financial community, had become so obsessed with the constant press reports of great winnings that the movement was uncontrollable."[9]

DEMOCRATIC ASCENDANCY

After the American dream had been shattered for so many different constituents, a Democratic victory was virtually ensured. Despite its recognition of the problem of excessive speculation, the Hoover administration was powerless to prevent the inevitable crash. Public opinion was solidly on the side of Democrats, who would subsequently expand on the 18-point program of Hoover. The bankers who were able to proclaim with Mitchell that good stocks were as solid an investment as bonds only six years before were consequently villified by William O. Douglas a few years later as "financial termites." Republicans would not grace the White House again until 1952. They did not regain a majority in the House of Representatives until 1947.

Although public reaction was firmly on the side of Democrats after 1931, the Roosevelt years were not necessarily good ones for the markets. The Dow recovered after the first Democratic presidential and congressional victories but fell sharply during the recession of 1937. Recovery thereafter was slow. Between 1936 and 1937, the Dow fell 79 points (38 percent) before recovering and again declining by another 36 points (19 percent) and remained in the same trading range until 1940. While the war years were especially good for the economy, the index did not respond correspondingly. Between 1940 and 1945, the GNP rose from $100 billion per year to $213 billion. Personal consumption and expenditure also rose but the stock market did not follow suit, rising from 152 to 195. The reasons for this lack of enthusiasm were discussed in Chapter 2. The new administration was good for the public confidence, but the markets took a dimmer view of many of Roosevelt's policies, which initially appeared inimical to their own interests.

The years between 1933 and 1940 were dominated by government rather than by the markets. As originally seen, new-issues activity was low, given the slow economy and the new regulatory environment created by the SEC, which itself was slow in gaining acceptance by the financial community. Much necessary capital was provided to businesses of different sorts and sizes by the Reconstruction Finance Corporation rather than by the stock or bond markets. The federal government was in competition with the financial community for much of that time and market activity reflected this. In addition, the chairmen of the SEC following the short tenure of Joseph Kennedy were somewhat hostile to the markets in general, especially William O. Douglas and Jerome Frank. In 1939, Frank defended himself against a published charge that he was a revolutionary whose purpose as SEC chairman was "to lay the ground for . . . federal control of almost every activity of American life." He responded by stating that "America will go to hell in a hack if there is a drive away from the essentials of our profit system. The SEC existed primarily to preserve the capitalist form."[10] This response was similar to remarks made in prior years by both James Landis and Douglas. Despite the avowed goals of the SEC chairmen, the markets took a different view, at least until the end of World War II.

The markets' response to the New Deal years marks a turning point in the evolution of U.S. market capitalism. While the markets responded enthusiastically to the first year of Roosevelt's presidency, their reaction was much more subdued over the next 12 years. In 1933, a typical market reaction was witnessed when the Dow began to climb as the new President asserted himself. Roosevelt's "fireside chats" were well received by the public in general, especially after several years of turmoil and bank failure. But his liberal politics and the consolidation of presidential power, the latter best witnessed by the ease with which the Banking Act and the Securities Act of 1933 were passed, brought charges of autocratic presidential power that created caution in the markets. While these charges came from many conservative quarters, they illustrate the fact that the old "money trust" had been replaced with a new coterie of financial policymakers who had no patience with the old order that had created the crash and the Depression.

The American Liberty League was one such organization that espoused ideas more akin to the heyday of the 1920s than to the new political order that Roosevelt and his advisors were fashioning. On the surface, it was just another movement that had sprung up during the early years of the New Deal. The best known of the popular movements were Huey Long's Share Our Wealth Society and Upton Sinclair's End Poverty in California campaign. Both espoused taxing the rich to provide a stipend of one sort or other to the common people. Of the two, Sinclair's was more avowedly socialistic, envisioning California, a state in which he ran for governor as a Democrat, as a proving ground for a U.S. form of socialism. But when compared with the Liberty League, both were quite radical in advocating socialist solutions to the Depression. The Liberty League, in contrast, was anything but popular or socialist.

The association was founded in 1934. Its members included prominent conservative Democrats as well as rightwing Republicans, all of whom had one common trait: they all opposed the basic tenets of Roosevelt's policies. On the Democratic side were Al Smith and several prominent members of the duPont family. The Republicans included a former governor of New York and representatives from the oil, steel, and investment banking industries as well as the chairmen of General Motors and Montgomery Ward. All were united by the belief that Roosevelt was spearheading a communist plot to subvert the U.S. Constitution.

Despite its influential cast of characters, Roosevelt was more worried about the growing popular discontent and organized opposition on the Left.[11] The Liberty League appealed not to the masses but to businessmen who shared its beliefs. Nevertheless, it did represent a growing distrust of Roosevelt on Wall Street. More indicative of the conservative money "trusters" of days past than the mass social psychology of the Depression, it nevertheless did not appeal to all of those who might otherwise have been originally co-opted in the movement. Herbert Hoover was invited to join and would have appeared to be a natural member of an elitist, business-oriented group. However, he turned down the invitation, remarking that the members were "hardly the type of men to lead the cause of liberty," and adding further that he had "no more confidence in the Wall Street model of human liberty, which this group so well represents, than I have in the Pennsylvania Avenue model upon which this country now rides."[12]

While the American Liberty League was out of tune with the tide of popular, left-wing movements of the period, it nevertheless contributed to the suspicion of Roosevelt in the financial markets. The markets viewed any intervention in their once exclusive domain as outright government meddling, more often than not regarding such interventionist policies as alien and subversive. But the 1930s were still a period of innovation because of the administration-fashioned agencies, such as the original Fannie Mae, that would come to have a significant impact on the U.S. housing market. How then did the suspicious financial community come to embrace new financial institutions created by "subversives?"

During the period of massive bank closures of 1932–33, the real estate market collapsed. Many mortgage holders defaulted on their loans but many more remained solvent and their mortgages remained viable assets for lenders. One of the RFC's early objectives was to develop a market for these mortgages; however, initially there were few buyers. The market had depreciated so badly that existing mortgages were viewed as too risky for most institutional investors. As a result, the RFC Mortgage Company was created in 1935 in order to buy FHA mortgages and sell them to financial institutions. Following the limited success of this organization, Fannie Mae was created to continue buying and selling FHA mortgages to interested financial institutions.

But Fannie Mae was not an agency model created simply on a theoretical model. As Jesse Jones later related, "In setting up the Federal National Mortgage Association to work exclusively in the handling of FHA-insured mortgages, we again entered the mortgage field only after our offers to become partners with private capital had fallen on deaf ears."[13] The original intent of the RFC was to establish a private mortgage company, using government money to buy some of the initial stock, and assist the mortgage market on a private basis. But there were no takers of the RFC's offer. In Jones's words, "To aid some of them [potential investors], we offered . . . to match dollars with private capital by taking preferred stock. Nearly four years went by without our getting a single offer of cooperation."[14] The financial markets' reaction was quite clear; they were not willing to put up their own money for such ventures. That poor reaction necessitated the creation of Fannie Mae. But once the government-owned agency was established, purchasing and selling FHA-insured mortgages, the double guarantee proved attractive and Fannie Mae began to prosper. While the markets were suspicious of ventures with government that encroached on their traditional domain, they were more willing to accept encroachment if a government guarantee was provided along the way.

During the first Roosevelt administration, the GNP rose by 60 percent, from $56 billion to $91.3 billion. The Dow Jones average rose from a low of 50.16 to 194 before the recession of 1937, registering a 288 percent gain. Despite the skepticism that surrounded many New Deal policies, the market was still able to rise but, as mentioned in Chapter 2, the level of new financings remained on the low side. Some of the stock market's performance can be attributed to a change in the capital gains tax that was initiated in 1934. Beginning in that year, gains registered on securities held over one year again were given preferential treatment. A sliding scale was introduced that taxed only 80 percent of the gain on a security held between one and two years. The longer it was held, the lower the tax became. The actual tax rate on those long-term gains also declined. Gains of less than one year were still taxed at 100 percent, as they had been since 1916.[15]

The second Roosevelt administration witnessed a different pattern. From 1938 to 1942, the GNP continued to rise, from $85 billion to $159 billion, for a 87 percent gain. The stock market did not follow suit. Despite some wide trading swings, on average the Dow actually declined during the period. In 1938, its high was 158; in 1942 it managed no more than 119. Some of the market torpor in late 1941 can be attributed to the "crowding out" effect of government bond financings during the early years of the war. After the first full year of U.S. involvement in the war, it managed to reach a high of 145 in 1943 and then touched 152 in 1944. But again, the capital gains treatment contributed to the market's growth. Beginning in 1938, the treatment of gains held at least 18 months was lowered, as was the tax paid on those gains. But the most preferential capital gains treatment to date was instituted in 1942 when the holding period for a long-term gain was lowered to six months. Any gain on a security held longer than that period was taxed at only 50 percent of the profit and the highest tax rate applied to the gain was only 25 percent. While the taxes paid on long-term gains would change many times over the next 35 years, the six-month holding period remained in effect until 1977.[16]

Interest rates on high-grade corporate bonds continued to decline during the first two administrations, falling from 4.49 percent in 1933 to 2.72 percent ten years later. Government long-term bonds were only marginally lower, averaging about one-quarter of 1 percent lower than the corporates. While these yields appeared to be a positive note of public endorsement of Democratic policies, it should be remembered that the Federal Reserve began pegging interest rates in 1942. After that date, the rates on Treasury bills and bonds, and consequently all debt securities, remained in a range dictated by the Fed. Although corporate yields especially were low, the levels did not necessarily create capital market activity on the news issues side. As the market became flooded with Treasury securities to support the war effort, commercial banks' funds became heavily invested in government securities. As a result, borrowing from commercial banks was actually cheaper than raising funds in the bond market, so Wall Street did not boom despite the low level of interest rates.

Comparisons between market performance and behavior during the Republican years of the 1920s and the first two Roosevelt administrations are difficult because of the far-reaching economic and social effects of the New Deal. Gone were the days of laissez-faire markets and dreams of quick riches. In their place was a more somber atmosphere of social legislation designed to ensure that wealth could be accumulated without resorting to practices that produced such chaos in the past. The practical utilitarianism preached by Wall Street in the 1920s, where speculation and conflicts of interest were tolerated because panics "could no longer occur" under the watchful eye of the Federal Reserve, was replaced with a new social philosophy with additional watchful eyes that many true conservatives deemed subversive. Nevertheless, the American dream remained intact, waiting for all parties to cast off the past and again turn their attention toward the future.

During the fourth Roosevelt term, the market began an improvement over previous years. The Dow gained about 10 percent to touch a level not seen since 1940. Long-term government bonds remained in their 2.25 percent range due to pegging, and the GNP grew by only 6.25 percent, its slowest rate of growth since 1939–40. For the first time in the decade, the market's overall growth exceeded the growth in the GNP. Although hardly euphoric, the market's growth can be attributed to the Allied gains made during the year, especially the D-Day invasion, the defeat of the Japanese fleet at the Philippines and the Battle of the Bulge. Equally important was the United Nations Monetary and Financial Conference held in July 1944 at Bretton Woods, New Hampshire. At the conference, representatives of 44 nations met to plan for postwar economic recovery and the restoration of trade. The two most important developments of the meeting were the founding of the International Monetary Fund and the International Bank for Reconstruction and Development (World Bank). In the latter two cases especially, the international economic news had become brighter than at any time in the previous 20 years.

At the Democratic convention in Chicago in 1944, Harry Truman was chosen to run with Roosevelt in place of Vice President Henry A. Wallace, who would subsequently become Secretary of Commerce in Roosevelt's last administration. While Roosevelt registered a landslide victory over Democratic opponent Thomas E. Dewey by 432 electoral votes to 99, the margin of popular votes was only 2.4 million; his smallest margin in four elections. Truman, a two-term senator from Missouri, was selected to run over Wallace because he appealed more to Southern conservative voters and organized labor. When Roosevelt died on April 12, 1945, Truman succeeded him. Business and Wall Street again had a President in whom they lacked faith.

The new President had established a reputation that suggested a strong anti-business bias. As a senator, Truman had led an investigation into the condition of U.S. railways. Particularly hard hit by the Depression, many railroad companies had been organized into holding companies. The finances of these holding companies and their impact on interstate commerce and organized labor became the focus of congressional investigation. Truman led the Senate investigation into the Allegheny Corporation, a holding company that had acquired the Missouri Pacific Railroad in 1930. One of the main financeers of Allegheny was J. P. Morgan and Company, which acted as its investment banker prior to the passing of the Banking Act. The investigation itself took place in the mid–1930s and gave Truman the reputation of being opposed to Wall Street while at the same time favoring small business and labor—in short, the precise profile of an advocate of the New Deal.

Several speeches Truman had made gave an indication of his attitudes toward the Wall Street coterie that was still under attack from many quarters. In a Senate speech given in 1937, he likened the railway financeers to Jesse James, an outlaw who had caused considerable trouble for the Missouri Pacific in the previous century. The bankers, as he saw it, "used no guns, but they ruined the railroad and got away with $70 million or more. They did it by means of holding companies. Senators can see what 'pikers' Mr. James and his crowd were alongside of some real artists."[17] In another speech later in the same year, his barbs became sharper. As he said,

It is a pity Wall Street with its ability to control the wealth of the nation . . . has not produced some financial statesmen. No one ever considered Carnegie libraries steeped in the blood of Homestead steel workers, but they are. We do not remember that the Rockefeller Foundation is founded on the dead miners of the Colorado Fuel and Iron Company and a dozen other similar performances.[18]

Truman had established himself as a classic New Deal liberal alongside other better-known contemporaries such as William O. Douglas and Louis Brandeis.

Ironically, after Truman assumed office, the Dow had one of its better years in recent memory, touching a high of 196 and registering a low of 151, almost the same as the high of the previous year. But between 1945 and 1946, GNP also slowed for the first time since 1937–38 and registered a loss of about half of 1 percent. Much of the decline was attributed to a slowdown in government purchases of goods and services as the war finally came to an end. The drop in government spending was the largest since the 1929 crash, with total spending falling from $74.8 to $19.2 billion.[19] In the following year, 1947, GNP again resumed an upward pattern but the Dow did not follow suit, remaining at the same levels. Federal spending continued to slow and did not register a positive gain until 1948–49. The Dow did not resume an upward pattern again until 1950.

Although there is no precise correlation here between the Dow's performance and the levels of government expenditure, it can be seen that as federal spending declined, the Dow did not perform particularly well. This generalization only holds for two specific periods in the Democratic administrations of Roosevelt and Truman, 1937–38 and again in 1945–46. Personal consumption expenditures, however, do not display the same pattern. Spending for durable goods, nondurable goods, and services did decline in 1937–38 but not in the later period. Part of the financial folklore originates in numbers of this sort. When governments spend, the market rises, or at least holds it previous levels, until spending decreases. Federal spending increased dramatically in the last two years of the elected Truman administration, doubling between 1950 and 1951, and the Dow responded with a 15 percent rise.

On the purely political side, Truman's administration gave Wall Street some cause for hope, although not necessarily the sort engendered by the President himself. In June 1947, the Labor Management Relations Act (Taft Hartley Act) was passed over his veto, helping to swing the pendulum of power in labor–management relations away from the unions, which had accumulated a sizable amount of power during the New Deal years. The Korean War, which officially began in June 1950 when North Korea invaded the South, also put the country on a war footing again. In September of the same year, Truman signed into law the Defense Production Act, giving him the power to stabilize prices and wages. Within a year, government spending again increased and caused the Dow to rise.

After the November 1948 election, in which Truman defeated Republican Thomas Dewey by a popular margin of slightly more than two million votes, the markets fared badly. The day before the election, the Dow stood at 190. On the next trading day, it fell seven points and continued to fall for the rest of the month, finally closing the month at 172. The presidential election had proved a surprise, especially since the eightieth Congress had returned a Republican majority in the House by a margin of 245 seats to 188 for the Democrats. For the first time since the presidential election of 1924, when Robert LaFollette, a Progressive, had gathered almost five million popular votes, a presidential election had seen some strength registered by candidates from minor parties. In 1948, Strom Thurmond, running on the States' Rights platform, drew about one million votes; Henry Wallace, running on the Progressive ticket, received only slightly less. Between them, they drew almost the same number of popular votes that cost Dewey the election. The markets were not pleased with the outcome and the Dow's subsequent performance showed it.

Bond and money market yields remained in the same range as they had been in for the previous eight years. The yield curve was still subject to pegging and corporate yields overall were still only about three-eighths of 1 percent higher than their Treasury equivalents. Truman was insistent that the markets give their full support to the Korean war effort as they had done during World War II. He made certain that both the Federal Reserve and the Treasury were fully informed of the financing needs of the government, but the Federal Reserve Board was always not fully cooperative when it came to providing central bank support for the war effort. As Truman later related, when it came to discussing financial support for the war effort, "my approach to all these financial questions always was . . . to keep the financial capital of the United States in Washington. This is where it belongs—but to keep it there is not always an easy task."[20] If Truman still clung to a bit of New Deal bias against Wall Street, it would soon disappear when Republicans gained the White House in 1952.

RETURN OF THE REPUBLICANS

The 19 years of Democratic dominance of the presidency and Congress were accompanied by a resurgent but not particularly strong stock market. The Dow Jones Industrial Average reached a high of 194 in 1937 and by 1952 had only climbed to 294, for a gain of 52 percent. During the same period, GNP had risen from $56 billion to $352 billion. Federal government spending rose from $2.2 to $52.7 billion while personal consumption rose from $45.8 to $232.6 billion.[21] By 1952, the economy again was driven by personal consumption expenditures. Two-thirds of the GNP was, and has remained, driven by personal consumption. Despite many claims over the years that the Roosevelt administration particularly was a prolonged attempt to steer the U.S. political system toward a subversive European form of collective socialism, in collaboration with the Wall Street banking community, the historical evidence suggests that Wall Street took a different view. The many investigations of the securities business, discussed in Chapter 2, the pegging of interest rates, the aggressive expansion of commercial banks in lending, and the strong anti-Wall Street bias of the public in general all had a decidedly negative effect on the markets. But with the advent of the Eisenhower administration, the financial climate began to change.

The eight years of the Eisenhower administration were the greatest boom years for the market since the 1920s. The Dow rose from 294 in 1953 to 686 by 1960. At the same time, interest rates also began to rise; long-term Treasury bonds originally yielded, on average, 2.94 percent and rose to 4 percent. Corporate bond yields rose by a similar proportion. Corporate financings increased, especially after the SEC investigation of the Truman years had failed to prove collusion among investment bankers. Gross national product rose from $371 billion to $515 billion but federal spending remained relatively flat. Government purchases of goods and services stood at $58 billion in 1953 and began to decline marginally thereafter, totalling about $54 billion in 1960.[22] Regardless of the sort of events that caused rises or falls in federal spending, the market folklore was now beginning to take shape. Democrats were spenders while Republicans were more frugal. In

1945, federal spending amounted to 35 percent of GNP; by 1955 it amounted to only 11 percent.

These numbers belie the fact that Congress was predominantly Democratic for most of the Eisenhower presidency, with the exception of the eighty-third Congress, sitting between 1953 and 1955. The growth of the economy and the markets during the 1950s is more easily attributable to the peace that followed the Korean war than to the ideology of the Republicans or Democrats. Neither can the exercise of exceptionally strong presidential power be directly attributed to the market's growth in the 1950s because no other U.S. President wielded the power that Franklin Roosevelt possessed during his four terms. Nevertheless, the myth began to emerge: Republicans were better for the markets than their counterparts, despite the fact that Democrats dominated Congress between 1933 and 1960.

Any continuity behind the market myth rapidly disappeared after the election of John Kennedy in 1960. Until the consecutive Republican victories of Ronald Reagan and George Bush, neither party was able to sustain a hold on the White House in the following twenty years for two uninterrupted terms. The markets registered gains until the mid–1960s; thereafter, gains only occurred with heightened volatility at the same time. Beginning in 1965, the stock market entered a period of essentially zero growth accompanied by wide price swings, which had not been experienced since the years immediately following the 1929 crash. The original period of growth, between mid–1961 to the end of 1965, occurred during Democratic administrations. The period between 1966 and 1981 was oblivious to party labels; neither Democrats nor Republicans were able to raise the markets to new heights.

Kennedy's narrow victory over Richard Nixon in 1960 had little immediate effect on the Dow. It began the month of November at 589 and closed at 603. Interest rates remained essentially flat, with long-term bonds actually declining several basis points immediately after the election. If Democrats were reputed to be big spenders, the credit markets appeared to take little notice. During the two years of the Kennedy administration, the GNP rose form $533.8 billion to $607 billion and federal spending rose by a similar 13 percent. The Dow responded with a gain of 86 points after experiencing some wide price swings—almost the same percentage gain as the GNP and federal spending.[23]

During Lyndon Johnson's first two years in the White House, the Dow managed its highest level in history. Late in 1965, the index touched 995. But at the same time, money market rates began to increase, with the yield on three-month Treasury bills rising to almost 4.5 percent by the end of 1965. While the Dow had reached new heights, so too had the yields on debt securities. The year end 1965 was notable for two separate but not unrelated phenomena. Probably more important than the stock market average was the fact that the yield curve had become flat for the first time since the end of World War I. The "go-go" years 1961–65, as they were colloquially known, had brought with them a rise in inflation that continued throughout Johnson's presidency.

Between 1964 and 1965 inflation almost doubled, from 1.5 to 2.7 percent. During most of the 1960s, the index had remained in the 1.00–1.50 percent range.[24] While the absolute levels appear quite small when compared with the inflation of the following decade, rates of return in the financial markets were affected negatively because the nominal yields on short- and long-term debt obligations were also relatively low. A bond or Treasury bill returning about 4.5 percent in nominal terms returned only 1.80 percent on a real basis after the rate of inflation had been subtracted. While the real rate remained in about the same range as it had for the previous ten years, the absolute levels were rising and continued to do so for the rest of the decade. The stock and credit markets were facing their greatest challenge since interest rates had been set free by the Fed 15 years before.

The primary cause behind the rise in inflation, and consequently the rise in interest rates, was the increase in federal spending between 1964 and 1967. Spending increased by 40 percent while the GNP grew at a rate of 25 percent. Personal consumption remained as a similar proportion of GNP throughout the period, approximately 63 percent. As the markets reacted to the increase in spending, the folklore became more entrenched: Democrats were big spenders and the spending was creating a new inflationary environment and weaker markets. A second aspect of the myth also began to appear: part of this increase in spending was due to U.S. involvement in Vietnam, especially after 1965. Democrats were also "warmongers." The presidencies of Roosevelt, Truman, and now Johnson had all committed the country to war and the financial pressures that accompanied full or partial mobilization.

The inflationary effects of this spending were recognized by the Johnson administration, which at various times proposed tax increases to offset the effects of increased government spending. Johnson was fully aware of the impact that inflation would have both economically and politically, long before he faced massive demonstrations condemning the Vietnam war. As he later wrote in his memoirs, the Tax Adjustment Act of 1966 was passed after intense pressure on the Congress from the administration. It was that sort of occasion, regardless of the success of the outcome, that best demonstrated the essence of the American dream in political terms. As Johnson later noted, "A sense of national urgency is perhaps the most important source of cooperation. When the national interest is clear and the need for action compelling, the separate constituencies of the President and the Congress come together."[25]

Following the rise in the Dow, which led to the high of 995 being maintained through early 1966, the market dropped dramatically later in the same year to touch a low of 744. As the war intensified, the market again rallied to reach the 1966 level again in 1968 after several periods of intense volatility. But after the rally, it registered another precipitous drop during 1969 that continued into 1970. If market folklore was to believed, Johnson's decision not to seek a second full term in the spring of 1968 would have rallied the markets. However, the opposite effect occurred. After the 1968 election, in which Richard Nixon defeated Hubert Humphrey by less than 500,000 popular votes, the market remained relatively stable, rising by only seven points immediately after the election (952 to 959) before reaching its historic peak of 995 again in December.

The Democratic interregnum had come full circle. From Kennedy's narrow defeat of Nixon in 1960 to Johnson's landslide victory over Barry Goldwater in 1964, Republicans again tasted a narrow victory. The eight Democratic years had proved to be perhaps the most socially significant since the New Deal. The Civil Rights Act of 1964 and the Voting Rights Act of 1965 had been passed and were beginning to be implemented. The Great Society programs of 1965 were also underway as the Johnson administration declared "war on poverty." This program includes the privatization of Fannie Mae and the founding of Ginnie Mae as part of the newly created Department of Housing and Urban Development. But at the same time, opposition to the Vietnam war and the social unrest it caused domestically foreshadowed a political change that would occur in the 1968 election. In the financial markets, a change also occurred that was less socially significant but nevertheless would have equally long-standing consequences. The next decade would become known as the decade of inflation and the markets became more volatile than ever before. Accompanying the volatility was the demise of the market folklore that had been present since Franklin Roosevelt was president. The superficial but powerful psychological link between Republicans, Democrats, and the markets was effectively severed after 1968. None of the administrations of the 1970s would be able to claim that it had been beneficial to the markets. And the American dream would again be under attack.

THE DECADE OF INFLATION

In the latter 1960s, inflation remained in the 5.0–5.5 percent range. As the new decade began, it declined to about 4.5 percent in 1971 before beginning to gain thereafter. Yields on Treasury bills also dropped while longer bonds remained stable at about 6 percent and the yield curve again assumed a positive slope. But after 1972, inflationary pressures began to build and inflation doubled from about 4 percent to 8 percent by 1974. In this instance, the markets' predictable reaction was caused by a series of international events and domestic politics that could not have been foreseen.

In August 1971, President Nixon was forced to sever the convertible link between the U.S. dollar and gold, effectively ending the Bretton Woods system of foreign exchange parities that had been used since the original Bretton Woods Conference in 1944. The devaluation had been caused by the U.S. running balance-of-payments deficits in previous years, which had put pressure on the dollar in the markets. In the late 1960s, imports had exceeded exports for five consecutive years. By 1971, imports exceeded exports by $40 billion, the largest trade deficit in history to date. By cutting the dollar's convertibility to gold, the currency was effectively devalued. The trade effect was not immediate since the foreign exchange markets continued in turmoil until 1972. However, the effect of the devaluation could be seen in the trade figures for 1974, when imports and exports were almost equal.

The floating exchange rate market that succeeded the Bretton Woods system did not help create international financial stability. On the contrary, the dollar continued to fluctuate, sometimes widely, and when it did fall against the other major currencies an inflationary effect was created. Imports became more expensive and if the trade balance was negative, inflation could be imported through the exchange rate mechanism. Even the immediate effects of the new environment could not be anticipated. In the same year, Nixon also imposed wage and price controls, initially for a three-month period. Price controls were then extended for another year before effectively collapsing.

But the foreign exchange market was not the only culprit adding to inflationary woes. The rise in the international price of oil and the Arab embargo of shipments of oil to the United States in late 1972 and 1973 also caused the U.S. oil import bill to rise. The price of oil increased tenfold over the following ten years, having its most pronounced effect on inflation in Jimmy Carter's administration. But the combination of the floating of dollar and the increased import bill set the stage for an inflation rate that would almost triple its 1971 level.

The first Nixon administration was beset with economic problems and the markets did not react as they had to Eisenhower. The Dow plunged to 630 in 1970, its lowest level since 1963. After gaining over 300 points, it again fell from 950 early in 1971 to 800 by year end. After several other bouts of volatility, it reached another high in 1972 of 1036 as inflation abated temporarily. As the Vietnam war came to a close, government spending also began to fall, temporarily easing some of the inflationary pressure.

Investors began to vote with their pocketbooks in 1974 as the yield curve became negative once again. Short-term rates exceeded long-term rates by about 100 basis points, or 1 percent, for the entire year. Credit market conditions caused the largest fall in the Dow Jones Industrials since 1972 when the market fell by over 300 points, from 892 to 577. That drop prompted Nixon to remark that the market was a buy at those levels and the subsequent, yet volatile, rebound proved him correct. It would be early 1976 before the market would again reach 1000, after having weathered the Watergate crisis.

In addition to the oil price rise and the floating of the dollar, two other developments also added to inflationary pressures in the early 1970s. In 1972, social security payments became indexed to the inflation rate, ensuring that payments rose as consumer price inflation rose. In the same year, a new yet untried financial product was created that subsequently led to an erosion of the Federal Reserve's ability to control credit. This was the money market mutual fund, a fund created by investment companies that offered investors prevailing money market rates of interest on their investments. Since bank savings accounts were still limited by Regulation Q of the Federal Reserve, the money funds offered higher yields than banks and other depository institutions were able to offer, allowing savers and investors to keep abreast of rising interest rates. By investing in them, investors were able to preserve a portion of their savings against inflation. As discussed in Chapter 3, these new instruments proved troublesome to the Fed as it attempted to control money supply growth and credit creation toward the end of the decade.

Although the market finished the eight Republican years between 1969 and 1976 at about the same level at which it had begun, the intervening period was characterized by the most extreme volatility since the beginning of the Depression. In 1930, Herbert Hoover complained that much of the financial crisis that beset his administration could be attributed to international economic factors. But that argument fell mainly on deaf ears due to the isolationist position the country had taken since the end of World War I. Almost 50 years later, the argument would be well taken and better understood. The markets fared poorly during the Nixon and Ford administrations for a combination of international and domestic reasons. One point, remained indisputable, however: the myth that had died during the Kennedy and Johnson administrations did not reappear when the Republicans regained power. Neither party appeared good for the markets. The one-term administration of Jimmy Carter only helped underscore the point.

Contrary to popular opinion, the Carter administration was not the worst period for the stock markets in modern financial history. That distinction still belongs to Hoover. On balance, it was no worse than the markets' performance under Richard Nixon between 1972 and 1974. Immediately after the November election of 1976, in which Carter narrowly defeated incumbent Gerald Ford, the market immediately fell by almost 40 points from 971 to 933 in the following week. But within a month, it regained its momentum and rose to slightly over 1,000 by the year end. It touched its low of 742 in March 1978, reacting to increased rises in the price of oil. On balance, this performance is about standard for the decade. But the one market that did treat the Carter administration poorly was the credit market, where yields continued to rise until they reached their historic peaks in the first year of the Reagan administration in 1981.

Interest rate levels and inflation quickly became the millstone around the neck of the Carter administration. They provided the lever by which Reagan would unseat his opponent in the 1980 election. During the four Democratic years, consumer prices rose by almost 36 percent, the greatest four-year price rise to that date. The problem, however, was obviously inherited; the rate for the four Republican years immediately preceding was 28 percent. The major problem confronting Carter was the yield levels in the money and bond markets. Yields on Treasury bills and bonds rose every month of his administration. In January 1977, the rate on a three-month bill was 4.7 percent and the long Treasury bond yielded 7.35 percent. By November 1980, a similar bill yielded 14.38 percent while a 30-year bond yielded 12.30 percent. The yield curve had slumped to its most negative slope in the twentieth century. While rates continued to rise in the first year of Reagan's presidency, the political and economic damage had already been done.

Equally severe damage was done by rising interest rates in the corporate sector, where the yields on BBB-rated bonds rose as high as 16 percent on average in 1980 and 1981. Commercial paper rose to yields exceeding 17 percent and capital investment began to decline as companies put their expansion and investment plans in abeyance. As a result, balance sheets began to change. Corporate balance sheets became more heavily skewed in favor of short-term debt. Government borrowing also underwent a change as the average maturity of Treasury debt began to decrease. Investors were opting for shorter-term bonds rather than the longer term and Treasury debt fell from an average of 12 years to maturity to around six years. The demand for long-term bonds did not reappear until interest rates had fallen back to lower levels and resumed a positive slope.

Various legislative remedies were attempted during the Carter administration to bring interest rates down and to offset the damage done by inflation. As mentioned in previous chapters, the Depository Institutions Deregulation and Monetary Control Act was passed in 1980 after a short period of special credit restraints. The credit restraints themselves were imposed at the same time as a worldwide economic slowdown began. Although short-term interest rates subsided temporarily, the recession undermined economic growth and contributed to a rise in unemployment.

While the Monetary Control Act contained provisions to lift the interest rate ceilings of Regulation Q and provide for better Federal Reserve control over the creation of credit, its immediate effects were not felt until after Ronald Reagan took office in 1981. As a result, the Carter administration was left with the legacy of inflation, rising unemployment, historically high interest rates, and decreased production. Another legacy of this turmoil was the reappearance of the myth that Democrats were bad for the markets. The myth would be given further credence by the markets' improved performance during Reagan's two terms.

THE REPUBLICAN DECADE

The magnitude of Reagan's victory over Carter, 489 electoral votes to 49, gave a clear indication of public dissatisfaction with the four preceding Democratic years. The immediate financial legacy of the 1970s was the high inflation rate, a recession, the Monetary Control Act, and a relatively new Federal Reserve Board chairman in Paul Volcker. As Theodore H. White noted, the U.S. public had begun to reject the Democrats generally for the reasons already noted and had come to view Jimmy Carter as the apotheosis of all that was ineffective in U.S. politics in the face of international pressures.[26] While the Republican administration preceding Carter was not held in high esteem, stemming mainly from the Watergate affair, the Iranian hostage crisis and the failed rescue attempt weighed equally heavily on voters in the ensuing election as yet another example of the increasing impotence of U.S. presidents and the country's waning power and influence abroad.

The two Reagan terms furthered the American dream in traditional terms by attempting to return it to its simpler elements. The original budget proposed by the new administration provided for cuts of more than $30 billion from the original Carter projection for fiscal year 1982, but it was still larger than the last full Carter budget of 1981 by some $42 billion.[27] While trimming some areas of expenditure, the budget allowed others to increase along with the implied inflation rate. Originally, the tension between expenditures and potential revenues was to be offset by a reliance on supply-side economics, an idea that faded as the administration became more entrenched in its second term. By allowing taxpayers to keep more of their paychecks rather than taxing them to the extent that previous administrations had, the net benefit to the individual would eventually find its way back into the public coffers via taxes that would be paid on new investments or savings. This policy also represented an attack on some of the cherished institutional stipends on which Americans had come to rely in previous years.

One of the areas that came under budgetary constraint was federal aid to higher education. While the Reagan cuts in the higher education budget were not particularly substantial, economies were nevertheless mandated for the first time in many years. The student loan default rate, discussed in Chapter 6, became the focus of attention. By cutting the student loan aid packages by slightly less than 10 percent in the first budget, the Reagan administration made it clear that a cherished U.S. tradition was under attack. The amount of dollars available for grants and loans, now subject to change, were far less important than the questions they raised, immeasurable in dollars. What would be the future measure of entitlement? Were all students entitled to loans or only the best and the brightest?[28] The American dream, as it had evolved over the years since 1958 in this respect, was coming under a functional, if not structural, attack.

   Some of the elements of what became known as the "Reagan revolution"
could be found in one of the first pieces of legislation passed under the new
administration, the Economic Recovery Tax Act of 1981. This legislation was
aimed at creating new investment by cutting tax rates so that new investment
and jobs would be created. The maximum individual tax rate was cut from
70 percent to 50 percent and a host of new tax measures, including accelerated depreciation allowances and investment tax credits were introduced.
Tax brackets were adjusted for the effects of inflation in order to protect
against what is known as "bracket creep" inflation: the tendency of inflation
to push individuals into higher tax brackets. By allowing individuals to keep
more of their incomes, the hope was to stimulate investment.

   One of the accompanying measures was to cut the level of tax on long-
term capital gains from 40 percent to 20 percent on assets held more than
12 months. This individual measure was responsible for stirring the stock
market to one of the largest rallies in its often tortured history. From an
immediate post-Republican victory level of about 1015 in 1980, the Dow
continued an upward course to reach its new historic high of 2,722 in October
1987. This was the largest movement in the Dow in a two-term period since
the Eisenhower presidency. It was also the second largest rally in stock
market history to date, exceeded only by the rally after Franklin Roosevelt
became president in 1933. The myth was resurfacing.

   At the same time, interest rates began to subside from their historic
high of 1981–82. A combination of the fall in the price of oil, triggered by
the recession of 1980–82, and a tight monetary policy pursued by the Volcker-
led Federal Reserve brought interest rates down and returned them to a
positive slope by early 1983. Rates continued to fall until 1987, when they
reached their lowest levels since 1978. This was the period of bond refinancings discussed in Chapter 2, which many borrowers took advantage of
to lower their cost of debt capital.

   The general improvement in the economic climate was clouded, however,
by an increase in the "twin deficits" that characterized the Reagan years:
the budget deficit and the merchandise trade deficit. A balanced budget had
been a platform plank in Jimmy Carter's campaign in 1976 but had not been
successfully achieved. By 1983, the deficit had increased to some $207 bil-
lion, almost five times the deficit recorded in 1976. The Economic Recovery
Act could be partially blamed for the size of the deficit in that it had reduced
government revenues through tax cuts. Between 1981 and 1983, government
revenues remained flat, actually declining between 1982 and 1983, while
expenditures increased by 19 percent.[29] Congress made several attempts to
reduce the size of the deficit through the Deficit Reduction Act of 1984,
also known as the Gramm-Rudman-Hollings Act. The act mandated reduced
deficits each year until the budget deficit was trimmed significantly. While
some progress was made in reducing the deficit, controversy still arose in
the latter years of the Reagan presidency because critics contended that

much of the deficit was actually being disguised by a surplus in the social security system. If that surplus was not factored into the budget, the deficit remained much the same as it had throughout the first Reagan administration.

The financial markets were also affected by the merchandise trade deficit. This deficit was created in large part by the increase in the value of the dollar on the foreign exchange markets, which made imported goods cheaper as the currency rose. In 1980, the deficit was about $25 billion. By 1986, it rose to almost $150 billion, paralleling the strength of the dollar, which rose by some 40 percent in the markets. The size of the deficit caused considerable volatility on the stock and bond markets and became a contributory factor to the market break of October 1987. The combination of the two deficits exerted more pressure on interest rates than ordinarily would have been expected, given the overall state of the economy.

Although interest rates had fallen from their highs recorded in the earlier part of the decade, the real rate of interest was still in the 4.0–4.5 percent range during the last years of the Reagan administration and the early years of the Bush administration. As that sort of spread became standard in the credit markets, money market and bond prices became extremely sensitive to changes in the inflation rate, as they had been in the late 1970s. While it is obvious that the markets reacted favorably to the Republican administration on balance, the volatility that had appeared in the 1970s was still present as the markets rose.

One of the major contributors to the market volatility, especially in the stock market, was the Tax Reform Act of 1986. Passed through Congress with bipartisan support and considerable compromise, the legislation reduced individual income tax brackets from the levels established by the Economic Recovery Act. The maximum level of tax was reduced from 50 percent to 28 percent, with the minimum level set at 15 percent. New depreciation allowances were established and investment tax credits for purchases of capital goods were abolished. Corporate tax rates were also reduced from 46 to 34 percent. But perhaps most important for the markets was the abolition of the long-term capital gains tax, which had been an integral part of the economic landscape for decades. All gains from the sale of securities or other capital assets were to be taxed at ordinary rates of tax, the tax liability being established in the year the gain was realized.

In market terms, this meant that investors lost the motivation to hold assets for more than 12 months in order to take advantage of the lower tax brackets established by the Economy Recovery Act. Since there was no longer any motivation to hold securities for the long-term, more short-term trading ensued. Stock market volume began to rise and the market indices began to show greater volatility. This new market environment culminated in the market break of October 19 and 20, 1987. Because of this investor reaction, the market circuit breakers discussed in Chapter 2 were instituted.

The new environment required a discipline that the markets, somewhat protected by the old capital gains tax, had never before required.

The Republican years between 1981 and 1989 gave additional credence to the notion that Republicans were good for the markets. However, in the later part of the decade, traditional Republican principles were offset to an extent by older principles that have come to transcend both parties. While the Garn-St. Germain Depository Institutions Act, Economic Recovery Act, and Tax Reform Act of 1986 were all passed during the Reagan administration, so too were the Agricultural Credit Act of 1987 and the Financial Institutions Reform, Recovery and Enforcement Act of 1989. These last two pieces of legislation were designed to restructure the Farm Credit System and Federal Home Loan Bank Board respectively and were based on traditional, well-established agency lines dating back to the 1930s. In institutional terms, many Depression-era remedies were still being used to bolster certain sectors of the economy. But by the latter 1980s, these agencies had finally lost their ideological origins and were accepted as standards of U.S. financial practice.

The Republican years of Ronald Reagan appear to have resurrected the market myth. Despite circumstances suggesting that market behavior is based on many more factors than the political stripe of the party in the White House, the markets have nevertheless witnessed their greatest growth in two Republican administrations, as compared with only one extended period for the Democrats. While this history is far from conclusive, it is the stuff of which myths are made.

NOTES

1. Robert E. Lane, *Political Ideology* (New York: The Free Press, 1962), p. 439.

2. The actual slope of the yield curve, or the percentage difference between short-term rates and long-term rates, is equally important. Historically, long-term rates normally exceed short-term rates by about 1.5–2.0 percent. If the gap is narrower, an element of uncertainty is present, indicating that investors expect a change to occur at either end of the curve.

3. When stock prices remain depressed over long periods of time and companies refuse to issue new stock at less than optimal levels, borrowing in the bond markets will increase if firms still need funds for expansion. In these sorts of cases, firms will borrow at high costs with the intention of refinancing at a later date when yields decline.

4. *Moody's Municipal and Government Manual*, vol. 2 (New York: Moody's Investors' Services, 1988). All corporate bond yields mentioned in this chapter are based on the same source.

5. All Dow Jones Industrial Averages cited between 1920 and 1980 are taken from Phyllis Pierce, ed. *The Dow Jones Averages, 1885–1980* (Homewood, IL: Dow Jones Irwin, 1982).

6. Herbert Hoover, *The Memoirs of Herbert Hoover*, vol. 3 (New York: Macmillan, 1952), p. 110.

7. Ibid., p. 111.

8. Milton Freidman and Anna Schwartz, *A Monetary History of the United States, 1867–1960* (Princeton: Princeton University Press, 1963), p. 260.

9. Hoover, *Memoirs*, p. 19.

10. Kenneth S. Davis, *FDR: The New Deal Years, 1933–1937* (New York: Random House, 1986), p. 371.

11. Ibid., p. 400.

12. Ibid., p. 401. Hoover's refusal to join is also inconsistent, given his later remarks about Roosevelt and the New Deal. In his *Memoirs*, he likened many of Roosevelt's programs to fascist or socialist ideologies pursued in Europe during the 1930s. The Tennessee Valley Authority was characterized as an "introduction to socialism through electric power." The abandonment of the gold standard was described as "collectivism comes to the currency," and the Agricultural Adjustment Act of 1933 as "fascism comes to agriculture." Similarly, the National Recovery Act of 1933 was "among the early Roosevelt fascist measures." The kernel underlying all of these stark analogies was his belief that "the anti-trust acts had emancipated and protected the American people (common man, if you will) from the vicious growth of laissez faire economics inherited from Europe." The New Deal measures were thus seen as a return to nineteenth-century U.S. practices of noncompetitive collusion. See Hoover, *Memoirs*, Chapters 36–40.

13. Jesse Jones with Edward Angly, *Fifty Billion Dollars: My Thirteen Years with the RFC* (New York: Macmillan, 1951), p. 151.

14. Ibid.

15. Henry Aaron and Joseph Pechman, eds. *How Taxes Affect Economic Behavior* (Washington, DC: Brookings Institution, 1982), Table 11.

16. Ibid.

17. Quoted in Harold F. Gosnell, *Truman's Crises: A Political Biography of Harry S. Truman* (Westport, CT: Greenwood Press, 1980), p. 130.

18. Ibid.

19. *Survey of Current Business* (Washington, DC: U.S. Department of Commerce, September 1988).

20. Harry S. Truman, *Memoirs by Harry S. Truman*, vol. 2 (Garden City, NY: Doubleday & Co., 1956), p. 45.

21. *Survey of Current Business*, September 1988.

22. Ibid.

23. Ibid.

24. As measured by the gross national product implicit price deflator. See *Survey of Current Business*, September 1988.

25. Lyndon Baines Johnson, *The Vantage Point: Perspectives of the Presidency, 1963–1969* (New York: Holt, Rinehart & Winston, 1971), p. 443.

26. Theodore H. White, *America in Search of Itself: The Making of the President 1956–1980* (New York: Harper & Row, 1982), especially Chapters 8 and 9.

27. Ibid., p. 420.

28. Ibid., p. 421.

29. *Survey of Current Business*, September 1988.

Bibliography

Aaron, Henry, and Joseph Pechman. *How Taxes Affect Economic Behavior*. Washington, DC: Brookings Institution, 1981.

Anderson, Maxwell, Russell Kincaid, Caroline Atkinson, Eliot Kalter, and David Folkerts-Landau. *International Capital Markets: Developments and Prospects*. Washington, DC: International Monetary Fund, 1986.

Atkinson, Thomas. *Trends in Corporate Bond Quality*. New York: National Bureau of Economic Research, 1967.

Bank for International Settlements. *Annual Report*. 1969.

Beim, David. "Rescuing the LDCs." *Foreign Affairs*. July 1977.

Brady, Nicholas et al. *Report of the Presidential Task Force on Market Mechanisms*. Washington, DC: U.S. Government Printing Office, 1988.

Break, George, and Jack Guttentag. *Federal Credit Agencies*. Englewood Cliffs, NJ: Prentice Hall, 1963.

Brown, Brendan. *The Dollar–Mark Axis on Currency Power*. London: Macmillan, 1979.

Brown, Brendan, and Charles R. Geisst. *Financial Futures Markets*. New York: St. Martin's Press, 1984.

Burns, Helen. *The American Banking Community and New Deal Banking Reforms, 1933–1935*. Westport, CT: Greenwood Press, 1974.

Carosso, Vincent. *Investment Banking in America: A History*. Cambridge, MA: Harvard University Press, 1983.

Clendenning, E. Wayne. *The Euro-Dollar Market*. Oxford: The Clarendon Press, 1970.

Cooper, James Fenimore. *The American Democrat.* Edited by G. Dekker and L. Johnston. Baltimore: Penguin Books, 1969.

Coppock, Joseph. *Government Agencies of Consumer Installment Credit.* New York: National Bureau of Economic Research, 1940.

Davis, Kenneth. *FDR: The New Deal Years, 1933–1937.* New York: Random House, 1986.

Davis, Richard. "The Recent Performance of the Commercial Banking Industry." Federal Reserve Bank of New York, *Quarterly Review,* Summer 1986.

deTocqueville, Alexis. *Democracy in America.* New York: Vintage Books, 1955.

Douglas, William O. *Democracy and Finance.* New Haven: Kennikat Press, 1969.

Eccles, George, and Sidney Hyman, eds. *The Politics of Banking.* Salt Lake City: University of Utah, 1982.

Farm Credit System. *The Federal Land Bank System, 1917–1967.* Washington, DC: Farm Credit System, 1967.

Federal Reserve System. *Bulletin.* Various issues.

———. *Flow of Funds Accounts, Assets and Liabilities Outstanding 1959–1982.* Washington, DC: Federal Reserve System, 1983.

Ferrell, Robert H., ed. *The Eisenhower Diaries.* New York: W. W. Norton & Co., 1981.

Fisher, Lawrence, and James Lorie. *A Half Century of Returns on Stocks and Bonds: Rates of Return on Investments in Common Stocks and on U.S. Treasury Securities.* Chicago: University of Chicago Press, 1977.

Friedman, Benjamin, ed. *The Changing Roles of Debt and Equity in Financing U.S. Capital Formation.* Chicago: University of Chicago Press, 1982.

Friedman, Milton and Anna Schwartz. *A Monetary History of the United States, 1867–1960.* Princeton: Princeton University Press, 1963.

Geisst, Charles R. *A Guide to Financial Institutions.* New York: St. Martin's Press, 1988.

———. *A Guide to the Financial Markets,* 2nd edn. New York: St. Martin's Press, 1989.

Gosnell, Harold. *Truman's Crises: A Political Biography of Harry S. Truman.* Westport, CT: Greenwood Press, 1980.

Hamilton, Alexander, James Madison, and John Jay. *The Federalist Papers.* New York: New American Library, 1961.

Hayes, Samuel, A. M. Spence, and D. Van Praag Marks. *Competition in the Investment Banking Industry.* Cambridge, MA: Harvard University Press, 1983.

Hendershott, P. H., and K. Villani. *Regulation and Reform of the Housing Finance System.* Washington, DC: American Enterprise Institute, 1977.

Hoag, W. G. *The Farm Credit System.* Danville, IL: Interstate Publishers, 1976.

Hofstadter, Richard. *Anti-Intellectualism in American Life.* New York: Alfred A. Knopf, 1970.

Homer, Sidney. *A History of Interest Rates.* New Brunswick, NJ: Rutgers University Press, 1963.

Hoover, Herbert. *The Memoirs of Herbert Hoover,* vol. 3. New York: Macmillan, 1952.

Interim Report of the Working Group on Financial Markets. Washington, DC: U.S. Government Printing Office, 1988.

James, Marquis, and Bessie Rowland James. *Biography of a Bank: The Story of the Bank of America.* New York: Harper & Co., 1954.

Jefferson, Thomas. *Political Writings.* New York: Bobbs-Merrill, 1955.

Johnson, Lyndon Baines. *The Vantage Point: Perspectives on the Presidency 1963–1968.* New York: Holt, Rinehart & Winston, 1971.

Jones, Jesse, with Edward Angly. *Fifty Billion Dollars: My Thirteen Years with the RFC.* New York: Macmillan, 1951.

Jones, Lawrence, and David Durand. *Mortgage Lending Experience in Agriculture.* Princeton: Princeton University Press, 1954.

Krooss, Herman, ed. *Documentary History of Banking and Currency in the United States.* New York: Chelsea House Publishers, 1969.

Lane, Robert E. *Political Ideology.* New York: Free Press, 1962.

Lawrence, Joseph Stagg. *Wall Street and Washington.* Princeton: Princeton University Press, 1929.

Marshall, Jack, and Ken Kapner. *Understanding Swap Finance.* Cincinnati: South-Western Publishing Co., 1990.

Massaro, Vincent. *The Equity Market: Corporate Practices and Issues.* New York: The Conference Board, 1979.

McDonald, Forrest. *Novus Ordo Seclorom: The Intellectual Origins of the Constitution.* Lawrence, KA: University of Kansas, 1985.

Meltzer, Allan. "Regulation Q: The Money Markets and Housing and Monetary Policy." Federal Reserve Bank of Boston, 1970.

Meyer, Charles H. *The Securities Act of 1934 Analyzed and Explained.* New York: Francis Emory Fitch, 1934.

Moody's Municipal and Government Manual. New York: Moody's Investors' Services, 1988.

Morgan Guaranty Trust. *World Financial Markets.* Various issues.

National Center for Education Statistics. *Digest of Educational Statistics.* Washington, DC: U.S. Department of Health, Education and Welfare, 1972.

———. *Digest of Educational Statistics.* Washington, DC: U.S. Department of Education, 1988.

New York Stock Exchange. *Supply and Demand for Equity Capital.* New York, 1975.

———. *Marketplace: A Brief History of the New York Stock Exchange.* New York, 1982.

———. *Fact Book, 1988.* New York, 1988.

O'Connor, J. F. T. *The Banking Crisis and Recovery Under the Roosevelt Administration.* Chicago: Callaghan and Company, 1938.

Peach, W. Nelson. *The Securities Affiliates of National Banks.* Baltimore: Johns Hopkins University Press, 1941.

Phaup, Marvin. *Government Sponsored Enterprises and Their Implicit Federal Subsidy: The Case of Sallie Mae.* Washington, DC: Congressional Budget Office, 1985.

Pierce, Phyllis, ed. *The Dow Jones Averages, 1885–1980.* Homewood, IL: Dow Jones Irwin, 1982.

Pool, John Charles, and Steven Stamos. *The ABCs of International Finance.* Lexington, MA: Lexington Books, 1987.

Rasmussen, Wayne, ed. *Readings in the History of American Agriculture.* Urbana, IL: University of Illinois Press, 1960.

Richardson, Pearl. *The Tax-Exempt Financing of Student Loans*. Washington, DC: Congressional Budget Office, 1986.

Schlesinger, Arthur M., Jr. *The Age of Roosevelt: The Crisis of the Old Order*. Boston: Houghton Mifflin, 1957.

———. *The Age of Roosevelt: The Coming of the New Deal*. Boston: Houghton Mifflin, 1959.

Seidler, Lee, F. Andrews, and Marc Epstein. *The Equity Funding Papers: The Anatomy of a Fraud*. New York: John Wiley, 1977.

Seltzer, Lawrence. *The Nature and Tax Treatment of Capital Gains and Losses*. New York: National Bureau of Economic Research, 1951.

Solomon, Robert. *The International Monetary System, 1945–1976*. New York: Harper & Row, 1977.

Stanford Research Institute. *Preliminary Findings on Hedging Demand for Domestic Interest Rates and Foreign Currencies*. Stanford, CA: Stanford Research Institute, 1978.

Stoll, Hans. *The Stock Exchange Specialist System: An Economic Analysis*. New York: New York University, 1985.

Teplitz, Paul. *Trends Affecting the U.S. Banking System*. Cambridge, MA: Ballinger Publishing Company, 1976.

Thorsen, Niels Aage. *The Political Thought of Woodrow Wilson, 1875–1910*. Princeton: Princeton University Press, 1988.

Truman, Harry S. *Memoirs*. Garden City, NY: Doubleday & Co., 1956.

U.S. Department of Commerce. *Historical Statistics of the United States: Colonial Times to 1975*. Washington, DC: 1979.

U.S. League of Savings Institutions. *Fact Book, 1973* and *1988*.

———. *Source Book*. 1985.

U.S. Office of Education. *Report on Collection of National Defense Student Loans*. Washington, DC: U.S. Government Printing Office, 1965.

U.S. Secretary of Agriculture. *The Farm Debt Problem*. Washington, DC: U.S. Government Printing Office, 1933.

van Cleveland, Harold B., and Thomas Huertas. *Citibank, 1812–1970*. Cambridge, MA: Harvard University Press, 1985.

Weicher, John. *Housing: Federal Policies and Programs*. Washington, DC: American Enterprise Institute, 1980.

White, Theodore H. *America in Search of Itself: The Making of the President, 1956–1980*. New York: Harper & Row, 1982.

Whittaker, J. Gregg. "Interest Rate Swaps: Risk and Regulation." *Economic Review*. Federal Reserve Bank of Kansas City, March 1987.

Wickens, David. "Developments in Home Financing." *The Annals of the American Academy of Political and Social Science*. March 1937.

Wigmore, Barrie. *The Crash and Its Aftermath: A History of Securities Markets in the United States, 1929–1933*. Westport, CT: Greenwood Press, 1985.

Willis, Parker. *The Federal Funds Market: Its Origin and Development*, 3rd edn. Boston: Federal Reserve Bank of Boston, 1968.

Wilson, John Donald. *The Chase: The Chase Manhattan Bank, N.A., 1945–1985*. Boston: Harvard Business School Press, 1986.

Woerheide, Walter. *The Savings and Loan Industry*. Westport, CT: Quorum Books, 1984.

Index

ABOUT THE AUTHOR

CHARLES R. GEISST is the author of several other books on finance and politics, among them *Raising International Capital, A Guide to the Financial Markets, A Guide to Financial Institutions,* and *Financial Futures Markets* (with Brendan Brown), as well as *The Political Thought of John Milton.* He is also the author of many articles on financial and political topics that have appeared in journals and periodicals ranging from *Political Studies* to *Euromoney* and the *Neue Zurcher Zeitung.*

He received a Ph.D. from the London School of Economics and Political Science and did further study at the Yale Law School and Balliol College, Oxford. Originally a political scientist, he has taught both political science and finance and has worked as an investment banker for a number of years.